THERE'S ROOM FOR ME HERE

Literacy Workshop in the Middle School

For three years he had been planting trees in the wilderness. He had planted one hundred thousand. Of the hundred thousand, twenty thousand had sprouted. Of the twenty thousand he still expected to lose about half, to rodents or to the unpredictable designs of Providence. There remained ten thousand oak trees to grow where nothing had grown before

Jean Giono, *The Man Who Planted Trees*

THERE'S ROOM FOR ME HERE

Literacy Workshop in the Middle School

Janet Allen

University of Central Florida
Orlando, Florida

Kyle Gonzalez

Lakeview Middle School
Winter Garden, Florida

Stenhouse Publishers
York, Maine

Stenhouse Publishers, 431 York Street, York, Maine 03909

www.stenhouse.com

Library of Congress Cataloging-in-Publication Data

Allen, Janet, 1950–
    There's room for me here : literacy workshop in the middle school
  / Janet Allen, Kyle Gonzalez.
        p.   cm.
    Includes bibliographical references (p. 231) and index.
    ISBN 1-57110-042-3
    1. Language arts (Middle school)—United States. 2. Reading
(Middle school)—United States. I. Gonzalez, Kyle. II. Title.
LB1631.A388 1998
428'.0071'2—dc21   97–30613
                                                         CIP

Cover photo by Janet Allen and Kyle Gonzalez

Manufactured in the United States of America on acid-free paper
03 02 01 00 99   9 8 7 6 5 4

For Rick, who found a place for me—a home of peace, friendship, caring, and hope—especially every other Thursday!

For Troy, who continues to be my uncommon friend—my laughter—my place of dreams and adventures.

Janet

For my husband, Robbie Gonzalez, who has continued to believe that I can do anything I set my mind to, even when I don't believe I can. JKL, honey.

For my grandfather, Paul B. McNamara, who taught me about the joys of life and laughter.

Kyle

Contents

Acknowledgments

I would like to first acknowledge Janet Allen, to whom I am grateful for so many things: her mentorship, her ability to listen, and her ability to switch from the role of colleague, friend, and spiritual mother. Her belief in children and in teachers truly inspired me to forge ahead in education, a place I doubt I would have remained had it not been for her teaching and encouragement. Thanks, Janet, for everything. I love you. You *are* the Q.O.E.

I would also like to acknowledge my principal, Hugh Hattabaugh; without his support this project could not have happened. I thank him for his dedication to literacy and at-risk students. In addition, I thank him for hiring and having faith in a first-year teacher for the initial Reading Pilot Program.

I thank Orange County Public Schools, especially Deputy Superintendent Bob Williams, Superintendent Donald Shaw, and Rose Taylor for making the initial Reading Pilot Program and the subsequent Literacy Project a reality. I hope they realize how many students' lives have been changed as a result of these classrooms and the many excellent Literacy Project teachers.

I thank Sheila Ryan and Bess Hinson for all the books and encouragement they brought each time they came to my classroom.

I thank Philippa Stratton for not running out of my classroom the day she came to visit and have a tea party with fifteen eleven- and twelve-year-olds. I thank her for seeing this vision as important and acknowledging students who struggle.

I want to acknowledge my friend and colleague Lee Corey. She has listened to me babble during two years of carpooling to our graduate classes. I appreciate her support, her forthrightness about teaching, and her sense of humor when I take life too seriously. I also appreciate her help with this book—proofreading, offering suggestions and comments. Thank you, Lee-Lee, for being such a great friend.

I thank my wonderful in-laws, Angel and Margaret Gonzalez, for cooking barbecued chicken and ribs for our academic dinners and other student gatherings until they couldn't see straight. Thank you for raising such a wonderful son, who has loved me and been involved with and supportive of my students beyond the call of husbandly duty.

Last but not least I would like to thank my students from the past three years. They have redefined the terms perseverance and courage for me. I thank them for being *my* teacher—for making me laugh and cry as we learned together.

Kyle Gonzalez

Kyle Gonzalez has been *my* teacher in many ways. I thank her for allowing me to share her classroom and her students; for reminding me of the realities of a teacher's life; for being willing to take on roles that would scare many veteran teachers. Most of all I thank her for giving me a glimpse into motherhood. As a teacher, I'm proud to call her a colleague; as a mother, I'd be proud to call her daughter.

Anne Gaither has been my friend and colleague throughout this writing project. She daily offers alternative perspectives on education, writing, and life and has many times cleared the path and run interference so I cold find time to write. Her friendship brings sanity on the craziest days, and her care brings me hope.

Julie Joynt, my first University of Central Florida graduate student, my colleague and friend—she has made my life in Florida a home. Each day I am thankful for the ways she shares her family and her home. She has cooked countless meals, decorated my house, and listened. I've been honored to have the gift of her friendship.

April Henderson made the foolhardy decision to move into my neighborhood, and her life hasn't had many sane moments since. I'm thankful for her thoughtful ways—the all-night overhead marathons, the last-minute errands, and the laughter.

I'd like to thank the teachers in Florida and California who opened their classrooms and their hearts as they showed me effective teaching and learning at the middle school level. Thanks to those students, teachers, and administrators at Holland Middle School in Baldwin Park, CA; Jefferson Middle School in Long Beach, CA; Eliott Middle School in Pasadena, CA; and Slauson Middle School in Azusa, CA for the incredible models they have shown me of the things that can happen when schools rethink teaching and learning.

My thanks to Florida's Orange County Public Schools for the difference they are making in the literate lives of their students. It has been an honor to work with county-level and school-level administrators, teachers, and students in many of OCPS's schools. These people have been my colleagues in the best sense of the word: I learn from them, they help me rethink, and they show me that my work is meaningful.

My thanks go to the talented people at Stenhouse. Nicole, Martha, Tom, and Philippa make authors feel as though their work is significant, and they endeavor to turn that work into a product we can be proud of. They are thoughtful and witty, kind and patient (except for Philippa's occasional threat to disconnect my cable TV). I'm proud to be a Stenhouse author because of these people.

Finally, I thank my family for caring about me first, even before my work. They make every trip to Maine memorable—they remind me that there is no place like home.

Janet Allen

Chapter 1

In Pursuit of Hopefulness

You know, Giono said to me, there are also times in life when a person has to rush off in pursuit of hopefulness.

Norma L. Goodrich, afterword to *The Man Who Planted Trees*

Partnerships for Learning

I met Kyle Gonzalez in 1992. It was my first year of teaching at the University of Central Florida, and Kyle was an undergraduate there. I was then the only English education professor, so Kyle took several classes with me. With each subsequent class, I became more impressed with Kyle's focus on the students who would be on the receiving end of our ideas and plans. Her quiet ways and intense interest in the whys of education garnered my respect from the beginning.

In 1993, during the fall term of Kyle's final undergraduate year, I began talking with Orange County administrators about the increasing number of public middle school students who were unable or unwilling to read. These administrators read my dissertation (published in 1995 as *It's Never Too Late*), which chronicled my work with secondary students at risk in terms of literacy, and together we began to plan the Orange County Literacy Project. In the fall of 1994 the county would institute special classes attempting to replicate and modify for middle schools the classroom practices I had written about. The one change was the addition of a computer software program created by Vanderbilt University professors.

By the summer of 1994, three middle schools had been chosen to pilot the Literacy Project and two of the three teachers who would conduct the newly created classes had been hired. However, the principal of the third school called and asked me to recommend someone to teach these classes in his school. He wanted someone who had recently graduated from the English education program in which I was teaching, so that the philosophy and methodology would remain consistent. Kyle had just graduated in May and had begun her master's program immediately. She was the first person who came to my mind.

I had talked with Kyle often during her senior internship and watched her work with at-risk students in the Orlando Shakespeare Festival's Young Company. I was always struck by the high level of respect with which she treated students. In spite of the newness of her role as a teacher, she seemed to have a keen sense of responsibility for meeting students where they were. I knew that in spite of her lack of classroom experience, these characteristics would serve her well in dealing with students who were reading several years below grade level, failing almost all their courses, and spending a great deal of time in administrative offices because of discipline problems. Since I was a consultant with the project, I also knew that I would be working closely with Kyle to help her establish the literacy workshop in her classroom. And so, our collaborative research and writing began.

Writing and Reading *There's Room for Me Here*

During the first year of the Literacy Project, I spent a great deal of time observing Kyle's classes, talking with her, and helping her adjust the practices that had been effective in my classes in order to meet the needs of her students. We kept journals, collected samples, and interviewed students as a way of furthering Kyle's teaching and learning. When Kyle's teaching life became too hectic for journal keeping, she started dictating into a handheld tape recorder as she drove to and from work (perhaps not the safest way to drive through downtown Orlando). She taped her classes, conferences with students, and students' reading so that we could discuss what was happening in her classroom.

This was a stressful time for Kyle, and I have often wondered whether I could have withstood such pressure during my first year of teaching. Kyle had taken on a job that would have intimidated many veteran teachers. Although her class sizes were small (fifteen to twenty students per class), she had only students who were previously unsuccessful in school. Pulling these students from their regular classes, putting them all together in one classroom, and requiring them to be in class for twice as long as other students created a unique set of dynamics. In addition, this was a new project for Orange County and its success or failure would influence whether the project would be expanded to other schools and classrooms. Kyle's classroom, therefore, received frequent visitors: county administrators, school board officials, Florida Department of Education personnel, teachers and administrators from other schools and counties, and me. All this during her first year of teaching in a program that had no specific curricular guidelines with students that others had written off. It is a tribute to Kyle that she survived.

The following year, Orange County expanded the Literacy Project to ten additional schools. I met with new teachers and enlisted Kyle to help them move from traditional classrooms to the literacy workshop. Speaking with these teachers helped Kyle think carefully about the decisions she made in her classroom and the impact those decisions had on students' learning.

At the beginning of Kyle's second year of teaching, Philippa Stratton visited Kyle's classroom and the idea for a book was born. My observations and our conferences that year took on a dual focus: helping Kyle continue to refine her practice and documenting the journey that Kyle and her students were taking. That year of focused research led to the actual writing of this book, which began in the spring of Kyle's second year of teaching and continued throughout her third.

So, whose voice will you hear as you read this book? We want you to hear both our voices, as well as those of the students who have been in Kyle's classes for the past three years. Like other writing partners, we struggled with how to make the reading of this book coherent and consistent without making the writing anonymous. In all honesty, we also had to deal with issues related to Kyle's intimidation as a new teacher thrust into writing with her professor and my issues related to writing about a classroom not my own. Fortunately, we were asked to coauthor a chapter for an edited book, *Meeting the Challenges: Stories from Today's Classrooms* (Barbieri and Tateishi 1996) and were able to work through some of these issues in the context of a smaller project. I highly recommend this sort of trial run to those anticipating writing a book together.

Here's the writing pattern that worked for us. Together, Kyle and I reflected on the notes we had taken from our research and decided what topics should be chapters in the book. Before we began writing each chapter, we talked about the important issues in the chapter. Then Kyle went home, freewrote about that topic within the context of her classroom, and pulled samples of student work to support what she had written. When she finished, she gave both the freewrite and the samples of student work to me.

For Chapters 3 through 10, while Kyle was freewriting, I wrote the introduction for that chapter. I found research that supports the concepts the chapter deals with and then placed Kyle's classroom within the larger picture of that research. In each of these introductory pieces, the "I" is me.

At the end of these introductions, I cue the reader that we are moving into Kyle's classroom. After that point, the "I" is Kyle. These classroom sections are the heart of the book—in them we have tried to create a rich and specific context. However, not all the things in these sections actually come from Kyle's freewrite. They are compilations of Kyle's freewrites and student samples as refined by my observations and interviews. In some cases I used entire pages of Kyle's freewrites with only minor changes; in other cases, I added information that I felt was necessary for an accurate picture or moved material between chapters. Sometimes I added quotes or references, and sometimes I took out things that were too personal for public writing. There was no easy way to delineate which lines came from Kyle and which came from me without confusing us *and* our readers. In any case, after researching and writing together for almost three years now, we're not all that sure who said what anyway!

At the end of each of the chapters, we leave Kyle's classroom and reflect on what happened there. In those reflective pieces, the "I" once again is me.

Chapters 2, 11, and 12 veer from this pattern. In Chapter 2, I present a little necessary background. Chapter 11, "But What About...," is a list of questions. We compiled the list together, then Kyle wrote a response to each one. Later, I put them into categories and developed and edited them. So, although the "I" in those responses is me, we both contributed. I introduce Chapter 12, and then we each do our own reflections.

We feel this sandwich pattern is a realistic picture of the book: Kyle's freewrites are the meat and my introductions and reflections hold the chapters together. We hope that our writing is clear enough to achieve a larger goal: that you will be able take what we have learned from our teaching and researching and adapt it to your particular teaching context as you work with adolescents in your school.

Chapter 2

From "Hey, Crackhead!" to *The Lion King*

Almost anything can become a learning experience if there is enough caring involved.

Mary MacCracken, *Lovey*

Adolescence and the Literacy Workshop

Days spent with adolescents are challenging, tender, anxious, angry, loving, and exciting times for teachers. Unfortunately, in a middle-level classroom, all these emotions can be experienced in a ten-minute period, and no one who has spent a significant amount of time with middle school learners would ever accuse *anyone* of exaggeration. Each day with these young people moves our perception of normal a little further off-center. The older I get, however, the more I value that shifting ground adolescents are forced to tread. Adolescence is a unique time. Don't misunderstand me; I have no desire to return to that age. In fact, I seldom meet a reminiscing adult who yearns for his or her adolescence. There is good reason adolescents long to get out of that stage and adults don't want to return to it: it is a time filled with uncertainty and anxiety. Middle-level learners try everything they can to prove they are no longer children, yet one foot is still squarely planted in childhood's door.

Each time I'm with middle school students, I am newly struck by this phenomenon. One day in Kyle's classroom, I watched two young "men" come crashing into the classroom, calling a fellow student "Crackhead" and discussing a fight that was to take place later in the day. Within minutes those same two "boys" were curled up in one chair, sharing a set of headphones and listening to *Disney's The Lion King* on tape. One of them was cuddling a teddy bear, and they were both totally engrossed in the recording. It was both painful and heartwarming to watch.

The literacy workshop was designed to help students not only survive this stage of their lives but flourish in it. If we take individual things students say as our cues for what they want or need, we can become confused:

> Ms. Gonzalez, could you put *Beauty and the Beast* on the tape recorder for me?
> I don't need to learn to read. I have a hundred thousand dollars waiting in the bank for me when I turn eighteen.
> Would you read *Mr. and Mrs. Bo Jo Jones* to me?
> From a geophysicist's point of view, I'd like to diaphragm this poem for you.

Obviously, each of these students in the literacy workshop is in a different place—developmentally and academically. That range of adolescent needs and abilities is the hallmark of teaching and learning with middle-level learners. Adolescence brings about its own set of physical, cognitive, and emotional changes; when these changes are combined with the at-risk characteristics that many adolescents exhibit, the result can be challenging. Our design for the literacy workshop is based on not only understanding this difficult time in these students' lives but also using that energy and tentativeness to once again try to hook these learners as readers and writers.

Perhaps the first step in creating effective literacy programs for middle-level learners is understanding the changes adolescents are experiencing. Middle school teachers observe learners in the throes of these changes hundreds of times each day, and good teachers recognize that these changes influence students' ability and willingness to learn. In *Adolescence* (1993), Laurence Steinberg identifies the fundamental changes of adolescence as biological, cognitive, and social transitions. Each of these transitions has a major impact on what curriculum can and should be in the middle school.

Biological Transitions

One of the things that Kyle has noticed as she watches her students progress from sixth through eighth grade is their awareness of themselves and their bodies. For example, when her current eighth-grade boys were in sixth grade, they often shared cushions and cuddled together as they read. Two of the boys even continued to share one set of headphones for recorded books when they went into the seventh grade. Now that students are in the eighth grade, however, every student has his or her own place during independent reading. Some students still congregate in the same areas, but they always make sure there is a safe amount of distance between them so that no one will think they are touching.

Such actions are characteristic of adolescents who are experiencing biological transitions: "The adolescent's changed physical appearance may elicit new sorts of behavior from peers, parents, and others, and these new reactions may prompt the adolescent to adjust his or her behavior and self-image" (Steinberg 1993, 38). For adolescents in the throes of such intense physical changes, school can be a frightening place. Each day some student or other awakens with a different body than he or she had the day before. Comfort or discomfort with this new person has everything to do with how successfully he or she negotiates school that day. A school day and curriculum that allow for some choice of learning, a place where one can be alone and quiet or work with others, a way to find the care and feedback of a supportive adult, and resources that will answer the questions and worries that are always present will help students feel safe. A curriculum that is too structured, too lockstep, will add to students' feelings that there is no room for them and their needs in school.

This is not to suggest that students should be free just to hang out and find themselves. It is a reminder of the responsibility we have to help students learn to make reasonable and meaningful choices from a range of options. Literacy workshop allows teachers to set up classrooms in which these options can occur simultaneously: some students can be reading independently or with recorded books; others can be working together on a research project; a few can be at the computers writing or conducting research; students who need the teacher's individual attention can be receiving that through "check-ins" and conferences. This structure (and it does take organization to have so many things going on at once) allows for some of the messiness that comes with real learning. In *bird by bird: Some Instructions on Writing and Life* (1994), Anne Lamott reminds us of the importance of such messiness: "What people somehow (inadvertently, I'm sure) forgot to mention when we were children was that we need to make messes in order to find out who we are and why we are here" (32). There needs to be room in the literacy workshop for students to "make messes."

Cognitive Transitions

Kyle spent a considerable amount of time deciding whether or not to do a unit on segregation with her eighth graders. There was a diverse group of students in her class and race had been a big issue, but discussions about tolerance had not been very effective. In fact, the students who had been in the Literacy Project for two years were extremely intolerant of five students who were new to the project. She finally decided to assign Melba Beals's memoir *Warriors Don't Cry* as shared reading and use this literary experience to discuss fairness, tolerance, and segregation. During the shared reading and discussion, Kyle was not always sure whether students were internalizing the events and transferring them to their own lives. They still called each other hateful names and often showed intolerance for differences ranging from physical traits to cultural background.

While students did not immediately appear to be learning anything about tolerance, as the weeks passed, they continued to circle back to their reading and discussion of this book. One day Chanelle asked, "Is Chink a racist word?" When Kyle told her it was, she returned to her reading. Shortly after that, students who had been calling each other "Nigger" began catching themselves, looking at Kyle, and apologizing to her. Epithets like "porch monkey," "cracker," and "honky" began to be heard less. By the end of the year, when Kyle asked students to write about one important thing they had learned, a large number of students chose something related to segregation. These students had begun to step outside themselves in order to look at issues from multiple perspectives.

Steinberg (1993) lists five areas in which we can begin to see changes in adolescents' thinking: thinking about what is possible instead of just what is real; thinking about abstract things; thinking about thinking; thinking about multiple issues; and, seeing things as relative rather than absolute (58). The literacy workshop is designed to immerse students in problem solving, complex reading and writing tasks, critical thinking, reflection and self-assessment, real-world connections, and extended goal setting. Each of these is undertaken with the support of teachers, peers, and knowledgeable others so that students begin to internalize a process for thinking through complex issues.

The balanced literacy program in literacy workshop is modeled after Margaret Mooney's *Reading to, with, and by Children* (1990), which suggests that teachers need to provide time and support for the four stages of Vygotsky's zone of proximal development: performance is assisted by others; performance is assisted by the learner; performance becomes automatized/fossilized; and the process is repeated when new levels of difficulty are encountered (Tharpe and Gallimore 1988). Time and instructional support are built into the workshop for reading to students (reading aloud), reading with students (shared and guided reading), and reading by students (independent reading). The same balanced model is used for writing. Students have opportunities to see learning processes modeled by their teachers and their peers, time to continue learning these processes and strategies with one another, and time to practice independently to gain fluency. As new or more difficult materials and concepts are encountered, the teacher returns to the modeling stage. In this way, the students receive the scaffolding they need.

Social Transitions

A poignant story from Kyle's classroom illustrates the range of social transitions that adolescents experience. During Jeff's second year in the program, he was reading aloud in a small group of seventh- and eighth-grade guys. (This was a particularly rough group, and Kyle had talked with them about practicing before reading out loud and being sensitive to other students when they are reading.) Jeff soon started stumbling over words, and Carl jumped all over him. There was a moment of silence, and then Jeff started sobbing. Twenty minutes still remained in the class, and here was this big boy sobbing while his classmates stared at him. Not sure what she should do, Kyle took Carl out into the hall to talk with him about how his comments had upset Jeff. Although she was really angry, she tried to remain calm. In the midst of her talk with Carl, *he* started to cry. Kyle was now really worried that the eighth-grade boys would make fun of both boys outside class—a sure invitation for disaster. She left Carl where he was and came back into the room to console Jeff, patting his shoulder and reassuring him that his hard work in reading was helping him improve. Jeff's entire body was shaking with his sobs. Finally, he said, "I feel like I work so hard and I'm still so far behind everyone else." Then the most amazing thing happened. The eighth-grade boys Kyle had worried about the most gathered around Jeff saying, "Come on, man, it's okay." Contrary to what Kyle had expected based on their past behavior, the whole class supported Jeff and Carl, either by encouraging them with words or walking over and standing near them.

Jeff, Carl, and the other students in this class were redefining the kind of people they would be in relation to others. Steinberg sees this as one of the fundamental changes we can expect during adolescence: "The presence during adolescence of some sort of recognition that the individual's status has changed—a social redefinition of the individual—is universal" (1993, 90). While the characteristics of this change will vary by person, gender, and culture, it is a necessary step toward adulthood. Social redefinition is promoted when students connect with fictional adolescents who are also in transition.

In many societies, the rites of passage from childhood to adulthood are clearly marked. Ceremonies end one period and begin another. Tasks and behavior are expected depending on the stage of life one is in. In Lois Lowry's *The Giver*, Jonas waits for the Ceremony of the Twelves to receive his adult work; in Michael Dorris's *Sees Behind Trees*, Walnut uses his skills to gain his adult name. In our society, those passages are much less clear, and the disequilibrium caused by that lack of clarity causes a lot of upheaval in a lot of middle schools. Adolescents are aware that they are in transition, yet the work inherent to that transition is seldom talked about.

The literature, activities, and personal and academic goal-setting work in the literacy workshop are geared to provide time to read, write, think, and talk about what this time in adolescents' lives can mean. The literature we read focuses on issues that middle-level learners wonder and worry about: relationships, survival, being different, being alone, and physical appearance. The goal-setting activities and projects help students develop the habit of working toward personal and academic achievement. The integration of reading and writing across content areas helps students discover their areas of strength, and those strengths are used as a foundation for success. Each concept, lesson, or theme starts with the knowledge students bring and moves outward from there.

The learner is at the heart of the literacy workshop curriculum. When I work with teachers who are implementing a literacy workshop, I ask them to let go of some (not all) of their planned units, so that they will be able to ask the students what they are interested in learning. The things teachers want students to know and be able to do at the end of their time together and the questions students bring to the classroom can be combined to create a response-based curriculum that is student-centered. As Philip Schlechty (1990) reminds us, "Equal access to knowledge does not mean the same curriculum for each child; rather, it means a highly differentiated curriculum aimed at common learning. The uncommon curriculum for common learning may be a more appropriate slogan for schools of the future than is the concept of core curriculum" (70). It is that "uncommon curriculum" that Kyle and I document in this book.

Kyle's Classroom and Beyond

Today, there are Literacy Project classrooms in all middle schools in Orange County, as well as in many intermediate and high schools. Two middle schools in Orlando are Literacy Prototype schools, where the literacy workshop components are being tried by teachers across the curriculum. Bilingual programs, exceptional programs, and alternative schools here have followed the same model. Teachers in other counties in Florida—and in other states—are also modifying and implementing the literacy workshop in their schools and classrooms.

Each of Kyle's classes consisted of between fifteen and twenty students who were enrolled in a pullout program that lasted for ninety minutes each day. She structured the work they did together based on a balanced use of the components of the literacy workshop. There are teachers with whom I have worked in California who are using these same components with classes of thirty-five or forty students who meet for only fifty minutes each day. In some secondary schools with block scheduling, teachers incorporate the same components in classes that meet every other day.

Kyle and I wrote this book knowing that each reader will bring to it her or his own teaching context. With any book on education, there is never an exact match between the writers' and the readers' classrooms. This is as it should be. We should worry when all our classrooms begin to look alike. We see this book not as a pattern to be copied, but as a way for teachers to be validated in what they are currently doing, to be challenged to look at new ways of doing, and to be motivated to share their own ideas with others on the journey.

Chapter 3

Connections Within and Beyond the Literacy Workshop

Human beings are territorial animals, and they are ritualists. It seems that our minds adapt to the kind of place we are in, as soon as we recognize our surroundings.

Aidan Chambers, *The Reading Environment*

The Workshop Approach: Rethinking Curriculum

The workshop approach is hardly a new topic in today's professional literature. Nancie Atwell's *In the Middle* (1987) and Linda Rief's *Seeking Diversity* (1991) changed the way many middle-level language arts teachers used time and resources to invite adolescents into what Frank Smith (1988) calls the "literacy club." I don't believe any of these teachers would advocate that other teachers copy exactly what they did in their classrooms, but their successes helped many rethink curriculum and their roles within the classroom.

The literacy workshop builds on what we have learned about the value of reading and writing workshops. Central to workshops is the importance of a safe learning environment overseen by a committed mentor working with all learners. I learned the truth of that when I interviewed the ninth graders in my reading/writing workshop in Maine. Rachel and I reminisced about the early days when she had first joined the class, after several previous years of academic failure. It had taken weeks to break down the walls and get her involved in any of the literacy activities in our classroom. Once she began reading, however, there had been no stopping her. I asked her why she thought she had been successful in school during our year together. She sat quietly for several moments, obviously pondering my question. Finally she said, "There was room for me here." When my puzzled look obviously asked for more, she continued. "It seemed to me that everyone else had a place in school. The rich kids hung out together and did sports, but I wasn't rich. The smart kids did clubs and stuff, but I wasn't smart. The teachers didn't hate me or anything, but I wasn't special to any of them. That's it—I wasn't special anywhere till now."

That feeling of not belonging anywhere, of not having a place where one is special, can have a lasting impact on any adolescent. Sadly, for many students in our classrooms, there is no physical space in their lives that belongs to them. Joan Kaywell, in her book *Adolescents at Risk* (1993), cites a statistic from Linehan's research: "Estimates of the number of children in America who are homeless on any given night range from 68,000 to half a million" (148). Many of these children are in our classrooms each day. When we add to them the children who live in poverty and probably lack most, if not all, aspects of a positive environment conducive to literacy and language learning, the importance of a supportive classroom environment becomes very clear.

Many educators and researchers have written about the importance of classroom environment as a condition for learning for middle-level learners. Nancie Atwell (1987), Linda Rief (1991), Mary Krogness (1995), and Deborah Butler and Tom Liner (1996) all paint pictures of middle-level teachers who know the importance of building an environment that supports both the teachers' and the students' continued learning. Five components of that environment are critical to the literacy workshop: time, choice, resources, support, and connections. There is no magic formula for the proportion of effort that needs to be spent on each aspect of the workshop: success comes from the balanced integration of these pieces.

The roles of environment and mentorship and the way the components of time, choice, resources, support, and connections fit within that foundation in Kyle's classroom are illustrated in the next sections of this chapter. These ingredients are not specific to a certain number of students in a class nor to a particular class length. I balanced the same components in my secondary classes with thirty students; teachers in Orlando and Los Angeles are balancing their classes for thirty or forty students using the same criteria. The chart in Figure 3.1 has been helpful to these teachers as a way of looking at the activities in their classrooms in relation to the elements of time, choice, support, resources, and connections. These elements are artificially separated for ease of discussion, but in Kyle's classroom, we see that it is the connections among the elements and the struggle to maintain those connections that form the balanced literacy program.

A Balanced Literacy Program					
	Time	Choice	Support	Resources	Connections
Read-Alouds					
Shared Reading					
Guided Reading					
Independent Reading					
Shared Writing					
Guided Writing					
Independent Exploration					
Goal Setting					
Community Building					
Assessment					

Figure 3.1 *A chart that helps ensure that the components of literacy workshop are in teachers' programs*

In the Classroom with Kyle

Creating a Safe Environment

When I imagined my first job and my first classroom, I don't think I realized how crucial the classroom environment would be nor how difficult it would be to achieve an environment that would be safe for my students. Janet had written at length about how she had set up her classroom and the ownership that her students felt there. I had no idea how much impact that sense of ownership would have on my students' reading. I just wanted to create a beautiful place that would be so inviting that my students couldn't resist reading. Not surprisingly, creating a positive physical environment proved far easier than building a safe emotional environment for students who had developed coping strategies of anger, violence, and verbal abuse as a way of surviving in a place where everything had previously represented failure.

Before my students arrived, I set out to create an inspirational environment geared specifically to the students who would be inhabiting it. I hung as many motivational posters on the walls as I could find: Zora Neale Hurston would stare down at us while we read, and surely the image of Shaquille O'Neal reading a book would prove to be a great model for my students. As Martin Luther King Jr.'s "I Have a Dream" speech found its place in between a proclamation of self-esteem and Portia Nelson's poem "Autobiography in Five Short Chapters," I looked forward to the change all these words would make in the lives of the students who would soon enter Room 116. I wanted students to see that this was going to be a place of success for them—that I expected them to succeed rather than repeat past failures.

Between my vision and middle school reality, however, was a vast gulf. The only poster that caught anyone's attention was the one of Shaquille O'Neal sitting in a child's chair reading a book.

"That chair is too little for that man," Corian commented.

"Aw, that dog is a chump," Corey said, scoffing at the poster.

My favorite poster, the one proclaiming the "I Am Me" decree of self-esteem, was too long on words and too short on illustrations to get a glance. Alas, none of them even recognized poor Zora. The best-laid preschool plans...

Establishing Classroom Rules *with* and *for* Students

I knew that I was immediately going to have to show these students that our classroom would be different from the classrooms in which they had experienced failure if I wanted them to return the next day. (Although by the end of our first day together, I wasn't all that sure that even I wanted to return!) I had read about and discussed with Janet how she had asked the students to help her write the classroom rules. When I was a student, I had never had a teacher who shared this responsibility with us. Some classroom walls were colorfully decorated, others were bare, but the rules were already posted on almost all of them when we got there. Those rules interposed a definite barrier of authority. I remember feeling that the classroom was just a stopping-off place before we could spend time with our friends in the hallway.

However, rules were a way to set standards and maintain control, and as a first-year teacher, my biggest fear was losing control of my classroom. I had nightmares about students rebelling and walking out, throwing obscenities at me as they passed. I remembered Atwell's words: "I didn't know how to share responsibility with my students, and I wasn't too sure I wanted to. I liked the vantage of my big desk" (1987, 11). I, too, took comfort in the fact that even if I didn't look much older than their brothers and sisters, I had a big desk and the title of "teacher."

In spite of my growing apprehension, I had to create a way for trust to find its way into our classroom. Where to begin? On the second day of class, I took a deep breath and opened the floor for a discussion about rules. It did not go as I had planned. I stood at the front of the class and said, "Okay, what do you all think about rules for our class?" Blank stares. Giggling. Shifting around uncomfortably in chairs. Several moments passed with no suggestions. Finally, Tabitha spoke up.

"What do you mean? Aren't you just going to give us the rules? I mean, that's what they usually do." All the students in our middle school are assigned to a grade-level team, each team made up of four teachers. These four teachers set up their own rules and consequences at the beginning of the school year and post them in their classrooms. The first week of school is usually devoted to going over the team rules, the school rules, and the county rules. I was not on a team, and I had students from every grade-level team in my classes. No wonder they weren't thrilled with the prospect of discussing rules!

"Well, I'm not going to make up the rules by myself. We all have to spend time in this classroom and we should be able to work comfortably in here...all of us together. What rule do you think would be a good one to start off with?"

"Dang, why is that lady asking so many questions," Jason said as he rolled his eyes back in his head. The boys around him burst into the long, loud laughter he had obviously been hoping to get.

"Shut up!" Ruth yelled. "You guys are so stupid. Let the lady talk. I swear!"

Jason stood up and looked at her menacingly. "Come over here, girl, and make me shut up," he shouted.

Ruth, all eighty-five pounds of her, jumped out of her chair. I quickly made my way over to her, gently placing my hand on her shoulder. Jason smirked, and the boys around him once again burst out laughing. So much for the safe environment I was hoping to create. I waited for the boys to calm down. After what seemed like an eternity, they were quiet and sat waiting to see what I would do or say next.

"Okay, how can we figure this out? I don't think calling people stupid is an effective rule for our class." I glanced first at Ruth and then over at Jason.

"Man, *this* is stupid," he said. Several more encouraging laughs. I realized that I had fallen into the very teacher-versus-student stance I wanted to avoid.

I took a deep breath. "Jason, I appreciate your expressing how you feel about this activity, but could you express it in a way that doesn't disrespect me? I mean, have I called anything you've done in the past two days stupid?"

He glared at me. "Nah, man."

"Well, I'll never call you stupid. I can promise you that." I paused and continued to look him directly in the eyes. He kept glancing away. "I'd appreciate it if you didn't call me or something that I do stupid, either. Okay?" This time he looked back into my eyes and glared at me with both disbelief and disgust.

"I don't think people should ever be told that they're stupid. Do any of you?" A couple of students shook their heads, and I even heard someone say no. "All right, let's get some rules for our class. Corey, could you please write down our suggestions. Grab a marker and write down on the board what people say. Joey, how about typing on the computer for us? That way we won't miss anyone's comments." I waited for a moment, praying that they would both cooperate. I knew this was a turning point. If these two students refused to take on the tasks I had just given them, others would follow. I breathed a sigh of relief when Corey moved toward the board and Joey sat at the computer.

The first suggestion was, No fighting. A good place to start. We spent the rest of that day and all of the next compiling our list of rules. The list was decorated and posted at the front of the classroom (see Figure 3.2).

Playing by the Rules

I quickly learned that creating a safe environment and maintaining that environment are two different things. Students' initial interest in establishing classroom rules and defining roles lasts only as long as their attention span. The bigger task is helping them find ways to make better choices in avoiding or resolving conflicts.

I've decided that seventh grade is perhaps the oddest age in middle school. Mentally, many of my students are still children; physically and hormonally, I'm not sure what they are. My seventh graders revel in what Nathan McCall (1994) calls "jonin'" (23). Jonin' essentially involves kids

Figure 3.2 *A sample of the student-designed rules in Kyle's classroom*

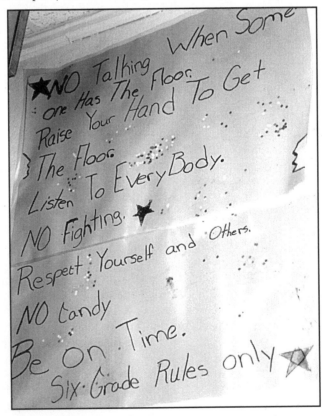

looking at one another's dress, mannerisms, etc., to find something, anything, that can be made fun of. My seventh graders are experts at jonin'. This practice erodes the safe environment of the classroom; when it gets out of hand, real problems occur.

One day one of my seventh-grade boys stayed after class to ask for help dealing with another boy who would not leave him alone. As he was talking, he broke down in tears because the other boy had made fun of his clothes and because "he called my daddy a drunk." Making fun of someone else's parents is the ultimate middle school insult. I was livid.

The next day I asked the entire class to gather on the floor for a class meeting. I could hardly believe I was about to take this risk: anyone who has ever worked with middle-level students knows how quickly these discussions can turn into fights and chaos.

"Okay, you guys, I am going to be honest with you. I have to tell you that I am sick to death of you all cracking on each other. I hear it all the time in here. This classroom is supposed to be a community. People in communities support each other, not tear each other down. Isn't there enough of that junk in the halls and in your other classes?" A few nodded. Several laughed uncomfortably. I told them I wanted to talk this out because I was going crazy seeing some of them leave class every day with hurt feelings or a lot of pent-up anger. Then I waited for what seemed far too long, but I was determined that we were going to work through this together.

Finally, Charlene suggested that we go around the circle and let people talk. "I know I got some bones to pick with some of ya." She glared menacingly around the circle. We agreed on some ground rules: the person who was talking should have complete respect—no comments, no mumbling, no nudging your neighbor. Tristen, usually pretty timid when it came to confrontation, went first.

"I want Ulysses to stop making fun of me. Every day he's got somethin' to say and I'm sick of it!" Ulysses sat shaking his head the entire time that Tristen spoke. When Tristen was finished, I asked Ulysses if he had anything to say to Tristen. He shook his head.

"Okay, Tristen, what is it that you need from Ulysses?" I asked, praying that no one was going to yell at Tristen to stop being a wuss and act like a man. Luckily, no one did.

"Ulysses, I want you to leave me alone."

No response from Ulysses.

"Ulysses, can you do that?" I asked.

He raised his head. "Yes."

The rest of the meeting did not go this smoothly. There were several points when I had to intervene. Defenses went up. The majority of the students, however, were honest and got what was bothering them off their chests. Charlene surprised me the most. She tends to verbally bully people, especially when she is protecting the interests of the class—which is most of the time. When I ask for quiet in the class, whoever ignores me faces the wrath of Charlene. While I sometimes appreciate her reinforce-ments, the students do not appreciate her yelling at them or bossing them around. In the midst of our "bone-pickin'" session, Jerry made the mistake of talking out of turn.

"*Shut up, Jerry!*" Charlene screamed.

"See, man, that is exactly what I'm talking about," he said.

"What you talkin' about? If you got somethin' to say, you better say it right to my face, boy!" Charlene glared as she bellowed at poor Jerry. All the students were intimidated by Charlene's size and voice, and Jerry decided to pass on her invitation. Later, however, when Charlene's turn came, she said, "I think that people won't pick a bone with me because they're afraid of me." At that point, Jerry admitted he did not like the way Charlene bossed him around and she agreed that she could stop being so bossy.

This kind of negotiation is one of the most difficult things I have had to learn. I still feel intimidated as I try to help students take responsibili-ty for their words and actions by establishing a place and a procedure for dealing with conflicts. When I first imagined myself as a teacher-mentor, I would have defined mentorship in terms of helping students find the right books and modeling positive attitudes for learning. I now recognize negotiation as a unique aspect of committed mentorship, one that is tied directly to creating a safe environment.

The Committed Mentor

As I faced the students who had been selected for the literacy workshop on that first day of school, I immediately felt overwhelmed. School for them had traditionally been a threatening place, and they had no reason to believe that this class would be any different from all of the other lan-guage arts classes they had hated. If anything, they probably figured this class would be even worse, because they now had to spend two periods in English instead of one!

The seventh- and eighth-grade boys in my morning block spent the entire class laughing loudly together, usually at the expense of the small-est, skinniest boy in the class. Todd cursed at how dumb everything was. At first, the three girls in the class sat quietly together. It didn't take long, however, for Ruth to launch into the exploits, mostly sexual, of her six-teen-year-old boyfriend, who had recently been released from juvenile detention. The remaining students stared aimlessly at the walls. Everyone appeared to have only one question in common—why do I have to be here?

The sixth graders weren't much better. Three of them literally could not stay in one place for more than two minutes at a time. I had already spoken with one boy's grandfather for more than thirty minutes, during which time he told me there was absolutely nothing he could do with this boy or his three brothers. The grandfather, who lived alone, was struggling to keep the children together after the state had removed them from their father's care because of his abusive behavior. The records of nearly all the students in this class revealed personal histories that made school seem insignificant.

I was beginning to understand what Janet meant when she said that the personal mentoring I did with students in the first few weeks of school would be more significant than what I taught them about literacy. It would take a drastic contrast from what they were used to for students to buy into a class that lasted twice as long as their other classes. I wondered what I could possibly offer these students that would convince them to believe that they could all become great readers and writers. My first task was getting to know the students well enough to help them become successful. Mentors know where their students are and what they hope to accomplish; I used the conference as a way to build trust as well as help students find a focus.

Conferences

In this smaller class setting, it was easier to have conferences with individual students. I began by scheduling a conference with each student at least once a week. At first, this was a formal conference in which I helped the student set academic and personal goals. Eventually, however, the conferences took on a life of their own. They became a nonthreatening way for us to talk, question, and get to know each other. In a very short time, some students began to initiate conferences.

Naturally, several of my students had discipline problems, not only in my class but also in their other classes. I realized that they had begun to view me as a committed mentor when they began coming to me to help them figure out altercations that had occurred outside our classroom. Typically, there would be a knock on the door while I was in class. It would open a crack, and a head would pop in. "Hey, Mrs. G., can I talk to you for a sec?" If I could, I would step into the hall to find a student clutching a crumpled pink referral slip. (Not surprisingly, most of their other teachers didn't mind letting these students out of class to come and meet with me.) I'd take a few moments to chat and figure out what had happened and how it could be resolved. If the student needed more time than I could spare at that moment, I asked him or her to seem me during my planning period.

Listening and open discussion were the biggest commitments I offered to my students, whether to an individual or to the entire class. Our class meetings became a way to resolve conflicts, offer encouragement, and celebrate success.

The Physical Environment

I spent a great deal of time creating comfortable seating areas, thinking that would be a sure way to entice my students to read. My principal had been able to get tables instead of desks for my classroom, and I was sure

Figure 3.3 *Carl making good use of a comfy chair during independent reading*

this would add to the sense of community I was hoping to establish. When I added three comfy chairs I had painstakingly cleaned and positioned for quiet reading, I felt the room was complete (see Figure 3.3). I quickly discovered that the only thing complete in our classroom was the chaos these comfy chairs precipitated. Although the students were extremely excited about choosing where they would sit, they had never experienced classrooms without parameters for choice, behavior, and consequences before, and I was too naïve to realize that they wouldn't be able to handle it immediately.

The comfy chairs and tables proved the undoing of our class on many of those first days. I wanted students to feel they were free to choose where they would sit, but there were invariably heated conflicts about who got to sit where. When class meetings failed to generate any successful resolutions, I finally had to assign seats until I felt they were ready to try free choice again. The comfy-chair war was one of those classroom management issues that had never surfaced in my education courses.

Except for the indifferently received posters I mentioned earlier, I left my bulletin boards blank; I wanted plenty of wall space on which to display student work. One bulletin board became home to the students' personal and academic goals (see Figure 3.4). On another bulletin board, students began displaying photos of themselves and decorations they made. I think my favorite area was the wall beside my desk, where I displayed work that students gave me as gifts: notes, poems, colored drawings, paper flowers. I realized this area was important to the students as well when one of my sixth graders got angry with me and marched up and ripped his artwork down.

Figure 3.4 *The bulletin board where students publish their personal and academic goals for the year*

The length of one entire wall was devoted to our literacy banner. Each reading strategy, writing tool, or literary term that we discussed became an entry, written in large, bold print that students could read it easily (see Figure 3.5). The banner was a reference for students in their writing and discussion—as they needed reminders about terms such as *flashback* and *prediction* or concepts about print such as *italics* and *bold,* for example—as well as a concrete symbol of the cumulative nature of the work we were doing together. As students became more independent in their literacy quests, they began using other references as well, but they never lost their pride in our literacy banner.

The other walls and shelves in our classroom were eventually decorated with student poetry and projects. The sixth graders made some wonderful dioramas of *Weasel* after we read the book during shared reading. Hanging from the ceiling was a huge banner the sixth graders made as a tribute to *The Great Gilly Hopkins* (see Figure 3.6). Yet another wall held the colorful posters that the seventh and eighth graders had designed as they created character sketches for *The Outsiders.*

The walls and shelves in our classroom changed as the students changed. The room became theirs because I made sure there was room for them. Over time, as some students became eager readers, there was less art and more writing, but that didn't happen overnight. At the end of the year, after everything had been removed from the walls for summer painting, the principal walked in and said, "Wow, it looks so different in here." Even he had gotten used to the messiness of students finding out who they were.

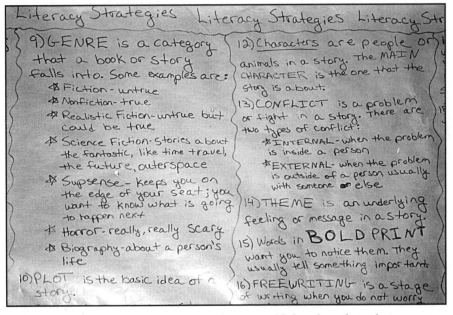

Figure 3.5 *The literacy strategies banner that was added to throughout the year*

Time

When Janet interviewed her incoming ninth graders, she found that one of the most common sources of their inability to read was not having been given enough time to complete reading and writing assignments. One boy told her that he had never completed any story in middle school: "I always flunked reading because I couldn't answer the questions. I could read the story. I just couldn't finish it. I would just start getting into the story and the teacher would say that time was up." I found the same to be true with my middle school students.

Time is probably one of the most essential factors in any classroom. In the literacy workshop, I try to make sure that when the whole group is working together, there is ample time for everyone to finish. During independent literacy exploration, time is never up.

Time is also needed to create a community. It takes time to feel safe enough to take risks with books, time to read books, time to talk about books together, and time to deal with frustration and failure. Most important, we also need time to celebrate our successes.

When I first started teaching in the literacy classroom, I felt an immense amount of pressure to turn these kids into readers as quickly as possible. I fed them strategies during shared and guided reading and attempted to integrate writing instruction in the midst of everything else. Some of the students did not even know how to identify the author's name from a book's title page; others couldn't walk into the classroom

Figure 3.6 *A banner made by students to illustrate the literary elements in* The Great Gilly Hopkins

without hitting another student. I would look at them and think, How am I supposed to teach them how to read when they don't even know how to pick a book? I quickly realized that reading was probably one of the last things on their minds when they came into the classroom. As a new teacher, I learned through their resistance, my defeat, and all our frustration that I had to slow down. My grand scheme of literacy instruction had to take a back seat to spending time listening to the students. When I began to build in time for us to talk, I saw that it was through this listening that I would learn how to help all of us take our next teaching and learning steps. When students began to feel safe because I was not rushing them through each activity, they began to take more risks with both their reading and their writing.

Choice

In Alfie Kohn's article "Choices for Children" (1993), he talks about the role of choice in helping students become committed learners. In talking with the other Literacy Project teachers, I have found that each of us has a unique schedule. The common denominator is that we each have found a way to build in time for students to choose the learning that matches their needs and interests. Choice is also built into shared reading, assessment, and independent research.

Before I began teaching, I always looked at student choice as a sure-fire way to undermine authority in the classroom. In retrospect, I realize that it all boils down to trust. The students have to trust me, and I have to trust them to make good choices. I also have to trust my ability to guide their decisions so that we can live with the choices they make.

In my third year of teaching, I now see a major difference, both for the students and for me. Classroom conflicts are not the major catastrophes they once were. I'm no longer writing detention notes and referrals every day or even every week, because I have learned other ways to help students when they have made poor choices. Now I send letters and notes home to parents or call or visit them as a way to help students make good choices before there is a problem. As we have become more trusting, it is easier for us to make strong academic choices. The students select their own texts for independent reading and then decide how they will demonstrate their learning. This is as much a sign of my own teaching growth as it is of the students' blossoming abilities to choose.

I think the reason it was so difficult for me to make choice a major part of the literacy classroom was that I hadn't been given much choice in my own schooling. It was not a big part of my K–12 education, and it had even less place in college. We were told what to read, what to study, and how to write papers and complete projects to meet the teacher's predetermined standards. My students mistrusted me because it was evident that I was uncomfortable with allowing them to choose the rules for our classroom. Their school experience so far had been of teachers telling them what to do. When they would not or could not complete the task given to them, they were punished in some way. To many of them, my offer of choice probably seemed a trick to get them to come up with their own punishments.

But because we persevered with the idea of choice, my students are achieving, not only academically but socially. Discipline and attendance are improving. They have been able to take our discussions about choices and goals with regard to independent reading and writing, literacy exploration, and assessment and transfer these concepts to other areas of their lives.

Support and Connections

Support and connections permeate the entire learning foundation of the literacy workshop. Direct support is given by teaching students literacy strategies that help them become more successful readers, writers, and researchers in language arts—and in other content areas (the strategies students learn for adapting their reading style to the type of text and their reason for reading also help them in their other classes).

Offering support and helping students make connections in their learning takes many different forms in our classroom. These students need a great deal of academic support in all their classes. In our language arts class, this support is provided during whole-class instruction, during shared and guided reading, as part of one-on-one guidance during independent reading and writing, and during individual conferences. The notes I take during our class activities and the journal I keep help me offer students the kind of individual and whole-group support they need to take their next steps. However, my greatest and most valid source of information about the kind of support students need comes from the students themselves.

During my second year of teaching, I realized that it wasn't enough for students to experience success in the class they had with me if they continued to fail in their other classes. Our middle school has two student "teams" in each grade level. Even though my students were not all on the same team and their content-area classes therefore varied, I knew all these classes would benefit from improved strategies and study habits. I decided to begin by asking the students to complete a "Here and Now" exercise (Kirby, Liner, and Vinz 1988): What do you find difficult in your content-area classes? What could I do to assist you in your content-area classes? Their responses follow:

Things That Are Difficult for Me

tests
difficulty understanding the teacher
the textbook
worksheets
getting along with the teacher
too many things to do at one time in class
subject is boring

Ways You Could Help Me

help me study for tests
help me understand the subject better
explain stuff to me
help me with homework
talk about the work with me
go through my work with me step by step
get me out of social studies and into art class
give me time to do homework
not have school at all
keep encouraging me
teach me to use my time properly
study with me and teach me the stuff ahead of time so I would
    already know it
show me some easier ways to do things
I can do it by myself

I wanted to help these students become proficient with all types of reading, but I didn't want to make the mistake I made during my first year of teaching. Even then I realized that part of my job was to help them become better readers in all their classes, but I spent so much time in class helping them with individual subjects and assignments that I ignored the types of reading that would hook them as readers. I was only reaffirming what my students already believed—that reading was a boring and tedious task that meant answering questions on a topic about which they had little knowledge and even less interest.

The second year, Janet and I came up with several short lessons to help students become more comfortable with their textbooks. I started spending twenty minutes each week modeling ways of reading textbooks. We talked about and worked through brief exercises on using context clues (graphics, headings, bold print), becoming familiar with vocabulary, using the index and the table of contents, and skimming and scanning. Independent literacy exploration became an important avenue through which many students got the support they needed to help them in their other classes. Some teachers let students complete their work in our class—that way, they had the extra time they needed and their classmates and I were able to help them.

A related problem for my students was their inability to get along with some of their other teachers. Their frustration at not understanding the material or not being able to complete assignments often turned into anger toward a particular teacher: why couldn't he or she give them the individual attention they needed to succeed? While I knew I couldn't solve the problems inherent to large classes, whole-group instruction, and text-driven curriculum, there were things I could tell my students about that would help them in these potentially disastrous situations. We talked about simple things like not interrupting the teacher's lecture to ask about makeup work or extra credit. We brainstormed appropriate ways and times to ask for help. We discussed finding seats where they might be more motivated to work and less distracted by friends or troublemakers. It was amazing to me that most of these students were totally unaware of the things they could do to develop good relationships with teachers so that they could get the help they needed.

While the connections that students learn to make with their peers, their teachers, and their other classes is important, the most important connection in our literacy classroom is the connection to story. Almost all readers can tell you about that first or that most significant story, about feeling that a book has been written especially for them. My students did not have that background of fond connections to books.

In order to select books that my students would connect with, I first had to find ways to connect with them. So I built time for talk into our schedule. We talked briefly each day about academic as well as personal issues, and I began to identify books that would meet them where they were. As time went by, I also used surveys, students' writing, my notes, and classroom activities as a way to discover books that might interest them.

Even after students found a great book, they still had trouble writing an authentic response to it. They were used to summarizing or merely telling me what they had read. As students searched for the right book, I searched for evidence of that connection in their writing. Students connected with books in a variety of ways: at an emotional level, at a sensory level (being caught up in suspense and action), and at an empathetic level (identifying with a character or situation). I knew when a student had found a book that was right for him or her when I read a response that moved away from summary and into something more visceral. Once that connection has been made, it is easy to help students find their next great book.

This year, I used my attendance at NCTE's fall conference to connect my students to the larger world of books. Before I left for the conference, I listed the authors whose books we had read that I was now going to be able to hear speak. I told them about the ALAN (Assembly for Literature on Adolescents) institute, and we found books by the authors who were going to speak during those two days. I told them that the main reason I was going was to learn about new books for us to read. I think some of them thought that was pretty far-fetched, especially when I asked someone to go to the map and point out where Chicago was. This got them talking about being afraid to fly. They couldn't understand taking that risk just to talk about books.

"Man, Mrs. G., you're going all the way up there just to talk about books?"

"Don't you ever get sick of reading?"

"You're not going to see the Bulls?"

I returned from Chicago the day before Thanksgiving. Since we always need to ease back into the routine when I've been gone for more than one day, I decided that this time we would talk about books. First, however, I had to listen to the injustices they had suffered at the hands of the substitute and how I had left too much work for them. Finally, they were ready to see what I had brought back from the conference. I opened the boxes and bags of books and talked about the authors I had heard and the new books I had found. As I pulled out each book, I mentioned the students I had in mind as I bought the books. We spent the entire ninety-minute class period talking about and touching the new books—probably the best and most long-lasting teaching moment of our year together.

Literacy Resources

Having the right resources in the classroom can make or break a teacher's attempt to create a literacy workshop. A variety of resources is needed to support the various student groupings as well as independent reading and writing. These resources are the fabric out of which the strategies are cut. Even when literacy skills and strategies are taught through direct instruction, they must always be embedded in a meaningful context. For example, flashback can be taught using Gary Paulsen's *Hatchet;* prediction can be taught with Lois Duncan's *I Know What You Did Last Summer;* and spelling patterns can be examined by looking closely at the words in poetry such as Shel Silverstein's *Falling Up* or Ogden Nash's *Custard & Company.*

Of all the resources in our room, the literacy resources are the most vital in hooking students as readers. Since I am a reader, I can usually find several books that I want to read in any collection of them. For struggling readers, it takes book talks, displays, films, and art to help students choose what to read. Combined with this motivation, there has to be support for the student who can't read the books he or she might choose, as well as a balanced collection so that students can explore a variety of genres, styles, and authors.

The most essential items for our class are the young adult and children's literature collections: class sets for whole-group shared reading; text sets of four, five, or six copies of a single title for guided reading and literature circles; and a wide variety of books for independent reading and writing. In addition, assisted reading is fostered through the use of recorded, unabridged books.

Building the Collection

Young adult and children's literature is the primary way I bring the joy of reading to the nonreaders in my classroom. Chapter 4 examines the types of literature, ways to invite students to read, how to determine students' reading interests, and record keeping. Here, I want to highlight literature that has been successful in our classroom for both independent and shared reading. I offer this list with the strong suggestion that if you are setting up a literacy classroom for the first time, you start with a small selection of books. Then you can add to your library as the year progresses and you get to know your students and their interests. I made many mistakes in my first orders of both recorded books and books for shared reading because I assumed higher reading levels or interests than the students had.

I started our literacy classroom with a fairly meager selection of books, most of which I had purchased in college as I thought ahead to my future English classroom. Most of the young adult titles I had, however, were more appropriate for high school than for middle school—especially middle-level struggling readers. And I had very few picture books. However, my principal had allotted a small budget for the Literacy Project's classroom library. In addition, as I told friends, colleagues, and older students about my classroom, I began receiving donations. I applied for and received a grant from our PTSA (parent-teacher-student association) for funds that helped me buy both new books and books on tape.

Several other organizations, such as local chapters of both NCTE and IRA, offer grants that help teachers establish classroom libraries. Book clubs and local bookstores are also excellent resources because they offer discounts to educators. (Bookstores are often willing to offer additional discounts for class sets.)

As Janet and I were writing this chapter of the book, I asked my students to help me develop a list of books that had been successful in our classroom. The books we have used in shared reading are highlighted in Appendix C, along with my comments on difficulty, interest, or genre. Appendix D is a similar list of titles for independent reading, this time with a notation about whether or not a recorded version is available. Students proposing titles for the list made index-card advertisements for them (see Figures 3.7 and 3.8). As students became involved in the project, they began to choose their next books for independent reading based on the recommendations of their peers.

At the beginning of the year, new students are most comfortable with books that are interesting, have relatively brief chapters, relatively large print, and some illustrations. Books for shared reading must have a lot of action, suspense, or humor to which the students can relate. When I first began teaching, I made two major mistakes: I shared books that were too difficult for the students and I read them in increments that were too long for the students' attention span. Even though shared reading allows the teacher to compensate for the difference between students' reading and

Figure 3.7 *Tabitha's recommendation for others to read R. L. Stine's* Double Date

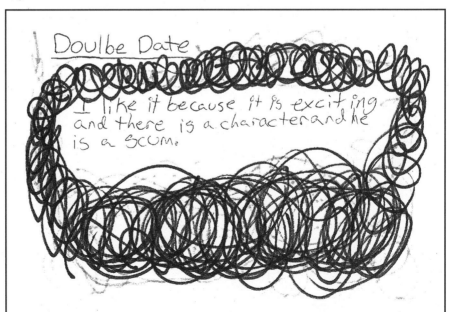

Figure 3.8 *Chanelle's advertisement for one of her favorite books*

listening vocabularies, struggling readers still need books that are not overwhelming. If the first books you choose for shared reading are too difficult, students will not be able to negotiate the physical elements of the text successfully and will miss the charm of a good story.

Storing and Displaying the Literacy Resources

In order to store our growing supply of literature, I scrounged as many bookcases as I could around the school and brought one from home. Our literature for independent reading is separated into the following categories: picture books, poetry, recorded books, young adult literature, reference materials, and magazines and comic books.

Class sets of novels for shared reading are stored in a cabinet when they are not in use. When a set is being used, they are stacked on a shelf in the classroom. At the end of each shared reading session, a student is responsible for making sure that all books have been returned to the shelf.

Displaying literature in our classroom has been a successful method for inviting students to try new books. There are several chalkboard trays in our classroom, which I use to display new books, often centered on a particular theme. I try to include picture books, young adult literature, and recorded books so that students are able to choose books both by interest and level of difficulty.

Recorded Books

Although I talk in more depth about the importance and use of recorded books in Chapter 5, I mention it here because I doubt that we would have met with the amount of literacy success we experienced in our classroom had it not been for recorded books. Recorded books allow students to experience the magic of a good book they are unable to read independently. Using unabridged recorded books as a form of assisted reading allows students simultaneously to see and hear both new words and commonly used words that may not have made it into their sight vocabulary.

While recordings of books can be costly, they are available from a variety of companies. We have used Recorded Books, Inc., almost exclusively for our titles because the recordings are high quality and unabridged. There are few things as frustrating for students (and their teachers) as tapes that do not match the books. It is difficult enough for readers who struggle with text to keep up if the recording is an exact match; if it isn't, it's almost impossible. The company also has an extremely generous exchange policy. In my first order (twelve titles), I chose books that were too far above the interest and reading levels of my students. I was able to exchange the entire order for more appropriate titles. And when tapes have been damaged or lost, a telephone call brings replacements.

The recorded books are shelved on top of the corresponding books (see Figure 3.9) so that students can quickly find both the books and the

Figure 3.9 *Some of the recorded books in Kyle's classroom library. The books and tapes are kept together.*

matching recordings. Students often base their choices for independent reading on whatever recorded books are available.

Portable Tape Players

In order to use the recorded books during independent or sustained silent reading (SSR), I needed portable tape players. These can be purchased at any department or electronic store as well as through companies like Recorded Books. I called and compared brands and prices before using the budget my principal had allotted for these purchases. I wiped out the entire budget because I decided to buy a good brand. While the tape players are a big initial expense, they are lasting resources. I purchased portable tape players (without radios) rather than tape recorders because they are truly portable and go where the students go when they read, which is not always next to a plug in the wall. Individual tape players also cut down on the distractions and allow for more choice during independent reading.

The tape players are stored in a locked cabinet when not in use, and we count them after each independent reading session. One student is in charge of the tape players each week, and no one is permitted to leave the room until they all have been accounted for. The students and I reached this decision after a few of our tape players disappeared never to return. As time passed, however, and the value of the portable tape players became clearer to the students, they were more careful about making sure that they stayed in the classroom.

Rechargeable Batteries and Chargers

In order to use the tape players most cost-effectively, we purchased rechargeable batteries and battery chargers. Again, when some of the batteries left our room and never came back, the students and I agreed that counting them at the end of each independent reading session would be the most effective way to keep track of them. Students take turns assuming this duty each week, which also includes charging the batteries. The batteries are usually left to charge overnight, and the student in charge in the morning block returns the charged batteries to storage. The batteries and chargers are stored in the cabinet when not in use.

Headphones

It might seem odd to waste space talking about headphones, but trust me—it will save you a lot of time, money, and headache to store them properly. After months of storing headphones in a bin in my cabinet and having to deal constantly with tangled and broken ones, I finally purchased small plastic hooks with adhesive backs. Hanging the headphones on these hooks preserves them. The cords don't get bent or damaged, and we always have enough to go around (see Figure 3.10).

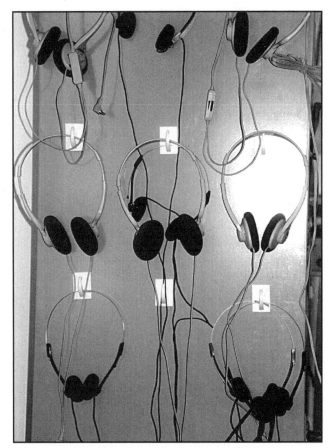

Figure 3.10 *Hanging the classroom headphones is a way to preserve them*

Art Supplies

In our classroom, we explore as many areas of literacy as possible. Art is an amazing tool for many nonreaders. As students began to make connections between art and writing that helped them with visualizing their reading, the number of art supplies we needed increased. We created a specific area of the classroom for keeping markers, crayons, paste, rubber cement, glitter, tissue paper, construction paper, scissors, and rulers. Sometimes, we all do projects together, such as the poetry projects we did with tissue-paper art after we had watched an Eric Carle video and studied the illustrations in his picture books. On other days, students use the art supplies to illustrate their writing, to work on their goals projects, or to respond to their reading. Students take turns taking inventory of art supplies, and everyone agrees to be frugal enough with them so that there will be enough to last us through the year. As any teacher might guess, the art area has prompted more than a few minutes of group meeting time: everyone's agreeing and everyone's doing are two different things. For the most part, however, the students have been responsible in this area as well, and only minor interventions have been necessary.

Reflections by Janet

Kyle and her students have negotiated the difficult territory that comes with building a community that has literacy goals at its center. It's even more difficult when a teacher has thirty or forty students in a class, but it's still possible. In classes of any size, there are community-building activities that can be done. Several books Kyle and I have used have effective strategies for building community in middle school and high school classrooms. Many of these activities can be tied to specific content areas. Four extremely effective books are *100 Ways to Enhance Self-Concept in the Classroom* (Canfield and Wells 1994); *Quicksilver: Adventure Games, Initiative Problems, Trust Activities and a Guide to Effective Leadership* (Rohnke and Butler 1995); *Tribes: A New Way of Learning Together* (Gibbs 1994); and *Communitybuilding in the Classroom* (Shaw with Kagan 1992).

As Kyle's students began to feel safe as well as successful in the classroom, she began to see changes in them. An extended community emerged in which students took advantage of the time, choices, resources, support, and connections they made use of *in* class *outside* class. In the mornings before school started, a group of five or six students from Kyle's morning and afternoon blocks began to congregate in the classroom. They came in to talk, hang out, and even read. Gradually, they started to bring in their friends so that they, too, could experience that literacy classroom.

After a while, Kyle also began having daily lunch companions in her room. Initially, Kyle had instituted lunch detention as a punishment and deterrent, but she knew it wasn't working when some of her regular detainees began requesting permission to eat lunch in her room even when they hadn't earned a detention. Two of her seventh-grade girls began bringing three or four of their friends to eat lunch each day. They were then joined by some seventh-grade boys. It was a comfortable time, a time to chat and catch up on neighborhood and school gossip: who was in love, who was planning a fight. There was also a daily argument about who was going to make a second trip to the cafeteria to get everyone dessert!

How did all of this fit with the literacy components of time, choice, support, connections, and resources to achieve a balanced literacy program? In K–5 classrooms, where students typically stay with one teacher for the entire day, much, if not all, of the balance can be seen on any given day. In our middle school literacy classrooms, we support teachers in incorporating these components into read alouds; shared, guided, and

A Typical Balanced Literacy Week (90–Minute Block)				
Monday	**Tuesday**	**Wednesday**	**Thursday**	**Friday**
IR (45 minutes)	Read-Aloud & Talk (5–10 minutes)	Read-Aloud & Talk (5–10 minutes)	Read-Aloud & Talk (5–10 minutes)	IR (45 minutes)
	Languaging			
	Shared Reading • Coaching Through Texts • Developing Literacy Strategies	Creative Drama • Poetry	Shared Reading	
	Break			
ILE (45 minutes)	• Whole-Class LEA • GW	Writing Workshop	• Whole-Class LEA—Book Log • Discussion and Sharing	ILE (45 minutes)
	• Closure—What Have You Learned? (5–10 minutes)	• Closure—What Have You Learned? (5–10 minutes)	• Closure—What Have You Learned? (5–10 minutes)	

Legend	IR = Independent Reading	GR = Guided Reading
	IW = Independent Writing	GW = Guided Writing
	SR = Shared Reading	LEA = Language Experience Activity
	SW = Shared Writing	ILE = Independent Literacy Exploration

Figure 3.11 *A sample breakdown of a week in Kyle's classroom*

independent reading and writing; and independent literacy exploration. Teachers establish a place in their weekly schedules for each of these focused yet flexible groups.

Figure 3.11 illustrates the way Kyle structured her class time of ninety minutes each day for one week. Other teachers have maintained all these strategic groupings in forty-five minute blocks. This focus allows individual, small-group, and whole-group strategic teaching and learning. These areas are illustrated in detail in other chapters in the book: reading aloud and shared reading in Chapter 4; independent reading in Chapter 5; and, shared, guided, and independent writing in Chapter 6. Independent literacy exploration (ILE) is mentioned in several chapters and discussed in terms of planning and logistics in response to one of the questions in Chapter 11.

In her book *Label-Free Learning* (1996), Charlotte Keefe states, "We must view 'appropriate education' as that which truly meets the needs of individual learners from each learner's perspective" (5). We have found that by giving students (1) the opportunity to work within both large and small groups so that they can understand how others come to create meaning from a variety of resources, (2) the time and choice to explore answers to their own questions independently, and (3) the support they each need to make connections within and across content areas, we help create independent learners. Learners who are supported in this range of learning begin to know their needs and interests and how to get help from others when necessary. This kind of education is not only appropriate but generative. On any given day, we see students move between teaching and learning in a natural way—a way that will sustain them as they transform school learning into learning for life.

Chapter 4

Reading as the Foundation for Literacy: Whole-Group Strategies

In this classroom it is fun, Mrs. G. It is helping me with reading. When we have shared reading it helps me with hard words.

Tricia

Developing Strategic Readers

The testimony of students like Tricia points up two important aspects of shared reading: readers are invited into the magic of story and at the same time learn the important concepts of story grammar (Mandler and Johnson 1977; Thorndyke 1977; Rumelhart 1977). During shared reading, readers follow along in the book as a fluent reader reads aloud to them. I do not see this as a time for traditional round-robin reading, each student reading a paragraph in turn. This is a time for students to experience the beauty of language and consistency of voice as demonstrated by a reader who has practiced reading in public. Teachers who are not comfortable reading aloud themselves often use professionally recorded books for this purpose.

As I helped Kyle plan for her students, we chose to build on the meaning-centered nature of reading by extending this shared-reading experience through whole-group strategies. Margaret Mooney (1990) finds this focus paramount: "Right from the beginning children need to understand that readers read to find out what the author is saying, and that words are only a means to that end" (28). Developing strategies that were more than "just some worksheets" (which often distract students from reading), that were tools students could use to become more independent in their own reading, was a challenge. Over time, however, we found that most of the activities we designed helped students move toward deeper understanding of concepts related to print, author's purpose, and the interactive nature of reading.

Kyle used shared reading not only to model effective literacy behavior, but also to develop and extend literacy strategies, to share successes and challenges, to help students set goals and plan for future reading, to share literature that might otherwise go unread, and to help students make critical literacy-to-life connections. As we developed these strategy lessons, we were mindful of Mooney's caution: "Any readings for attention to details of vocabulary, structure, grammar, or other specifics should not interfere with that pleasure or with the child-author interaction" (1990, 27). Therefore, we designed most strategy lessons to take place either before or after shared reading. Those few that were presented during breaks in the reading dealt with checking for understanding, helping students maintain focus and make connections, helping students manage the text conventions, and explaining concepts or words foreign to the students' backgrounds.

Prereading Focus

Prior knowledge is the raw material for "building bridges between the new and the known" (Pearson and Johnston 1978). While all students sometimes need help accommodating new concepts, it is critical for older students who are nonreaders. Assessing the relevant prior knowledge that students bring to the text as well as creating strategy lessons that will develop that knowledge when it doesn't exist can make the significant difference between saying the words and understanding the words. Kyle and I are constantly looking for ways to give students this support before they begin to read a text.

The first strategy lesson Kyle attempted centered around using prediction to establish both a connection to and a purpose for reading. William Brozo and Michelle Simpson (1995) define predictions as "hypotheses that can be confirmed, refined, extended, or rejected using evidence from the text. In this process, original predictions give way to new predictions as new information from the text is encountered, thus setting further purposes for reading" (134). Predictions allow Kyle's students to access both the surface of a text and its meaning. In this chapter, you will see how Kyle continues to use basic strategies such as prediction while developing new strategy lessons to help her students achieve deeper understanding and increase their independence. The ultimate goal of all of the strategy lessons she has created is to help students become "self-winding readers and writers" (Mooney 1988).

In the Classroom with Kyle

Choosing the Text

In my admittedly short career as a teacher working with struggling middle school readers, there are few moments more rewarding than seeing a student who once despised reading curl up in a chair, totally engrossed in a book. That sense of satisfaction is rivaled by the joy I feel when students who once disrupted shared reading plead, "*Please* don't stop reading! I want to see what happens next." Getting struggling readers hooked, usually through some form of assisted reading, is the first step toward encouraging them to value literacy. That step usually occurs when I match a reader with the right book. Margaret Mooney says that the books we share with readers should have "charm, magic, impact, and appeal," which is all well and good. But finding a book for shared reading that will appeal to an entire class of students who hate reading and often appear apathetic about school in general is very difficult.

To find books for shared reading with students in the Literacy Project, I search through professional journals, texts, and book lists (see Appendix B). I also ask for recommendations from other teachers, both those in my graduate program and those who are teaching in Literacy Project classrooms throughout the county. And, of course, I use Janet's suggestions.

When I help a student find just the right book during independent reading, I base my recommendations on what I know about the student's interests and his or her history as a learner. When choosing texts for common, shared reading, I have in mind the general interests of the students as a class and their overall learning styles and needs. I have three broad criteria for the texts I choose for us to read in common: interesting information, an intriguing story, and rich language. I want books that capture my students' interest, convey the magic of a great story, and contain the language and artistic richness that supports strategy instruction.

That first year, I found several: S. E. Hinton's *The Outsiders;* Irene Hunt's *The Lottery Rose;* Lois Duncan's *I Know What You Did Last Summer;* Katherine Paterson's *The Great Gilly Hopkins;* Walter Dean Myers's *Scorpions;* Susan Shreve's *The Flunking of Joshua T. Bates;* and Beatrice Sparks's *It Happened to Nancy.* Encountering these books in shared reading helped my students see the beauty and excitement of a great story rather than concentrate on the tedious pronunciation of difficult words. They were also able to connect the lives of others to their own lives. The young characters in these books lived lives of desperation that were all too real to the students in the Literacy Project. It was the reading hook that many of them needed.

Unfortunately, adolescents need more than a hook; they need to be taught to use the kind of strategies that competent readers employ almost without thought. They need explicit, direct modeling of when and how to apply strategies effectively, and they need support when they try to use these strategies themselves. So, while I started with and emphasized the magic of a good book, I also used a variety of shared-reading strategy lessons to help move students toward independence.

Prereading: Predicting the Text

The first book I read as shared reading was Gary Paulsen's *Hatchet*. When I asked Janet for a suggestion, she said this had been one of her students' favorite books. As she talked about the enthusiasm of her students for this book, the chapters they wanted her to read again, and the hours they spent trying to plot on a map the exact location where it takes place, I knew this was the perfect book with which to lay the foundation for reading in our classroom.

I couldn't have been more wrong. My classroom was filled with nonreaders who lived in central Florida, hundreds of miles from a cold, snowy wilderness. Although I knew they would need help understanding the situation and plot of a book set in a territory so foreign to their background, I wasn't prepared for the negative attitudes that prevailed even before we began reading.

"Okay. What do you do when you first start a new book?" My question was met with laughter and a few unhelpful comments.

"We don't read books!"

"If you gave me a book, I'd throw it across the room."

Clearly, no one was willing to risk answering my question. They were still excited because I let them sit on the floor; who cared about reading?

"Why don't you look at the cover of the book. What do you see on the cover that might give you a clue to what the book's about?"

The somewhat abstract cover elicited some response; however, no one in the room knew what a hatchet was, so the title was of little help. Here are the predictions ventured by the class of fifteen students:

1. A boy going camping in the woods
2. Plane-crash survival
3. Lost
4. Committed suicide
5. Hatchet
6. Wolf howling, danger of being killed
7. He killed himself with a hatchet

The entire lesson seemed a flop. The kids didn't want to read this book and fought doing so from day one. Finally, I had to admit the book was not meeting my first goal—that students enjoy reading it—and I decided to abandon the text and show the movie version, *Cry in the Wild*, instead. I felt like a failure and was sure my students had learned nothing from my feeble attempt to share a really good book and at the same time help them see the importance of prediction in reading. Inadvertently, however, I had taught them a valuable lesson: readers sometimes abandon a book that doesn't meet their needs and purposes at the time. This is one of the tenets in Daniel Pennac's "The Reader's Bill of Rights" in his book *Better Than Life* (1994). This was small consolation at the time.

I was therefore understandably surprised and elated when I noticed many of the students making predictions before they started reading their books during independent reading (Constance's prediction in Figure 4.1 is only one of many). It was a good lesson for me: the ultimate suc-

Figure 4.1 *Constance's prediction before reading Jon Scieszka's* Knights of the Kitchen Table

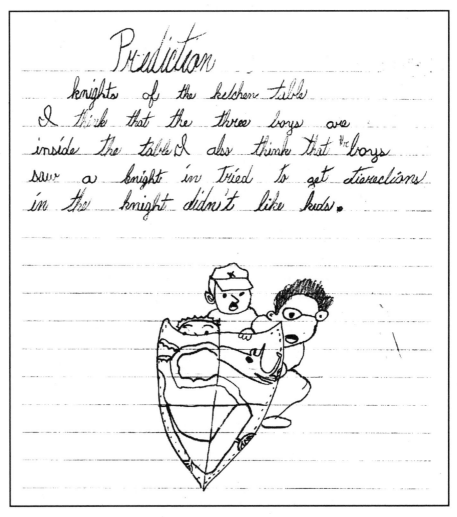

cess of any strategy lesson is that once students know when and how to use the strategy, it helps them read a new book. In future shared reading that more appropriately met my students where they were, we continued to use prediction as a before-reading strategy and talked about how what we find out when we read the book confirms or disproves our predictions.

I had fallen into the trap of believing that children would learn only what I taught and that we would all know what I thought I was teaching. It was a shock (and a wonderful surprise) for me to realize that learners can learn not only what you didn't intend, but also what you couldn't have imagined. The lesson has served me well.

Using K-W-L to Establish a Purpose for Reading

I read *It Happened to Nancy,* edited by Beatrice Sparks, as a shared text with my seventh and eighth graders near the end of our second year together. I was a bit hesitant about reading the book, because it deals with the date rape of a fourteen-year-old girl, Nancy, who then contracts the AIDS virus. When I initially mentioned the book to my students at the beginning of the year, the response had been extremely positive—not a surprise, since to them the book was about *sex.* Much to my students' displeasure, I decided to wait until the end of the year to read the book, because it focused on such heavy issues. I was beginning to realize that book choice is not only about content but also about timing. While my students had certainly far surpassed the reading levels with which they began that disastrous reading of *Hatchet,* I wanted to build more strategies as a reading community so that the challenging format (nonfiction, diary entries, little action, erratic time sequencing, and focus on thought/reflections) would not detract from the book's important message. I also wanted to have as much time as possible to build a safe classroom environment in which such significant social problems could be discussed.

I suspected that the students' knowledge of AIDS was limited and perhaps incorrect, so I decided to implement a prereading strategy that would reveal not only the information—and misinformation—they already had but also their questions about the disease, which would help them establish individual and group purposes for reading the book. The K-W-L technique (Ogle 1986; see Appendix A.9) allows students and teacher to brainstorm what students already *know* (K), determine what they *want to know* (W), and document what they've *learned* (L). Preparing a K-W-L chart gives individual readers the benefit of the larger body of knowledge held by the entire class and lets the teacher know what additional resources and support might be needed for the students to read the book successfully. It helps both students and teacher focus.

Of course, the students were eager to begin the novel and weren't thrilled with the prospect of first having to do something other than read. While that was a refreshing attitude, I tried to convince them there was an issue we needed to discuss before we began reading.

"What?" Jermaine eyed me suspiciously.

"Well, I want you all to think about what you know about AIDS."

"God!"

"AIDS. We know all about that. That monkey from Africa brought it over here," Corian declared with a knowing smile. I was suddenly very grateful we were doing this.

"Okay, look at the chart you have in front of you. Do you see the three columns? Look at the first one, labeled 'Known.' I'd like you to write down everything that you know about AIDS under this column. Ignore the other columns for right now."

"Can we work with someone else?" Jermaine asked.

"Of course. When you've listed as much as you can think of, we'll take some time to put your responses on the board." As I walked around the room, looking over shoulders, I listened to a snippet of conversation between Corian and Jermaine:

CORIAN: I want to know when they brought that monkey over from
    Africa to bite people. That's what spreaded AIDS and chicken pox,
    too.
JERMAINE (*laughing at Corian's agitation*): Man, you get it from sexually
    transmitted stuff and other people's needles.

After about five minutes, we were ready to share responses and have a discussion. Carl stood at the board, Corey and Corian were stationed at computers, all three ready to record the group's responses.

"Okay, who feels comfortable sharing what they know about AIDS?" Jermaine, of course, was ready to begin. Assuming the stance that preceded his long-winded answers and usually brought him both attention and laughter, he surprised us by saying only one word: "Sex."

While his response elicited the sought-after giggles and comments from the class, it also opened the door for other comments:

1 Sex
2. Using/sharing needles
3. Fighting/someone scratches you and has AIDS
4. It kills you
5. If someone has AIDS and bites your skin and breaks it
6. Does not hurt you
7. You can't get it by having contact with someone
8. I know it's a virus
9. Started by a monkey
10. You might get it from sex

The responses went unchallenged by other class members until Anthony said, "If you is fighting someone and they has AIDS and they scratch you and you can get it." While several students questioned the truth of that statement, no one had the knowledge to really argue the point with him. When another student offered that you can get AIDS if someone who has AIDS bites you, it looked as though these might be areas in which students had enough interest to do some research.

After everyone had an opportunity to share what they knew about AIDS, I asked them to think about what they wanted to know about AIDS. As soon as I said, "Take a few minutes to really think about some questions regarding AIDS that you'd like to have answered," the pencils began moving. Our discussion about what students knew had prompted lots of questions.

When everyone had finished, we again shared our responses:

1. When are those stupid scientists that we're paying our tax money going to find a cure?
2. How do they say the monkey started it?
3. Can you get AIDS from mosquitoes?
4. Can you get it from kissing?
5. How did it start?
6. Why?
7. Nothing
8. Are they going to find a cure?

We discussed these questions, and students attempted to answer them. Then I asked them to circle, on their individual K-W-L charts, the number one thing they knew as true about AIDS and the number one question that they wanted answered. I planned to use their circled responses/ questions as the basis for their research as we got further into the book.

Using Chapter Mapping as Reading Support

Soon into my first shared reading, I realized that my students definitely needed some help, both in sorting through all the words to find the themes and patterns and in recalling events and characters well enough to tie the segments together. They were having an extremely difficult time following the text as I read. Perhaps because they concentrated so on following along (those who attempted to do so, at any rate), they had a hard time distilling the chapter's significant events, character development, or memorable language and settings. Although they seemed to enjoy the language and the story, I had trouble getting a focused response. Their random bits of information and misinformation made our discussion somewhat nonproductive.

I went to Janet with my problem. As she and I talked, it occurred to us that perhaps the many years of completing worksheets and end-of-story questions, combined with labored reading, had made these students relatively incapable of synthesizing individual events into a whole story. Indeed, we had both found that these kinds of students had relatively little experience with longer texts. As their reading floundered, they had typically been given shorter and shorter texts and asked to answer simple, fact-based questions when they had finished.

Then Janet told me about chapter mapping (Armbruster and Anderson 1980). Here's how it works. The teacher gives each student a sheet of paper with empty boxes drawn on it, one for each chapter (see Figure 4.2). Then, after reading each chapter, she asks the students to use one of the boxes to illustrate what they feel are the most important aspects of the chapter. The teacher also asks the students to title each chapter, even if it already has one. This strategy not only enables students

Figure 4.2 *A chapter map form used to help students with comprehension*

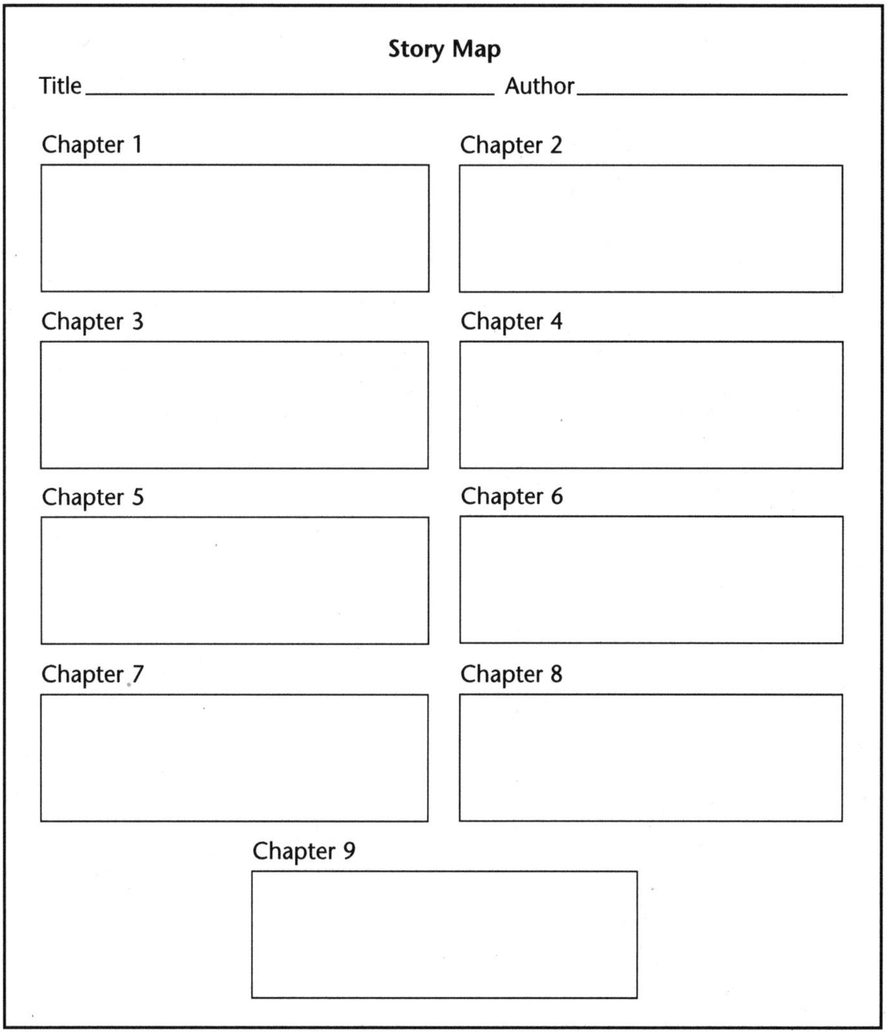

Story Map

Title _____ Author _____

Chapter 1

Chapter 2

Chapter 3

Chapter 4

Chapter 5

Chapter 6

Chapter 7

Chapter 8

Chapter 9

to begin recalling people or events from a story, it also allows the teacher to get immediate feedback about each student's comprehension.

The next day, I modeled chapter mapping on the overhead. I asked students to tell me the most significant parts of the chapter we had read the day before. Everyone had an opportunity not only to recall the previous day's reading from their own perspective, but also to hear what other members of the class had found significant. I realized the importance of titling each chapter when I listened to them trying to come to a consensus—the depth of their discussion was amazing. It was the perfect time to explain that while we were working as a group on a map for yesterday's chapter, from now on each of them would create an individual chapter map for each day's reading.

From then on, each day after we finished shared reading, I gave my students several minutes to complete a chapter map. Early on the students complained that the spaces on the preconstructed map I was using weren't big enough. They began dividing letter-sized pages into quarters and using a quarter of a page for each chapter. (Figure 4.3 is a chapter map Constance did for Jon Scieszka's *Knights of the Kitchen Table*.) Several days later, I began asking for volunteers to come up to the overhead and draw their chapter maps. Surprisingly, this became a coveted activity each day, and I was again struck by the richness of the other students' questions. Our talk led us all to a deeper understanding of the text.

Learning from My Mistakes

When a new group of sixth graders entered the Literacy Project in its second year, I didn't want to make the mistake I had made with *Hatchet*. Near the end of the first year, when I had finally managed to find several books they liked, I asked my students to tell me what made a good book. Here's what they said: the book shouldn't be too long; the chapters should be short; the print shouldn't be too big or too small; there should be some pictures; it should sound like real people; and it should have interesting stuff in it.

When Janet suggested Susan Shreve's *The Flunking of Joshua T. Bates*, I read it and realized that it had many of the characteristics on my students' list. As a bonus, I knew my students would sympathize with Joshua because they had so much in common with him. (At the end of my first year of teaching, Irene Hunt's *The Lottery Rose* had been a great success in part because the students identified with Georgie and could sympathize with his conflicts and problems.)

In *The Flunking of Joshua T. Bates*, the title character has failed third grade because his reading skill is not what his teachers think it should be. Joshua, however, feels differently about why he failed. He believes that his old teachers hate third graders, especially boys. In addition to its obvious connection to the lives of the students in our class (many of them had repeated a grade in elementary school), this book offers the kind of

Figure 4.3 *Constance's chapter maps for our shared reading of* Knights of the Kitchen Table

support my students said they needed. It has short chapters, pictures, and reasonably sized print; it's interesting; and it's not too long. They also empathized with Joshua's hatred of school and the torment he suffered at the hands of a bully named Tommy Wilhelm. Unfortunately, my students had encountered many Tommy Wilhelms in their lives.

The class quickly became engrossed in Joshua's life, and the solid literacy strategies they were developing, like chapter mapping, helped them with books they were reading independently. I was also learning how to use chapter maps to help me understand students' comprehension. After I looked at the maps, the students and I would discuss the traditional skills of finding the main idea, sequencing, cause and effect, summarizing, and inference.

Constance was one of the students who connected with Joshua the most. She loved to draw, but her talent had not served her well in terms of success in school. Chapter mapping became a way for her to showcase that talent and for me to build on the success she was experiencing to help her become a confident and competent reader.

Constance's chapter mapping of *The Flunking of Joshua T. Bates* (see Figure 4.4) showed that she not only had internalized the significant events in the chapters that had a lot of action, but also was able to articulate the essence of chapters that focused on Joshua's thoughts and feelings. She titled the first chapter, "When his mother told him that he feld." Joshua is surround by taunting voices: "You are going to the therd grade class...ha, ha," and "You feiled." In the second chapter, she illustrates more of Joshua's feelings of despair. Then in Chapter 3, when Joshua's frustration drives him to deck Tommy Wilhelm, his tormentor, Constance depicts a triumphant Joshua saying, "I won," while the bully is crying on the ground saying, "I can't breathe."

It was obvious that Constance had connected with Joshua, and that connection continued throughout the book. By looking at her chapter maps, Constance was able to retell the entire story. She had experienced the success of retelling in an environment that supported her success. Hazel Brown and Brian Cambourne (1990, 32) list the following environmental characteristics as contributing to successful retelling: social interaction, unpressured situations, an understandable purpose, role perception, and a risk-free setting. In addition, chapter maps and retellings became significant for me as ways to determine a book's readability and interest level.

I also found that chapter mapping helped students develop the ability to imagine while reading—a habit of mind they had never learned. Karen Ernst notes the value of this in her book *Picturing Learning* (1993): "Through reading literature...students learned how pictures and written language work together" (59). I was able to use chapter maps to teach the concept that language creates images in the mind and that these images can differ for each person depending not only on her or his reading of the text but also on the life experiences she or he brings to the book. Students began to internalize that readers both transform and are transformed by the books they read (Rosenblatt 1976).

Again, reading this book brought a benefit I had not anticipated. At the beginning of our reading, I worried that the negative attitudes Joshua had toward reading and school might reinforce the negative attitudes my students already had. And at first, that was exactly what happened.

Figure 4.4 *Some of Constance's chapter maps for* The Flunking of Joshua T. Bates

However, it was therapeutic for students to relate, in our discussions and in their writing, events in their lives that were similar to what happened to Joshua (see Figure 4.5). And while Constance and many of the other students initially connected with Joshua's failure, as Joshua became more successful, they also connected to that success. The literary image of Joshua's reading success was mirrored in the success they were experiencing in our classroom.

As the students progressed in shared reading, chapter mapping became less critical. For example, seventh and eight graders who were in their second year of the Literacy Project had a class meeting and decided they didn't need to do chapter mapping for our last shared reading of the year, *It Happened to Nancy*. While they all agreed that chapter mapping had really helped, they felt that "now that we're readers" it was unnecessary. I knew they'd made the strategy their own.

Figure 4.5 *Corey's response after we began reading* The Flunking of Joshua T. Bates

Understanding Characters

Creating images of scenes or events is an expression of a mental model (Johnson-Laird 1983; Sanford and Garrod 1981; van Dijk and Kintsch 1983). I think that's one reason children's picture books were such a hit in my classroom. The beautiful illustrations gave my students a mental model they were often unable to create for themselves because they were struggling with the words. Creating a mental model of a character requires even higher levels of inference. D. G. Morrow (1985) showed that readers actively construct mental models that reflect information relevant to the main characters. Students who are poor readers and avid television viewers have had little experience with creating mental images of characters independently. I knew that my students would need some help with understanding characters and their motivations.

When I discussed this with Janet, she suggested a graphic organizer as a starting place for helping students visualize characters. Textbook supplements and professional books are full of graphic organizers, but the one I found most useful is the stickman, which had been given to Janet by a teacher at a conference. Using the stickman strategy gives my students the opportunity to discuss a character by looking at categories: ideas, visions/hopes, feelings, what she or he did, strengths, and weaknesses (see Appendix A.8). I decided to use the stickman to help students look at Georgie, the main character in *The Lottery Rose.*

I gave everyone a blank copy of the stickman chart and placed a transparency of the form on the overhead. I decided to start with weaknesses, because during the reading so many students condemned Georgie for not defending himself against Steve, his abuser. They seemed to have a great deal of difficulty acknowledging that Georgie was physically incapable of defending himself against an adult. When I asked them what they would have done if they were six, Georgie's age, instead of their current ages, eleven to fifteen, they still could not comprehend Georgie's dilemma.

"I'd kick his butt!"

"I'd tear him up!"

"Man, Georgie was a wuss...what he doing letting that man beat on him like that?"

"He crazy. Why don't he tell somebody on that man?"

Then I asked the students to list what they thought Georgie's weaknesses were and write them on the weakness section of the stickman chart. Corey's chart (see Figure 4.6) is representative of the rest of the class. The first weakness he noted was that Georgie couldn't defend himself. Since Steve had threatened to kill Georgie if he told anyone what Steve did to him and Georgie's mother continually reminded Georgie of Steve's threat, I was curious why the students couldn't see Georgie's dilemma. They insisted, as Corey noted on his stickman, that he should have told someone. Perhaps some of these students were all too aware of

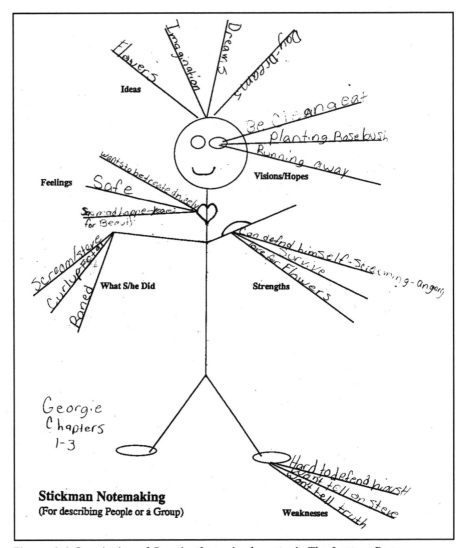

Figure 4.6 *Corey's view of Georgie, the main character in* The Lottery Rose

the dilemma of a six-year-old child who is being abused; they could finally be angry for Georgie.

When we moved on to Georgie's strengths, Corey agreed with some
of the other students that Georgie could defend himself against Steve in
one way: by screaming in terror whenever he saw Steve. Corey did point
out, however, that Georgie's screams only infuriated Steve and brought
more beatings. His other strengths, his love of flowers and surviving,
bring home Georgie's pitiful life.

At this point, I should have stopped. The students were having a difficult time with the chart, and each person's contribution was being dis-

cussed at length. They were restless and frustrated, and the magic of the story was quickly disappearing. As we worked through the remaining categories, the students became increasingly less interested. By the time we finished, I felt the strategy had been a failure. The students certainly gave no indication that they found using a graphic organizer a useful tool for their prewriting. In retrospect (I often think this is how the best teaching is done), I realized the activity should have been completed in pieces over several days and that I should have let the true responses of the students come through.

Even though I felt the strategy hadn't worked that day, I decided to try it again, this time with a video. Using the stickman chart with *Miracle on 34th Street* turned out to be a great success. Ironically, this time, rather than boredom, there was a volatile argument between the seventh graders who still believed in Santa Claus and those who didn't. I had to break up some potentially dangerous verbal conflicts and remind the class that we had to respect each other's beliefs even when they were different.

The subject of Ruth's chart (see Figure 4.7) was Susan, the central character, who does not believe in Santa Claus. She completed it with a great deal of ease compared to her previous attempt. I wondered if perhaps the immediate mental image the video provided helped Ruth move on to descriptions and inferences. I found especially interesting Ruth's including as a strength Susan's ability to ask for things from Santa even though she did not believe in him. There are hundreds of students in our classrooms who continue to come to school, asking for something —anything—from a system in which they seem to have no faith. Perhaps, like Susan, they believe just enough so that they can't give up.

Using this strategy was another learning experience for me as well. Although my purpose in using the stickman with a popular shared-reading novel had been sound, I had not given the students the support they needed to make the transition from literal answers to those requiring abstract thinking about inferences, cause and effect, and character analysis. Teaching the strategy in the context of something with fewer challenges— a short story, video clip, or television sitcom—allows students to transfer the strategy to shared and independent reading.

Postreading: Text Highlighting

When I became a teacher, I hoped that great literature would generate honest and thoughtful responses from my students simply because it was great. The reality was something else entirely. Either students were too intimidated to say anything that had to do with reading or they used their standard responses: This is dumb. This is boring.

In classes I took with Janet at the university, she had said that creating and maintaining productive discussions are one of the most difficult tasks that teachers face. After only a few weeks in the classroom, I couldn't have agreed more. When I asked for questions or comments about the

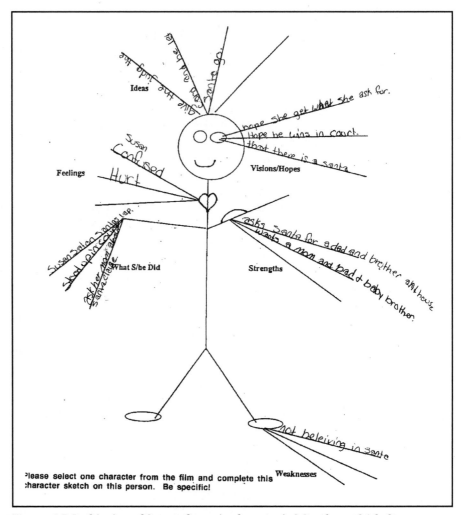

The figure contains the following handwritten and printed labels:

Ideas

Feelings

Susan
Confused
Hurt

Visions/Hopes

hope she get what she ask for.
Hope he wins in court.
that there is a santa

asks santa for a dad and brother and house.
wants a mom and dad & baby brother.

What S/he Did

Strengths

Please select one character from the film and complete this character sketch on this person. Be specific!

Weaknesses

not beleiving in santa

Figure 4.7 *Ruth's view of Susan, the main character in* Miracle on 34th Street

reading, dead silence usually followed or I had to prompt them so much that they ended up telling me what they thought I wanted to hear. Aidan Chambers (1996) calls this the "teacher-dictated model....It is about the readers discovering the book the teacher wants them to find rather than cooperative talk in which a community of readers make discoveries far beyond anything they could have found on their own" (69). After a whole a year of frustrating discussions, I knew I had fallen victim to that teacher-dictated model and needed to find a way to restructure the postreading time in our classroom.

Chambers designed a strategy called *highlighting* to help book talk become student rather than teacher directed. Highlighting is described in detail in his book *Tell Me: Children, Reading, and Talk* (1996), which I highly recommend. Basically, students are asked to respond to a book in four categories: likes, dislikes, puzzles, and patterns. After students have entered at least one item in each of the categories on their individual highlighting forms, the teacher (or the students) use an overhead projector, word processor, or a chalkboard to record the replies of the entire class in each of the categories (see Figure 4.8). After the responses of everyone in the class have been recorded, students look at the chart and draw lines to and from items that are repetitive across the categories (see Figure 4.9). The students are thus able to identify recurrent responses to the book and generate topics for class discussion. The items with the most lines drawn to them are the ones the students have the greatest interest in and/or the most questions about and are discussed first.

There were two days left in the year, we had just finished *The Lottery Rose,* and I knew that discussing it would be a struggle. Most of the students were reluctant to say anything aloud in class for fear of being laughed at. The few vocal students therefore dominated any discussion. The students had enjoyed *The Lottery Rose,* in part because Georgie, the

Figure 4.8 *Ruth recording what students liked about* The Lottery Rose

Figure 4.9 *Joey indicating for students items that are repeated in more than one column*

main character, had suffered some of the same physical and emotional abuse they had suffered. They also really identified with Georgie's hatred of school and his lack of success. Some of the students had actually cheered during our shared reading when it became evident that Georgie might have been responsible for setting a fire under his first-grade teacher's car! They nodded and made angry comments when Miss Cressman forced Georgie to read aloud and then permitted other students to humiliate Georgie when he couldn't. It was obvious that similar events had taken place in the academic lives of many of these students. However, as I knew from experience, students' liking a book did not mean there would be a successful discussion of it. When Janet suggested that perhaps this was the time to try text highlighting, I was game. I devised a simple organizer that students could use to record their brief responses in each of the categories (see Figure 4.10).

I tried to build on the momentum of the book's ending by explaining that we were going to try something new. The students grumbled a bit, claiming that other teachers—smart teachers—had stopped making them work because the year was over, but they showed less hesitation than I had anticipated. As always, I told them why I was using the strategy: I wanted to know what they thought about the book, I wanted them to hear what others in the room thought, and I wanted all of us to realize that we can learn new things about what we think by talking about our ideas. As I began to draw the chart on the board, however, the groans and panicked questions began in earnest.

Figure 4.10 *The organizer students use to record their individual responses at the beginning of the text highlighting strategy*

Likes	Dislikes	Puzzles "I wonder if... "	Patterns

"What is she making us do now?"

"What's a puzzle?"

"What do dislike mean?"

After I had answered those questions, the one big question remaining was, "You mean we have to talk out loud?" Todd groaned the loudest, until I told him that he had to put his opinions down but that he didn't have to share them unless he wanted to. The only time Todd had ever shared his opinion during the entire year was to tell me just how dumb the books and activities were.

Once we started, the students had few problems listing their likes and dislikes. When it came to puzzles, however, they were stymied. Janet was in the room that day and suggested that students complete that category by saying to themselves, "I wonder." This worked, because they had wondered a good deal about some of the things that had taken place in the book. I told them to ignore the patterns category for right now. The responses under each category varied greatly, but they were incredible indicators of their personal reactions to the book. When several students began to question not only why Georgie was abused but why abuse happens, I knew they had actually been thinking as they listened to the book.

I was surprised by how eager the students were to have their responses written on the board. It was as if their opinions became important because they had been written on the board for everyone to see. Once all the other responses were on the board, I returned to the patterns category. Did anyone know what a pattern was? It was clear from their responses that I had been wise to leave this category for us to work through together.

"What you cut clothes from."

"Something you trace."

Since students needed to see pattern as repetition, I glanced around the room for a concrete example. Carl's shirt was made from a patterned fabric, and I asked Jermaine to describe it.

"It's got a whole bunch of triangles and squares."

When I asked him what he meant by "a whole bunch," he looked at me as if I were crazy and then very patronizingly explained that a whole bunch was more than one. Success. I then asked if they saw anything else in the room that had "whole bunches" of something, and someone quickly pointed out another shirt, this one striped. Someone else mentioned the border around the walls of the room, which depicted people reading. When students had a concrete definition of repetition or pattern in their heads, I asked them to transfer the concept to *The Lottery Rose*.

"Do you see anything in the book that happened more than one time?"

Tabitha raised her hand and pointed to the first response under the likes category, which was, "He's brave." She explained that she saw a pattern between that entry and "When he showed Timothy his back." I drew a line from the first to the second "like" on our list.

"Does anyone else see anything connected to Georgie's bravery in any of the other categories?" After Ruth said it was brave when Georgie gave Robin his rosebush, others students quickly began identifying patterns of Georgie's bravery.

The students then identified other patterns they saw. For the first time all year, everyone participated. My role had changed; where before I had tried to elicit "right" answers from students, I was now truly facilitating effective brainstorming, thoughtful responses, and purposeful discussion. I saw to it that comments were offered in an orderly way so that they could be recorded, I helped students clarify meaning, and I made sure that everyone had a voice. When the brainstorming of patterns began to slow down, I prompted the students to move on to the discussion phase of text highlighting.

"Tell me which pattern seems to have happened the most?"

They immediately made the connection between Georgie's getting beaten, and anger and hate. Interestingly, Todd, who had protested most about both this strategy and the reading of the book, became the discussion leader. I couldn't believe how much he had been affected by this book. Had I tried any other method of assessment, whether traditional or alternative, I would have gotten his this-is-stupid response. Today he had a comment about every pattern listed and backed up those comments by referring to events in the book. One of the patterns he mentioned was Georgie's attempts to plant his rosebush. He said the rosebush was the only secure thing in Georgie's life. "It was something he could depend on—it was a source of love. Everywhere he went, the rosebush went." He also said he thought Paul, Mrs. Harper's son who had been killed in a car accident, was a symbol for Georgie because of the connections he saw between Georgie and Paul. At one point, he even moved to the board to make sure the recorder of the moment was getting down all of the class responses!

Our discussion continued for the entire class period. It was rich, both in content and in participation. I was impressed and amazed not only by the number of details from the book students were recalling, but also at how they were reading between and beyond the lines. As the discussion began to slow down, many of the students were still staring at their thoughts, which covered the entire wall of our whiteboard. Finally, Corey broke the short silence: "You know, we should draw a picture of an ice cube melting to show how Georgie was changing. It would show how he used to hate everybody, but all that's changing." It was a perfect image for this book—a perfect image for our year together.

Reflections by Janet

At the end of class the day they discussed *The Lottery Rose,* I told Kyle's students how impressed I was with their thoughtful comments about this wonderful book. I mentioned that even my high school students had struggled with parts of the highlighting strategy when I had read the book with them. They were basking in my praise, and then Joey said, "Yeah, we're gifted."

Kyle's use of whole-group strategies to extend the shared reading of a variety of books built on the strength of talk and collaborative learning. Students learned to use a variety of strategies to help them not only during shared reading but also during independent reading. In all cases, we were able to see the strategies transferred to other learning, not only in Kyle's class but also in their content classes. Their confidence also improved. Students who had been silent found their voices. Students whose voices had been strident and angry found other ways to express their opinions. Students learned to listen to and respect the opinions of others, and they learned the strength of the community and the individuals within the community. Fortunately for Kyle's students, all of this was done within the context of captivating literature. They left that year of classes knowing, at least in part, the truth of Robert McCammon's words in *Boy's Life* (1991):

> It seemed to me at an early age that all human communication begins with somebody wanting to tell a story. That need to tell, to plug into a universal socket, is probably one of our grandest desires. And the need to hear stories, to live lives other than our own for even the briefest moment, is the key to the magic that was born in our bones. (33)

Perhaps it is finding the magic that is in our bones that helps each of us find the ways in which we're gifted.

Chapter 5

Can't We Please Just Read? Independent Reading in the Literacy Workshop

Some books are to be tasted, others to be swallowed, and some few to be chewed and digested; that is, some books are to be read only in parts; others to be read, but not curiously; and some few to be read wholly, and with diligence and attention.

Francis Bacon

For many of us, the joy of finding the right book and the time to settle in and read is one of life's sweetest pleasures. Depending on how busy we are, we usually find at least some time to taste a new book, and sometimes we simply lose ourselves in one. Few have described this activity as beautifully as Victor Nell does in *Lost in a Book* (1988):

> Reading for pleasure is an extraordinary activity. The black squiggles on the white page are still as the grave, colorless as the moonlit desert; but they give the skilled reader a pleasure as acute as the touch of a loved body, as rousing, colorful, and transfiguring as anything out there in the real world. (1)

I've met many reading addicts who would certainly agree. They, like me, have stacks of books near their beds, lists of books to buy, and the ever-present paperback tucked away in purses or car consoles just in case they get caught somewhere with a few minutes to read. Time to read is and always has been a precious commodity in my life. I learned early in life the truth of Bette Greene's words in *The Drowning of Stephan Jones* (1991): "Inside every good book is a secret" (23).

Unfortunately, many of the students sitting in our classrooms have yet to experience the mystery or the pleasure of a good book. One of my students summed up her experiences with books in a letter to her middle

60

school teacher, experiences that are in direct contrast with Nell's words
and my experience:

> I'd like to tell you what happened with my reading. I was given
> reading assignments. I was told to read <u>this</u> book and I found no
> intrest in your books. They were boring with a big B! And what
> made it worse, you gave me a surtin time to do it, and I couldn't
> get it done.

When teaching and learning with students who feel this way about books,
one of our most critical tasks as middle-level teachers is helping them have
the kind of experiences with books that will entice them to further reading. Independent reading is that time during the day when students make
their own choices about what they will read, when the teacher gives the
support needed for readers to have successful experiences with the books
they have chosen, and when students take the time to enjoy the reading
experience. It is also a time when teachers can steal a few minutes to read
books themselves, perhaps ones students have recommended.

In Kyle's classroom, independent reading is several protected blocks
of time each week in which students read books they have chosen (see
Figure 3.11 in Chapter 3). Research supporting the advantages of such
extended opportunities with books is clear. In 1984, Richard Allington
stated that the amount of independent, silent reading that students do in
school is significantly related to gains in reading achievement. The
authors of *Becoming a Nation of Readers* (Anderson et al. 1985) found that
independent reading influences reading fluency. W. E. Nagy, P. A.
Herman, and R. C. Anderson (1985) state that independent reading is a
major source of vocabulary growth. If we connect these significant findings to L. C. Fielding, P. T. Wilson, and R. C. Anderson's research (1986)
showing that for the majority of students, reading from books occupies
only one percent or less of their free time, we see how critical it is to build
time into each school day for independent reading. While designating
time for independent reading is the necessary first step, many other components contribute to making that time productive—as we will see.

In the Classroom with Kyle

From Vision to Reality

I remember sitting as a quiet undergraduate in Janet's adolescent literature class. When my classmates and I saw the syllabus, we were convinced that either she was insane or she *really* knew what she was doing.
When I had finished reading the fifty required novels, I realized I had
begun to renew the love of reading I had somehow lost as I droned
through my undergraduate core classes. I also began to see the value of

books that meet students where they are. I took those beliefs with me when I began my first job as a middle school language arts teacher in Orange County's Literacy Project.

I felt totally prepared to implement a successful independent reading program. After all, I was armed with what I considered to be a pretty impressive knowledge of books. I had a growing collection of young adult books, some cast-off chairs, and a love of reading I was sure would be contagious. My only challenge would be providing an ever-changing collection of books. As I looked around my classroom the day before classes began, I was pleased. I saw the comfortable chairs, the big bookcase filled with books, the crate of books on tape, the Walkmans and rechargeable batteries, and thought smugly, Who wouldn't read with all this great stuff?

Our first day of sustained silent reading (SSR) was an eye-opener: my students were neither sustained nor silent, and they certainly had no intention of reading. Perhaps things might have been different if I had had a class of twenty readers and three or four nonreaders. Maybe then I could have managed to give the three or four nonreaders individual attention while the others settled in with their books. In my classroom, however, there were fifteen nonreaders. Fifteen students who all hated reading *and* school and found it highly entertaining to watch me run around like a maniac, trying to cajole them to read. I conducted interest surveys. I interviewed them. I scribbled lists of prospective books for each student. I was pleased when they showed some excitement about the Walkmans, then disappointed when I realized they were only interested in the radios they assumed were built into them. The magic did not happen. Sustained silent reading became a battle zone.

My students made no attempt to browse the wonderful collection of books I had gathered. (My days of pondering how to categorize the books had certainly been time wasted.) While a few of the students deigned to take the books I handed them, most were quick to tell me that the books were too long or too ugly or too boring. I was afraid that if I heard the word *boring* one more time, I would lose control.

The logistics of managing the classroom during SSR became increasingly nightmarish. When I attempted to have a conference with one student, five or six others would begin talking and disrupt the one or two who were actually trying to read. Reprimands and requests to wait quietly until I had time to help them triggered further disruption. Each day I thought, There has got to be a better way! When I finally stopped resenting the students for not stepping silently and gratefully into the beautiful SSR picture I had painted for myself and began listening to what the students were telling me, we began to find that better way.

I took as the foundation for that better way the "nos" that had been such a big part of my students' and my negotiations:

1. No books that are too long
2. No books without illustrations

3. No books that have small print
4. No old, tattered-looking books
5. No books without tapes
6. No boring books
7. No distractions during SSR (i.e., using the computer, writing, talk-ing, moving around)
8. No unfair treatment when someone breaks the rules

I discovered that many of the young adult novels and the recorded books that I had ordered were far too difficult for the students in our lit-eracy workshop. Anything that looked suspiciously long, even if it had an accompanying tape, was automatically rejected. I found that I needed more children's books, and I definitely needed more recorded books. If a student expressed interest in a book that wasn't available on tape, I took the book home and recorded it myself.

I had avoided most children's books because I thought students would see them as an insult. I purchased some Caldecott winners and a few that targeted older readers, but ignored traditional picture books. The students quickly proved the error of that thinking.

Seventh graders Anthony and Jason had initially given me problems, but things began to change when they fell in love with the oversized Disney books. After talking with them and realizing that they really were captivated by these classics, I offered to take the books home and read them on tape. Listening to these tapes was the first time either of them had been actively engaged during independent reading. It was also the first time that they had sat quietly, not disrupting others who were try-ing to read. They enjoyed not only the sound of my voice on the tape but the background noises as well—my dog Gonzo barking or the telephone ringing. For Jason and Anthony, the tapes were the bridge from shared reading to independent reading.

Books without illustrations were definitely too threatening for most of my students when they first entered our class. Some of the students would literally grimace when I offered them a book that contained only print: "Nah...that looks boring!" The thickness of the book and the appearance of the cover were what determined acceptance or rejection. It had never occurred to me the physical appearance of a book was so important to a nonreader. My students also quickly rejected some of the older books that were in poor condition: "This junk is ugly!" Once I real-ized that the external attributes of a book were critical, I was able to make better choices in the books I bought for our classroom collection.

Classroom Atmosphere

Distraction was a major hindrance during sustained silent reading. Class during those first weeks more often than not bordered on chaos. Some students struggled to find books with my help. Others complained loudly that they couldn't find the page numbers. A few brave souls actually tried to read in spite of the noise and arguments of those who were still not connecting with books. I knew that if I wanted to cut down on the distractions in the room and give students the kind of assistance they needed to help them move forward, I needed to develop some effective organizational strategies. I started keeping a weekly log (see Figure 5.1) noting the book each student was reading, the number of pages read during each SSR time, and the student's behavior. I asked students who were reading with the support of books on tape (assisted reading) to tell me the tape number and side of the tape they were working on at the end of class. I even asked a few students to write down the last sentence they had read. Before I started using this simple organizational technique, the students and I wasted exorbitant amounts of time trying to remember where everyone had left off. By making notes about stopping points, we were able to eliminate a great deal of anxiety at the beginning of each class and all have more time to read.

Figure 5.1 *A sample of Kyle's notes in her reading log.*

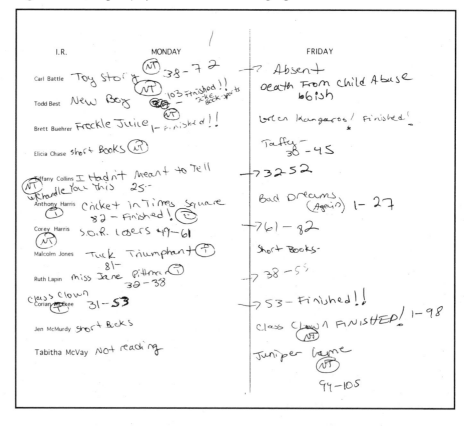

Finding a Place of One's Own

Another distraction during SSR was deciding who was going to sit in the three "comfy chairs." One had come from my college apartment, and I found the other two along the side of the road. (My fiancé was put to the test when I dragged him into school to help me steam-clean these road-side treasures.)

These comfortable chairs quickly became the source of numerous verbal and even physical disputes. There were daily battles over who was going to sit in the comfy chairs during SSR. At first I very calmly asked the students to be considerate of one another and share the chairs. When that didn't work (are you surprised?), I raised my voice—a lot. I threatened to remove the chairs from the classroom. I began to lose my voice along with my patience. The final straw was a shoving match between two contenders. At my wits' end, I finally decided to give the problem back to the students. "Okay, what is a fair way for everyone to get the chairs?"

Corian immediately suggested that he get a chair every day and I forget about "the rest of these gits" (new students). This did not go over well. After much griping, someone finally suggested that everybody should get the chair on a certain day.

"That's a great idea," I praised. "But how are you going to know which day is yours?"

"We'll remember," yelled a voice from the back of the room.

"And what are you going to do when someone says that it's not your day? What are you going to do when there's a substitute?"

We finally agreed to post a chart assigning the chairs by period and student. Thus, the comfy chair seating chart (see Figure 5.2) came to be part of our lives, contributing greatly to the silent aspect of sustained silent reading.

Ironically, some of the students didn't even want to sit in a chair, they wanted to take a chair cushion to their own private reading place (Anthony's spot was under my desk; Corian's, under a table; and Brett's, under one of the computers). The sixth graders eventually began fashioning tents with the chairs and cushions (see Figure 5.3). These private spaces became an integral part of sustained silent reading, and class members respected their boundaries.

Support for Reading

Gradually, many of the students began to get interested in some of the books I offered them. Some, however, still didn't seem to be hooked. When I complained to Janet, she always gave the same reminder: "Be patient. Remember, these kids may have had negative school and reading experiences for their entire lives. Keep inviting them to read. They'll eventually find a book they like."

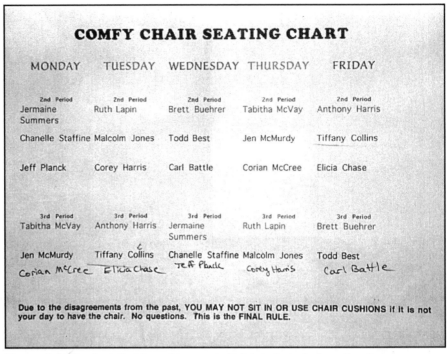

COMFY CHAIR SEATING CHART

MONDAY	TUESDAY	WEDNESDAY	THURSDAY	FRIDAY
2nd Period	**2nd Period**	**2nd Period**	**2nd Period**	**2nd Period**
Jermaine Summers	Ruth Lapin	Brett Buehrer	Tabitha McVay	Anthony Harris
Chanelle Staffine	Malcolm Jones	Todd Best	Jen McMurdy	Tiffany Collins
Jeff Planck	Corey Harris	Carl Battle	Corian McCree	Elicia Chase
3rd Period	**3rd Period**	**3rd Period**	**3rd Period**	**3rd Period**
Tabitha McVay	Anthony Harris	Jermaine Summers	Ruth Lapin	Brett Buehrer
Jen McMurdy	Tiffany Collins	Chanelle Staffine	Malcolm Jones	Todd Best
Corian McCree	Elicia Chase	Jeff Planck	Corey Harris	Carl Battle

Due to the disagreements from the past, YOU MAY NOT SIT IN OR USE CHAIR CUSHIONS if it is not your day to have the chair. No questions. This is the FINAL RULE.

Figure 5.2 *The chart that brought peace to Kyle's independent reading time*

I increased the number of children's books in my collection and ordered more-appropriate recorded books. I asked students to browse through catalogues and help me choose new books for our classroom. When Jermaine told a classroom visitor, "She'll even buy books for you," I realized that some of these students probably never had anyone buy a book just for them. This was the kind of support some of these students needed to realize the importance I placed on books and reading.

As individual students got hooked on books that matched their interests and needs, the support I provided changed. If I noticed a student not following along with the tape, having difficulty with the recorder, walking around, taking a long time to get settled, or repeatedly asking to go to the restroom, I checked in with that student for a minute or two to see whether I could help solve the problem.

A check-in differs from a reading conference in why and where they're held and how long they last: check-ins are brief, conducted on the run during independent reading, and meant to help a student maintain interest and focus in order to continue reading; reading conferences are usually held at my desk, last longer, and address reading challenges the student may be facing and the progress he or she is making. I usually schedule reading conferences during independent literacy exploration, so that students won't be distracted by my extended discussion with one person.

Figure 5.3 *Tristen and some other sixth graders in their space during independent reading*

In the beginning I usually initiate check-ins, but as students become more involved in their reading and have questions about the texts, they often approach me. The check-in scenarios that follow illustrate the range of time and attention they can require.

Tiffany's Check-In. Tiffany was reading Caroline Cooney's *Whatever Happened to Janie?* She had already read *The Face on the Milk Carton* by the same author and had struggled with text features such as italics and literary devices such as flashbacks. While *Whatever Happened to Janie?* didn't contain any dream sequences, which had troubled her in *The Face on the Milk Carton,* it offered a new challenge: the third-person narration took place at different points in the main character's life. At first Tiffany had decided the sequel was too difficult and confusing, even though she was eager to find out what happened. When I offered to take the book home and read the first few chapters on tape for her, she agreed to give it a try.

I brought the tape back later in the week, and Tiffany began following along excitedly. After she completed the first few chapters aided by the tape, she continued with the book on her own. The next day she approached me with a question:

TIFFANY: Is this Jennie or Janie?
KYLE: Do you mean which one is her name?
TIFFANY: Yeah.
KYLE: Well, who calls her Jennie?
TIFFANY: Her sisters and older brothers.
KYLE: Her real sisters and brothers or the ones that she has lived with?
TIFFANY: The ones (*pausing as she thinks*)...she don't have any at the
    other house.
KYLE: Right. So we're trying to figure out why the author keeps calling
    her two different names, Jennie and Janie, right?
TIFFANY: Uh-huh. I don't get it.
KYLE: What's her name at the beginning of the book?
TIFFANY: She calls herself this (*pointing at the name* Janie *in the text*) and
    they call her that (*pointing at the name* Jennie *in the text*).
KYLE: Do you think she likes being called Jennie? (*Tiffany shakes her head
    no*) Why?
TIFFANY: Because she thinks, um, that she's the Johnson's, not the other
    people's.
KYLE: Right. Okay, so the Springs are her real parents and the Johnsons
    are the ones who named her Janie, right?
TIFFANY: Umm-hmm.
KYLE: And now she's living with the Springs, the people who are her real
    parents, so they're calling her what they named her when she was
    born.
TIFFANY (*giving an encouraging nod*): Yeah.
KYLE: How do you think that makes her feel? I mean, how is she feeling
    now that she's living there with the Springs?
TIFFANY: She was happy for two hours. She said that when her sister Jody
    tries to talk to her at night, she just lies there, um, "like a stick."
KYLE: Okay.
TIFFANY: And she said that she wants them to be more like sisters.
KYLE: Who said that, Janie or her sister Jody?
TIFFANY: Jody.
KYLE: How would you feel if you were in Janie's shoes?
TIFFANY: I'd run away.

Because of our conversation, Tiffany realized that Janie's name changed depending on the family she was with. By using one or the other name, the author was giving her clues not only to the physical setting but also to Janie's state of mind. Tiffany left the check-in able to continue her reading independently.

Jermaine's Check-In. Jermaine checked in while he was reading Madeline L'Engle's *A Wrinkle in Time*. In spite of the fact that he was using tapes for this assisted reading, this was still a challenging text for him.

JERMAINE: I don't get this.

KYLE: Where are you in the book?

JERMAINE: I'm at the part where they are at their house. Do you know what I'm talking about?

KYLE: No. Tell me.

JERMAINE: I'm at the part where they went to that house and they met that boy who was real tall and he had on, like, those highwater pants (*giggles*). Then they all go into the house.

KYLE (*trying to get back to his original reason for calling me over*): Do you remember your question?

JERMAINE: No, I don't remember it now.

KYLE: Okay, can you call me back if you think of it?

JERMAINE: Yeah.

I moved away to help another student, but in less than thirty seconds, his hand was in the air again.

JERMAINE: Oh, oh. Hey, I remember now. I was gonna ask you. Is this thing right here (*pointing to the cover, which has a picture of the characters in the book riding a centaur with a rainbow over them*), whatever that is, is it gonna be in the book?

KYLE: What do you think?

JERMAINE: I don't know.

KYLE: Okay. If you looked at the cover of the book, what would you guess that it would be about?

JERMAINE: I don't know.

KYLE: Why would it be on the cover?

JERMAINE: I don't know.

KYLE: Make a prediction. You're good at those.

JERMAINE: I don't know. A time machine or something?

KYLE: Does that (*pointing to the centaur on the cover*) look like something that you see every day?

JERMAINE: No. What's the name of it?

KYLE: Ever heard of a centaur?

JERMAINE (*making a face*): What you say?

KYLE: A centaur.

JERMAINE: I'd call it a horse-man.

KYLE: Right. Why are these people riding it?

JERMAINE: I don't know. That's why I asked you.

KYLE: Do you think that it's going to be in the book?

JERMAINE: I don't know. What is it?

Jermaine kept up a barrage of questions about the centaur, while I tried to direct him back to the text and its characters. Although he initially wanted to clarify the connection between the cover illustration and the plot, he was drawing out our conversation because he needed some one-on-one attention. I finally had to leave the conversation unresolved, but I scheduled a conference with him.

Chanelle's Check-In. When I left Jermaine, I decided to take a minute to see how Chanelle was progressing. She had recently made the move from assisted to unassisted reading, and I wanted to make sure she understood what she was reading now that she was on her own. She was engrossed in Judy Blume's *Otherwise Known as Sheila the Great* when I approached.

KYLE: Has she passed the swimming test yet?
CHANELLE: Nah, she can do a dog swim.
KYLE: So she's actually gone in the water?
CHANELLE: Yeah, but she, ah, won't stick her head in.
KYLE: Does she have to stick her head under?
CHANELLE: If she wants to pass the test.
KYLE: Do you think that she will pass the swimming test?
CHANELLE (*nodding her head*): Yeah.
KYLE: Why?
CHANELLE: I don't know yet, but I just know she will.

I moved on, assured that Chanelle was making solid progress with her unassisted reading of this book.

Teacher Roles During Independent Reading

My primary roles during independent reading are:

- ★ Supporting transitions from assisted to unassisted reading.
- ★ Checking for understanding.
- ★ Giving individual literacy attention.
- ★ Responding to questions.
- ★ Posing questions to aid students' understanding.
- ★ Helping students find the right books.
- ★ Modeling positive reading behavior.
- ★ Coestablishing reading agendas.
- ★ Reinforcing reading strategies.
- ★ Helping with mechanical problems (tapes, recorders, etc.).
- ★ Helping students focus/modify their reading behavior.

Although each student in the literacy workshop has equal access to my time, my support, and the classroom resources, the reading progress of each differs. There are a variety of reasons for this: the degree to which they've previously experienced reading failure, their background as learners, and their motivation, to name a few. Therefore, looking at their progress over time individually helps me see their progress without making comparisons. The following case studies show my teacher roles in action.

Tabitha. Tabitha entered our classroom as a shy and reserved seventh grader. She was one of only three girls in the seventh- and eighth-grade section of the Literacy Project. She had long hair, always wore worn jeans, favored country music, and called herself a redneck. She was definitely not into school. She had never repeated a year, but her grades had always been poor. She was absent often, usually two or three days every two weeks. Even on the days when she came to school, it was difficult to keep her there. She frequently complained of stomachaches and headaches and would ask to go to the guidance office so she could call someone to come and get her. When in class, she sat in the back of the room and rolled her eyes at the boys' antics. She had two standard responses: "I'm sooo over this" or "Boooring."

When it came to independent reading, however, Tabitha was the exception. Like the other students in the class, she was not thrilled at having to read; unlike the others, she was willing to try some of the books I offered her. When I suggested that she try some historical romances, she wrinkled her nose. She took a couple, however, and appeared to begin reading. When I spoke with her a few days later, I expected to hear that she was enjoying the books in spite of her initial reaction. Instead, she confided that she was just reading them until I could find her something new. "These books just don't seem to be true. I mean, what kind of woman is going to get captured on a pirate ship and fall in love with the pirate who captured her?" Tabitha was a smart young woman and I had definitely missed the mark in matching her interests with the books we had.

It was time to begin again. This time I had the sense to ask her opinion. "Well, what would you be interested in reading?"

"Maybe some of those poetry books you read." She had loved Maya Angelou's poem "No Losers, No Weepers," so I handed her that book.

She went through the book quickly, choosing poems that she seemed to enjoy, and then asked for another collection of poetry. I gave her Stephen Dunning's new edition of *Reflections on a Gift of Watermelon Pickle,* and she spent days reading that. Then she began looking for her own books. She went through our classroom collection and found Eloise Greenfield's *Honey, I Love* and then discovered some Native American poetry: Nancy Wood's *Dancing Moons* and *Thirteen Moons on a Turtle's Back* edited by Jonathan London became two of Tabitha's favorite books.

Once Tabitha's success with poetry had given her a solid reading foundation, I wanted her to move on to other genres. Short stories, especially scary ones, had begun to click for several students in our class, and I thought Tabitha might enjoy them too. The stories were not threateningly long, the language was fun, and several of them still had illustrations. I offered her Alvin Schwartz's trilogy, *Scary Stories, More Scary Stories,* and *Scary Stories III.* They were an immediate hit. She read these collections several times and then moved on to short stories in Donald Gallo's *Connections* and *Visions* collections.

After Christmas, Tabitha seemed interested in moving on to some young adult novels. Since she had enjoyed Schwartz's stories so much, I assumed she would enjoy R. L. Stine. I offered her *The Thrill Club,* along with the accompanying tapes. Stine, however, was a no-go. "Like this would really happen," Tabitha laughed as she handed the book back to me. "Get me some more of that Indian stuff," she instructed.

Since I didn't have any novels that fit that description, I selected Suzanne Staples's *Shabanu* and the accompanying tapes and asked her to try those. Each day in class, Tabitha devoured the book. When she asked to take the tapes home, I knew I had her. Tabitha read every moment she could find and finished *Shabanu* quickly. Success with one book often breaks the nonreader cycle, and Tabitha was totally captivated with the magic that she had found in her "first real book." Her intense connection to the book is illustrated in her reader response letter to me (see Figure 5.4).

Next, I suggested that she read Lois Duncan's *Killing Mr. Griffin* until I could find some books and/or tapes with stories of the Native American culture. As I talked up Duncan's book, Tabitha seemed interested (I had a few moments of worry that perhaps she was *too* interested in a book

Figure 5.4 *Tabitha's response to her reading of* Shabanu

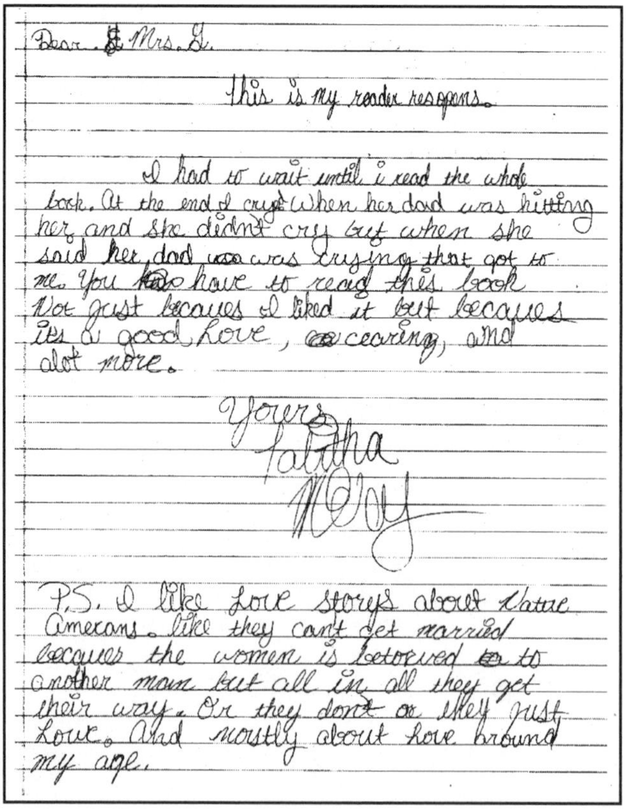
Dear Mrs. G.

This is my reader respons.

I had to wait until i read the whole book. At the end I cryd when her dad was hitting her and she didn't cry but when she said her dad was crying that got to me. You have to read this book Not just becaues I liked it but becaues its a good love, cearing, and alot more.

Yours
Tabitha

P.S. I like love storys about Native Americans. like they can't get married becaues the women is betorved to another man but all in all they get their way. Or they don't or they just love. And mostly about love around my age.

about killing a kidnapped English teacher!). After I jokingly asked her not to get any ideas from the book, she agreed to read it. Although the book wasn't on tape, the suspense kept Tabitha going, both in school and at home (reading at home had become a new habit).

After the success of *Killing Mr. Griffin,* I decided to continue offering Tabitha books that had a lot of suspense. I had just finished reading Duncan's *Ransom,* a tale of five high school students who are kidnapped and held for ransom, so I told her about it. She immediately took the book and settled into her favorite reading spot. She followed *Ransom* with another Duncan title, *The Third Eye.* In typical avid-reader fashion, Tabitha had become devoted to an author.

When Tabitha returned to my class for a second year, she was definitely a reader. She seldom asked for assistance in selecting new books and read independently far more than with the assistance of recorded books. She was still fascinated with Native American literature, so I stocked up on resources for her. She delved into Jean Craighead George's *Julie of the Wolves* and *The Talking Earth;* Jamake Highwater's *Anpao;* and went back to read Suzanne Staples's *Haveli,* the sequel to *Shabanu.* She took another major step toward reading independence by looking for books outside the classroom. She felt some pride in finding Linda Shuler's *She Who Remembers* and *Voice of the Eagle* without my assistance.

One day she came racing into class and told me breathlessly that she had had a dream the night before about a young Native American girl. In response to my questioning whether she had written it down, Tabitha began to write poetry (see Figure 5.5): after a year in my classroom, her reading had begun to influence her writing. With that connection, Tabitha's world began to expand. A next logical step was to write to tell a favorite author what an influence her books had been (see Figure 5.6).

During one of our reading conferences, I asked Tabitha to tell me how she perceived the changes in her literacy. She responded, "It's all more interesting because I can read anything and everything now. I didn't want to read before, because it seemed long and boring. I felt like I should be doing something else besides reading, like playing outside or something." We agreed that I had definitely kept offering her the "wrong" books at the beginning of our time together and remarked on how our weekly reading conferences had helped us find books and genres that were interesting to her. Tabitha was now a reader. She had needed more help finding the right books than developing the strategies to read them successfully. She definitely emerged as a reader and a writer once she had the right conditions for her growth: a supportive, risk-free environment, the right resources, and someone to help her make the connection that literacy can be life.

Anthony. Although Anthony's progress in no way resembled Tabitha's, he stole my heart. Just as students enter our classroom with varying backgrounds, they also vary greatly as to their ability and their literacy.

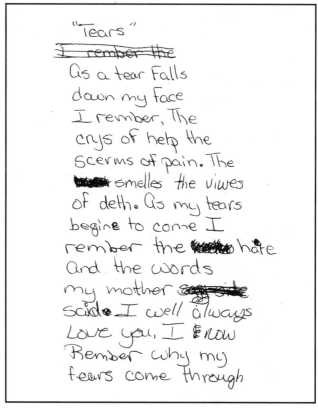

Figure 5.5 *Tabitha's poem written in response to her dream about a young Native American girl*

Tabitha needed a significant intervention to break down her initial non-reader facade, but once she began reading, she was able to take on the role of book finder, book chooser, and responder. Anthony's needs were significantly greater.

Anthony spent most of his time in class being far more interested in aping the behavior of his brother and several of the other boys than in doing anything that smacked remotely of reading or learning. In spite of that, I was touched by his gentle, quiet need for attention. Anthony never asked for attention, but as I held conferences with him each day, his sincerity and childlike core always emerged—something he never allowed to show around his peers. He looked several years older than he was; his physical strength and appearance hid his academic frustration and failure very well.

When Anthony first came into our classroom, he wouldn't open the young adult books that I offered him, even the ones with accompanying tapes. But I kept trying. Week after week, he would politely accept any book I offered, listen to my book talks, and then walk away. He would try

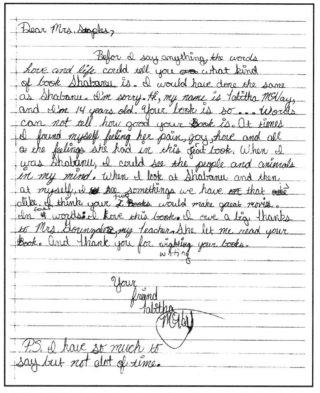

Dear Mrs. Staples,

Before I say anything, the words love and life could tell you what kind of book Shabanu is. I would have done the same as Shabanu. I'm sorry. Hi, my name is Tabitha McVay, and I'm 14 years old. Your book is so . . . Words can not tell how good your book is. At times I found myself feeling her pain, joy, love and all of the feelings she had in this great book. When I was Shabanu, I could see the people and animals in my mind. When I look at Shabanu and then at myself, I see somethings we have that is alike. I think your two books would make great movies. In words, I love this book. I owe a big thanks to Mrs. Gonzales, my teacher. She let me read your book. And thank you for writing your books.

Your friend
Tabitha McVay

P.S. I have so much to say but not alot of time.

Figure 5.6 *Tabitha's letter to her favorite author, Suzanne Fischer Staples*

to read one or two pages and then fall asleep. One day he picked up Martin Handford's *Where's Waldo?* and actually seemed to enjoy it. It wasn't the kind of reading I was hoping for, but in desperation I decided to build on that shred of success by buying all of the other Waldo books. As I looked back at my notes of the invitations to read that I had given Anthony, I realized both the significance of his choosing that first Waldo book as well as the significance of my not really seeing where he needed to start. Once he finally taught me that lesson, we were on our way.

My first success with him was the *Disney's The Lion King*, which I taped for him and he read several times. He even spent several days sharing the book with another student in the class. This time I knew better than to ignore his lead. I purchased several more Disney books: *The Little Mermaid, Aladdin,* and *Beauty and the Beast.* I put all of them on tape, and Anthony read them over and over again.

Once I let go of the books I thought he should be reading, Anthony began to browse through all the children's books we had and began making his own selections. One of his favorites quickly became Jane Resnick's *Original Fairy Tales from the Brothers Grimm.* The breathtaking illustrations and the classic stories of childhood seemed to captivate him. Every once in a while I would again offer Anthony a young adult novel on tape, but he would still read only a page or two and then put it aside. Instead of falling asleep, however, he would go to the shelf and get the book of fairy tales, pick up his tape player, and read. The book response in Figure 5.7, which he wrote after one of these sessions, told me what was working for him with the book of fairy tales and what was not working for him with the other books I had been selecting.

Anthony's next step was a natural progression from taped children's books to children's books without taped assistance. When he chose to read Elizabeth Koda-Dallan's *The Tiny Angel* without a tape, I was thrilled. That he was becoming more comfortable with prose, as opposed to the rhyming couplets typical of many children's stories and fairy tales, was also positive. In his response to the book he wrote, "The book I am reading is The Tiny Angel. I picked this book because of the pictures thay look good and look fun and another reason is because of the words thay are not that long like thay used to be." By virtue of the large number of children's books he had encountered through assisted reading, he was now able to recognize many words independently. I decided I would once again invite him to read a young adult novel now that he had developed both some competence and some confidence in his reading.

I bought Sid Fleischman's *Jim Ugly* and the accompanying tapes for what I hoped would be his first attempt. Anthony was immediately intrigued by the title, since one of his favorite adjectives was "ugly." Although he was a bit put off by the length of the book, it had illustrations and accompanying tapes, so he was willing to take a chance. When he finished it, he wrote:

> the boy name is jack. because jack dad found the dog and he named the dog Jim ugly becasue the dog look like a dog and a wolf. yes I like the book I wont to read another book like it. I like Jim ugly and jack because thay get to go every were to try to find jack dad and they run a way from home.

Figure 5.7 *Anthony's response to his reading of the picture book* Original Fairy Tales from the Brothers Grimm

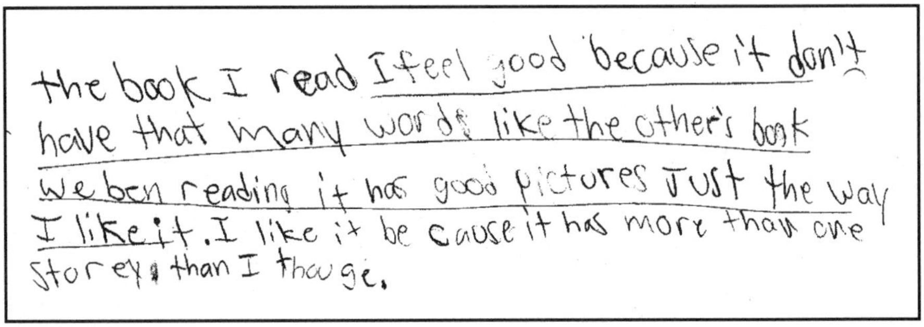

the book I read I feel good because it don't
have that many words like the other's book
we ben reading it has good pictures Just the way
I like it. I like it be cause it has more than one
storey than I thouge.

When I compared this response to Anthony's previous responses, I noticed two significant differences. In this response, Tony not only commented on his approval of the book, but began to talk about the details of the story. In fact, he began his response by giving significant story elements: characters, details about plot, and his opinion of the story line. In addition, this response showed Anthony's changing picture of himself as a reader: he signed himself "the best kid in your class."

Anthony's love of fantasy prompted me to offer him L. Frank Baum's *The Wizard of Oz* next and it, too, was a hit. He pulled the book off the shelf almost every day. When I noticed that he was reading voluntarily during times other than independent reading, I rejoiced. His response demonstrated his increasing ability to connect with and describe both the book and his understanding of his reading process (see Figure 5.8).

I then resolved to build on the earlier success Anthony had had with the young adult novel *Jim Ugly.* I spent days looking in bookstores and catalogues trying to find titles that would keep him moving forward. We communicated regularly through his written book responses. Unlike Tabitha, who preferred conferences, Tony seemed to feel proud of each new written response. These written responses helped both of us see the changes over time not only in his attitude toward reading but in his increasing confidence in his vocabulary and ideas.

As our first year together ended, I thought often of how enticing the world of fantasy must seem to him in the face of the harsh realities of both his home and school life. I was eager for Anthony to return in the fall so that we could continue to build on the reading habits and tastes he had developed. His confidence in taking risks with longer books—some without tapes or illustrations—was exciting, and I imagined how his reading might increase during our second year together.

When the eighth-grade Anthony returned, however, it was not to take up where we had left off in May. I felt we were almost back where we had started the previous August. I was heartsick that Anthony had lost so much ground. Then I noticed him going to the front of the room and

Figure 5.8 *Anthony's response to* The Wizard of Oz

The book that I am reading is the
wizard of oz.
What I like best about this book is the long walk
they had to take becouse they got in a lot of trubule.
I donot Nothing least about this book.
my favorite character is the tin wood man. becuse
he has a ax.

glancing at the new picture books I displayed there: Beatrix Potter's *The Tale of Squirrel Nutkin* and *The Tale of Peter Rabbit;* Audrey Wood's *King Bidgood's in the Bathtub* and *Rude Giants.* It seemed Anthony needed to reestablish himself as a reader by revisiting his earlier journey.

Fortunately, it only took a few days before he regained his previous confidence and was able to move back into the kind of reading he had been enjoying at the end of the previous year: Gary Paulsen's *Nightjohn,* Natalie Babbitt's *Tuck Everlasting,* and George Selden's *A Cricket in Times Square.*

After a few weeks, I introduced him to a new genre, horror and suspense, and Anthony found another area of reading interest and success. He had seen several of the other students reading R. L. Stine books and chose *The Thrill Club* as his introduction to the genre. This was quickly followed by *The Dare* and *Bad Dreams.* Success was written all over his face as the once-shy Anthony eagerly shared his opinions about these popular horror novels.

Just when I felt Anthony had finally overcome his struggles with reading—lack of confidence, unfamiliarity with words and story grammar, cumulative years of failure, lack of interest—he began missing school. Anthony, his brother, and his sister all became sporadic members of the Literacy Project classes. I was well aware of the negative effect this would have not only on Anthony's developing reading fluency but also on his confidence. Each time he was in class, I could see his enthusiasm for reading fading, just when I thought he might be ready to move from assisted reading to independent reading of young adult novels without illustrations. Supporting this transition was one of my key roles; however, with tentative readers like Anthony, I also understood the dangers of frustration and anger. For him to take this step would require an enormous amount of support—support that could not be sustained if he wasn't in school. Then, almost as quickly as his attendance had waned, it began to improve.

By February, it appeared that Anthony was back to stay—both as a student and as a reader. He was still using books on tape, but now consistently chose young adult literature without illustrations. A few weeks later I noticed he had begun spending a lot of time fooling with the tape player. Since this was usually either a sign of faulty equipment or a cry for attention, I began watching him carefully. What a relief to realize that Anthony was independently weaning himself from assisted reading. He would read a paragraph or two along with the tape, stop it, and then try to read a couple of paragraphs on his own. I was so thrilled with this sign of independence I wanted to hug him. I left him alone, but did tell him what I had noticed when he turned in his latest book response. As we talked, his shy smile confirmed the pride he was feeling. He left our conference, picked up another new book, and settled into the comfy chair. He was a reader.

Reflections by Janet

Tabitha and Anthony are two very different examples of how students learn from independent reading. Kyle's response to their needs and her support of their learning are important models of the teacher's role during independent reading. That role can easily be described in affective terms: Kyle was a mentor, a nurturer, an encourager, and a supporter. But I believe her role can also be described in terms of the theory underlying this kind of support. Vygotsky's zone of proximal development is important here: "The only good kind of instruction is that which marches ahead of development and leads it; it must be aimed not so much at the ripe as the ripening function" (1978, 104). It is in marching just slightly ahead of the learner that teachers can offer significant support to all readers, especially those who have struggled with reading for years.

John W. A. Smith and Warwick B. Elley (1994) list four stages of the zone of proximal development:

Stage 1: Performance is assisted by more capable others.
Stage 2: Performance is assisted by the learner.
Stage 3: Performance is developed and automatized.
Stage 4: Performance regresses, stages 1–3 are repeated.
(83–84)

I saw students in Kyle's classroom functioning at each of these stages every day. Kyle's support of Tabitha and Anthony is a concrete example of the varied roles and flexible strategies that teachers employ depending on the stage of the learner. Almost all readers in the literacy workshop are at stage 1: they need and depend on Kyle as the capable other who gives them support. They seek support in finding the right books and in using resources and strategies to help them become successful. Smith and Elley maintain that the teacher's role during this critical time is to "structure the situation" (83), which is what Kyle did. She established guidelines for independent reading, she provided time for reading, she set up parameters for productive behavior, and she established ways in which students could ask for her assistance.

After many demonstrations of when and how to activate appropriate strategies in both whole-group and individual settings, students begin to take on some of the responsibility for their reading success. The check-in Kyle did with Tiffany is stage 2 in action. Tiffany has begun to use the strategies she is familiar with to try to make sense of a difficult text. The text is just beyond her independent reading level, and as she struggles, she recognizes the point at which she is no longer making meaning from the text. Having used the strategies she knows, she returns to Kyle for more assistance. Once the assistance is given, she is able to move forward independently.

Tabitha is a wonderful example of stage 3. The many reading conferences, the strategy lessons Kyle provided during shared reading, and the support of books on tape quickly led Tabitha to a stage of independence in which her reading became automatized and "fossilized" (Vygotsky's term). Her letter to Kyle at the end of the year (see Figure 5.9) indicates not only that she can now read independently, but also that she sees the impact reading will have on her future life. The fact that this young woman, who could not or would not read two years before she wrote this letter, articulates the possibility of becoming a writer and a reading teacher reinforces for us just how important it is for teachers to meet students where they are and help them change.

If Tabitha encounters unsupportive teachers and environments such as Cyrene Wells describes in *Literacies Lost: When Students Move from a Progressive Middle School to a Traditional High School* (1996), she might well regress in her reading. She would then, as indicated in the description of stage 4, need some assistance from another reader, a mentor, or a comfortable book to get back on track. When Anthony came back after the

Figure 5.9 *Tabitha's letter to Kyle at the end of her eighth-grade year*

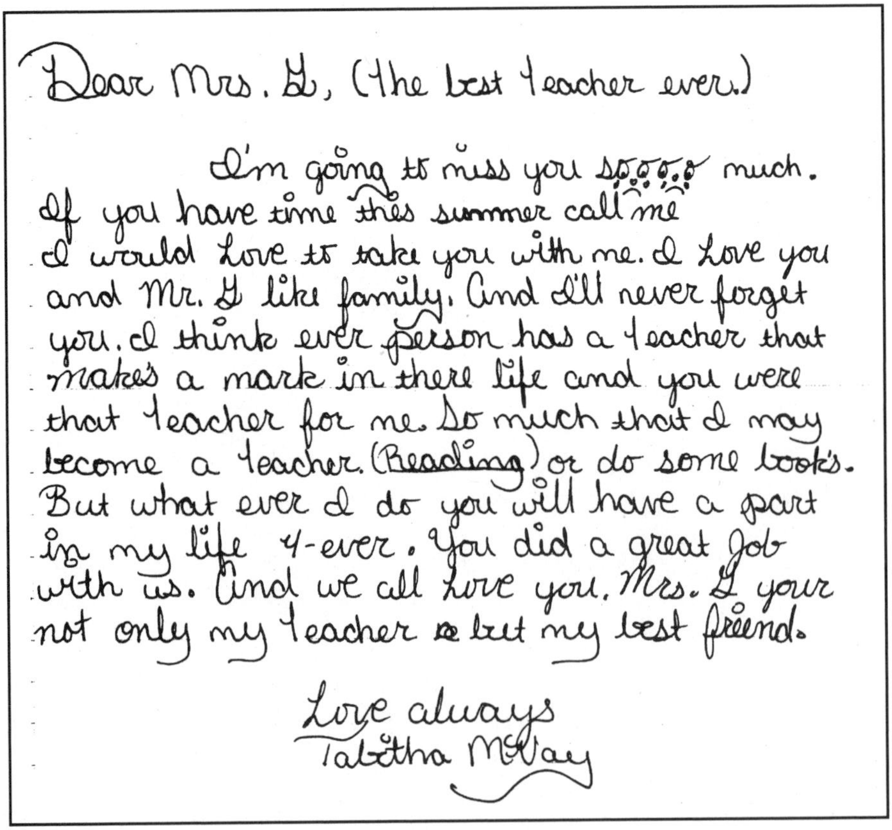

Dear Mrs. G, (the best teacher ever.)

I'm going to miss you sooo much. If you have time this summer call me I would love to take you with me. I love you and Mr. G like family. And I'll never forget you. I think ever person has a teacher that makes a mark in there life and you were that teacher for me. So much that I may become a teacher. (Reading) or do some book's. But what ever I do you will have a part in my life 4-ever. You did a great job with us. And we all love you. Mrs. G your not only my teacher but my best friend.

Love always
Tabitha McVay

summer break, he appeared to have lost ground and reverted to stage 1. However, without Kyle's having to intervene, he returned to the comfort level he felt with picture books until he had his sea legs again. Once he felt comfortable, he was able to move back into and through stages 1 through 3.

In her teaching journal, Kyle grappled with what these students were teaching her about independence and assistance during independent reading, and I believe she hit on the key to understanding this time in readers' lives.

> It's almost as if readers, with the correct environment and support, have an internal gauge that tells them when they are ready to make the next step in their reading. Whether it's from *Where's Waldo?* to a Disney book, or from reading a young adult novel with a tape to reading it independently, they seem to know. I guess it's up to teachers not only to provide the correct environment and resources for new readers, but also to allow time for students to discover their own literacy gauges.

I like the notion of allowing readers to find their gauges, but I also know that Kyle provided an incredible amount of support, direct instruction, modeling, and confidence building before the gauge became reliable. Each new student in the literacy workshop came with a gauge that said, "Avoid reading at all costs." Yet, amazingly, all of the students began to read. It took much longer for some than for others, but all the students made moves toward independence. It took about a year and a half for Anthony to read a novel independently; for Tabitha, it took only a few weeks. The chart in Figure 5.10 indicates the progress made by one class of fifteen students. At the beginning of the year, only four students were reading independently; at the end of the year, only three students were still being assisted by books on tape. The level of reading also changed: Ruth was reading Judith Viorst's *Alexander and the Terrible, Horrible, No Good, Very Bad Day* independently at the beginning of the year and reading LouAnne Johnson's *Dangerous Minds* independently at the end of the year.

These changes do not happen without considerable intervention on the part of a caring, knowledgeable teacher. As a new teacher, knowing when and how to intervene were skills Kyle had to develop. Over time, as Kyle learned to observe, document, and reflect on the changes she was seeing in her students, she became more knowledgeable about ways to help students progress more quickly. Nevertheless, in spite of Kyle's increasing efficiency and understanding, each student did appear to move in response to some inner gauge. Perhaps it is the growing knowledge of the truth in these words of Robert Coles (1989): "A story can possess, as it connects so persuasively with human experience" (204–205). In that growing knowledge comes the desire for more stories...and deeper stories.

The literature that Kyle invited young readers to share during read-aloud and shared reading introduced them to stories that were just out of

Name	Beginning of Year	Method	End of Year	Method
Carl	*Disney's Aladdin*	Assisted	*Little Lefty*	Independent
Brett	*The Escape of Marvin the Ape*	Assisted	*Scary Stories*	Independent
Anthony	*Disney's Beauty and the Beast*	Assisted	*Bad Dreams*	Independent
Ruth	*Alexander and the Terrible, Horrible, No Good, Very Bad Day*	Independent	*Dangerous Minds*	Independent
Tabitha	*Thirteen Moons on a Turtle's Back*	Independent	*Haveli*	Independent
Corey	*The Nightmare Before Christmas*	Assisted	*Stonefox*	Independent
Malcolm	*The Tale of Squirrel Nutkin*	Assisted	*A Cricket in Times Square*	Assisted and Independent
Chanelle	*Scary Stories—More Tales to Chill Your Bones*	Assisted	*I Hadn't Meant to Tell You This*	Independent
Jermaine	*Shark Beneath the Reef*	Assisted	*A Wrinkle in Time*	Assisted
Elicia	*Are You There God? It's Me, Margaret*	Assisted	*Dear Mom, You're Ruining My Life*	Independent
Jen	*The Tiny Angel*	Independent	*Death from Child Abuse and No One Heard*	Independent
Jeff	*Rude Giants*	Assisted	*The Thrill Club*	Assisted and Independent
Tiffany	*The Face on the Milk Carton*	Assisted	*I Hadn't Meant to Tell You This*	Independent
Todd	*Baseball Pals*	Assisted	*Canyons*	Assisted
Corian	*101 Super Sports Jokes*	Independent	*The New Boy*	Assisted

Figure 5.10 *This chart reflects the independent reading progress of one group of Kyle's students from the beginning to the end of the year*

their reach. Those stories gave them a reason to *want* to read; independent reading gave them *time* to read. It was during independent reading that Kyle and I began to see the breathtaking wisdom of Jane Yolen's advice: "We need to help students fall through the words and into the story."

Chapter 6

Reading to Write and Writing to Read

Put simply, in the whole range of academic course work, American children do not write frequently enough, and the reading and writing tasks they are given do not require them to think deeply enough.

Judith Langer and Arthur Applebee

When Writing Stops

In Donald Murray's book *Crafting a Life in Essay, Story, Poem* (1996), he says, "I began to write long before I could read, even before I could print my name—even before I was born" (1). If that had ever been the case for the students in our literacy workshop, most of them had long since abandoned the notion that writing was a natural process—something they had been doing all of their lives.

While most literacy educators agree that reading and writing are mutually supportive, parallel processes, I have found that for at-risk students writing is a far riskier venture than reading. The struggling readers and writers I encounter are similar to those Cathy Roller deals with in her book *Variability Not Disability* (1996). In discussing the difficulty she experienced getting students to write, she states, "Writing, unlike silent or oral reading, leaves behind a permanent record. Writing documents the children's 'deficiencies' in ways they heartily resist. They do not like to have traces of incompetence on paper for all to see" (84). Many of my high school students told me they absolutely could not write, but when I questioned them further, they meant they could not spell. If their penmanship was poor to boot, they felt the only thing to do was avoid writing altogether. The negative memories about writing that many adolescents bring to middle-level classrooms make it difficult for them to get past their anxiety. For struggling readers and writers, there are just too many things they can do wrong—spelling, usage, penmanship, syntax—and the errors on the page are tangible and permanent.

When I first introduced the literacy workshop into my own classroom, I quickly saw a positive correlation between students who became avid readers and those who wanted to write and improve their writing. A few students came into class saying they liked to write, but when they were given choices during independent literacy exploration, no one chose to do so. In fact, at the beginning of the year, the more writing prompts we did as a group, the less writing they seemed to do during independent writing. Over time, however, as students read more books during shared and independent reading and I modeled ways we could respond to that reading, I noticed that many of them started to experiment with writing. Their language became richer, and they were more likely to take writing and speaking risks.

Take Rachel, for example. Her response to our first shared-reading novel was two sentences of voiceless summary that took no language risks whatever. After one month of reading and being read to almost constantly, her voice as a writer began to emerge:

> "Teachers Pet" was an outstanding book. The book kept me on the edge. Just when I figered it out it wold change. I wish I was in Kate's place. I found it intreaging. A handsom man in love with her. A meeting behind every corner. The suspance was wild. The adventure that Kate went thurugh is what I always wished for. Love, horror, fear, running from someone, putting the puzzle pieces together. I really enjoyed the book.

Once Rachel made the personal connection to books, it was a natural extension for her to begin expressing that connection through her writing. *Plain Talk About Learning and Writing Across the Curriculum* (1987), a document published by the Virginia Department of Education, discusses this as a connection to thinking: "Writing is also the perfect tool to ensure that students do stop and think and make personal knowledge from a matter at hand" (3).

Like Rachel, Kyle's students needed the impetus of reading immersion combined with strong support from Kyle for them to take their first writing steps.

In the Classroom with Kyle

Reading to Write

If I could, I would always choose reading over writing as the primary focus of instruction, not only in my Literacy Project classroom, but in any classroom. After working with reluctant readers and writers for almost three years, I have concluded that I could explicitly teach elements of writing until I was blue in the face and it would have little impact on students' writing. Each year I am more firmly convinced that students will always struggle with writing until they have a reading history.

Until students become readers, it is difficult for them to know the beauty of a story, the rhythm that language holds, the voice writing can convey. My students come to me devoid of reading history (or if they have one, that history is negative), and their writing reflects that lack of reading. They see writing, like reading, not as a way to construct a story or communicate a message but as a device for tricking them into right or wrong answers. For my students, writing is capital and lowercase letters, subject-verb agreement, nouns, punctuation, paragraphs. They certainly do not see writing as a way to express themselves; rather, they see it as yet another impossible literacy task.

When they came into my Literacy Project class, almost all my students, who ranged in age from eleven to fifteen, did not even capitalize their sentences or use end punctuation. During my first year of teaching, I tried to help them become writers by teaching them the tools of writing. At some not-soon-enough point, I realized I was teaching them the tools of editing, not the tools of writing. In addition, I expected them to practice these tools on writing assignments that I got from other English teachers: Halloween stories, what-I-did-over-Christmas-vacation essays, etc. You can imagine the writing I got from this combination of lifeless prompts and decontextualized grammar lessons.

And after I thought I'd made all the mistakes there were to make in teaching writing, I added peer response and editing groups, which I modeled after the ones I'd been part of in my university writing classes. In those writing groups, the only problem had been limiting feedback so that everyone had a chance to share a piece of writing. In the literacy workshop peer response groups, nothing seemed to work. I kept trying to figure out what I was doing wrong. Was it classroom management? The wrong combination of students? Had I not been specific enough about how response groups should work? After weeks of struggle and an increasing sense of failure, I finally realized that these students could scarcely construct meaning from a published book, much less take on the challenge of a reluctant-reader-and-even-more-reluctant-writer's version of a Stephen King story. Most of the students were totally disengaged, and those who were still trying to participate gave less than helpful responses to their peers' writing:

"Man, your writing is too messy to read."
"You can't write and I can't read your writing."
"You don't even know how to use periods. What's wrong with you?"
"Looks fine to me."

Their feedback was reduced to the only kind of responses many of them had ever received from teachers: comments about grammar, punctuation, and handwriting.

After six torturous months during which I dreaded teaching writing and the students hated writing even more than they had when they entered the classroom in August, I gave up. I wanted my students to see writing as a tool for expression and communication, and nothing I was doing as part of my direct or indirect teaching of writing was accomplishing that. I decided that any writing we did in class would be for valid purposes: to express ourselves, to connect to our shared and independent reading, to explore new topics, to define our goals, to document our dreams, to get rid of frustrations, and to resolve classroom issues. It still took me many weeks to convince the students that they could just write. Every day I repeated, "We're not going to worry about spelling right now. Just get your ideas down." My students were finally able to begin at the beginning—using writing as a way to express and explore.

Writing to Resolve Classroom Issues

Issues often arose in the classroom that could not be addressed effectively or entirely through discussion, which sometimes became too heated, causing some students to retreat into silence and others to revert to bullying. In those situations we often used writing to prepare for a discussion or to ensure that each student took something away from our talk. For example, if students were not respecting our classroom rules, I might ask each person to write down at least one thing he or she wanted to bring out in a subsequently scheduled class meeting. Or after a discussion I would ask students to write down the most important points that had been made. At other times, I would ask students to write down what they thought the cause of a problem was and how it might be solved. I would weigh these opinions against what I was seeing and then share all points of view on the overhead.

At one point some students were being disruptive during shared reading. I told the class what I saw happening and asked them to write down what they were seeing as well. Corey's comments (see Figure 6.1) helped

Figure 6.1 *Corey's written response to the problems he was seeing in our classroom during shared reading*

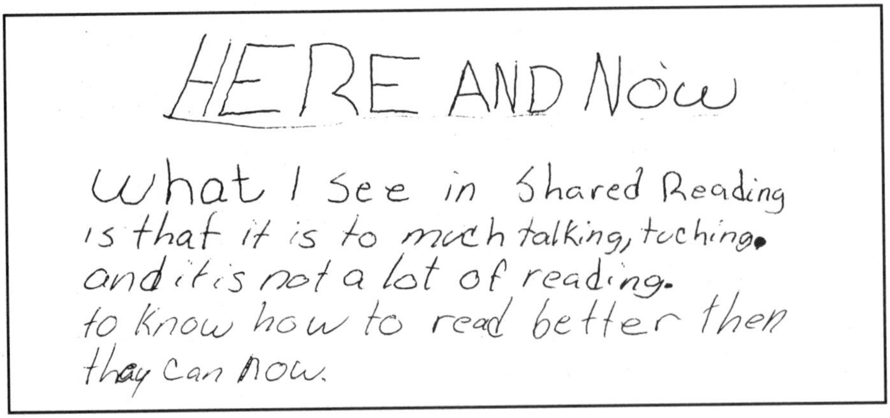
HERE AND Now

What I see in Shared Reading
is that it is to much talking, tuching.
and it is not a lot of reading.
to know how to read better then
thay can now.

me see what he was really thinking. In an open class discussion, Corey would have been concerned with maintaining his image and therefore have sided with those who were being disruptive. In his writing, he could be honest because his anonymous opinions were combined into a list with those of the other students.

Many of the students in my classes had never been allowed to go on field trips, so I was a bit nervous when we were planning to attend a live performance of a play followed by dinner in a restaurant. Attempting to discuss etiquette with them, I discovered that most of them had never been to a theater and several of them had never eaten in a restaurant. I decided to have them make "field trip etiquette" posters for our classroom (see Figures 6.2 and 6.3), and we then pooled our collective etiquette knowledge to create a single list of etiquette rules:

Sixth Grade Etiquette Rules for Field Trips

1. While on the school bus, do not say, "You stupid old man" to the bus driver or other cars on the highway.
2. While at the restaurant, say "Can you *please* give me the mustard." Do not say, "Hey, Stupid! Hey, you!" and do not scream around the table or hit people.

Figure 6.2 *Sharone's ideas for field trip etiquette*

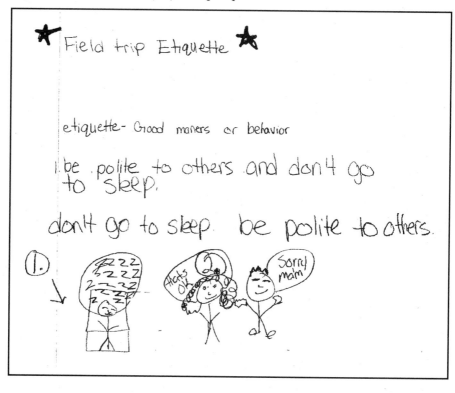

Figure 6.3 *Shel's ideas for proper behavior in the theater*

3. Be respectful to others while people are performing.
4. What to do: say thank you when somebody gives something nice. What not to do: shout out or call people names, such as, "You are ugly…I hate you…You are mean."
5. Don't go to sleep.
6. Be polite to others.
7. Don't stand up on the bus.
8. Don't talk when the actors are talking.
9. Don't kick the person's chair in front of you.
10. Things to do: say thank you and clap. Things not to do: burp when you're eating and say bad things about the performers.
11. What to do: do not be noisy. What not to do: talk out loud, like "You are ugly." "So are you."
12. What not to do: talk out and say that she is ugly. What to do: be polite.
13. What to do: listen to the teacher. What not to do or say or dress like: say, "I don't have to dress like her"; don't dress like a bum.
14. Do not be rude. Do not talk back to the teacher. Be respectful.
15. Listen to the teacher.
16. Pay attention to directions. Listen to the play. Be good on the bus.
17. Be nice to other people.

We also used writing to try to resolve students' problems with substitute teachers. Every time I had to be out of class, I dreaded coming back and receiving the substitute teacher's report. Finally, I decided to return the problem to the students. First, I asked them to write down the problems that occurred when a substitute took the class. When they finished doing that, I asked them to go back and brainstorm solutions to these problems (see Figure 6.4). As we had done with our field trip etiquette rules, we shared our writing and then one of the students typed all the suggested solutions into a list that each student kept in her or his individual notebook. Students had a set of solutions they had created, and I had a resource to which I could direct them on the days they had a substitute teacher.

Writing to Express Feelings

Many times students want and need to talk with me privately about problems they are having in their lives. Unfortunately, there is rarely time to do that. Therefore, I often ask students to write to me about their problems. This gives the students an immediate release, and I can deal with the problem when I have a quiet moment in which to give the issue some thought.

These writings range from the directive from Tabitha in Figure 6.5 to Charles's recounting of how he used writing to keep from fighting:

> Dear Mrs G,
> Thank you for the notebook you gave to me because I got mad today i wrote about it before i said anything and i realized that it would have been a stupid thing to argue or fight about and I just got up and ask the teacher could i change seats and she said yes.

Figure 6.4 *Jerry's thoughts on the problems that arise when a substitute is in the class. He also included possible solutions for those problems.*

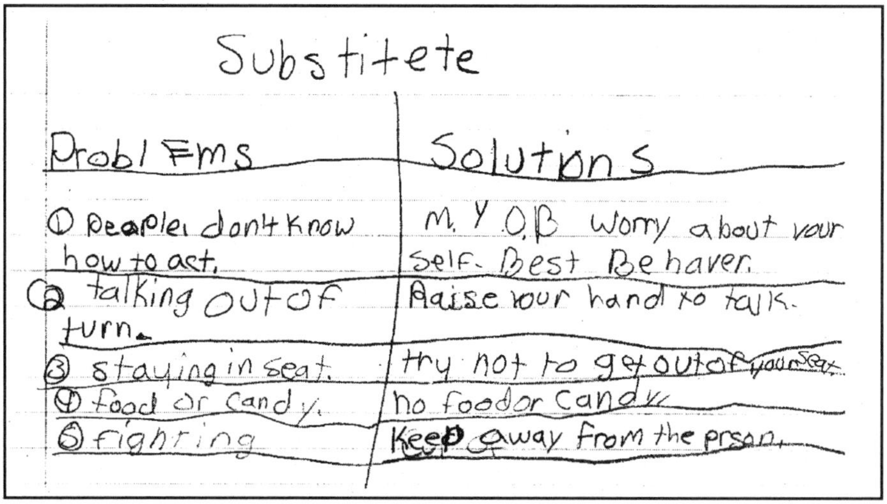

Substitete

Problems	Solutions
① peaple don't know how to act.	M.Y.O.B worry about your self. Best Behaver.
② talking out of turn.	Raise your hand to talk.
③ staying in seat.	try not to get out of your seat.
④ food or candy.	no food or candy.
⑤ fighting	Keep away from the prson.

Figure 6.5 *Tabitha's note to Kyle about a problem she is having in class*

Then the boy just look at me funny and turned his head i think i did a very good job on handling myself and i just wanted to thank you for all your help not just on school work but with life and reality. Thank you!

I find that encouraging spontaneous writing to serve a specific and authentic purpose is much more effective than asking my students to write in personal journals.

Middle school students love to write notes, and letter writing has become one of the most popular forms of writing in our classroom. It's a way for students to communicate with friends, strangers, and me when talking is not possible. These letters are a way to express emotions, share opinions, and even respond to books they are reading.

During this past year, my sixth graders and I faced one of our most difficult moments when Kances had to leave our school in order to live with her aunt. Kances had won the hearts of her peers with her infectious laugh and concern for others. Despite her history of difficulties in school and at home, she was a delight to have in class. On the day she was to leave, it seemed natural for Kances to say her good-byes by sitting at the computer and writing a letter to everyone in the class:

to yall

i am gonna miss you all but ill be back in december I hope that you will miss me to well half to go now see you in december

Shared Writing as a Connection to Reading

One of the most important ways I use writing in the classroom is to help students connect reading to their lives. I model shared writing after what I know about shared reading. During shared reading I "decode" the words on the page while the students follow along and develop mental images of the words being read. The risk for students is low, yet they develop reading strategies for pacing, using punctuation, checking meaning, deciphering words, using background knowledge, and monitoring their involvement with a text. Shared writing in our classroom works the same way. I do the actual writing, which keeps the risk low for students yet allows them to develop mental models related to story grammar, sentence structure, mechanics, voice, and style.

While virtually any print material can be used as a basis for shared writing, I often use picture books. Students see these as much less intimidating and can therefore focus their attention on the writing techniques used by the author.

One particularly inviting story I used is Elizabeth Hill's *Evan's Corner,* the story of a little boy who lives with his family in a small apartment with too few rooms for all the siblings. Feeling crowded, Evan tells his mother he needs his own place, but a corner turns out to be the only space available. He decorates it with his art, a plant, and other items that he treasures. As a class we discussed and wrote together about our classroom space in the school and then about students' spaces within our classroom. Students were then eager to create their own art and writing corners. Jermaine's first independent writing of the year (see Figure 6.6) was an offshoot of this shared writing experience. Although his computer-generated room drawing and the writing that accompanies it is primitive, this was a beginning step for him, one on which we could build.

Another piece of literature I found particularly effective in helping students learn to write the stories they love to tell is Judith Viorst's *Alexander and the Terrible, Horrible, No Good, Very Bad Day*. The theme of our class meetings was often the horrible injustice of life as a middle school student, yet when I asked students to write, they said they had nothing to write about. After reading this story aloud and looking for the patterns Viorst used in her writing to make Alexander's point, students brainstormed all the bad days they could remember. Then each chose one as the focus of his or her writing. One example is shown in Figure 6.7. Another is transcribed below:

Here and Now

I had a terrible, horrible no good very bad day when I was in the 3rd grade I woke one morning I got ready for school I was so mad

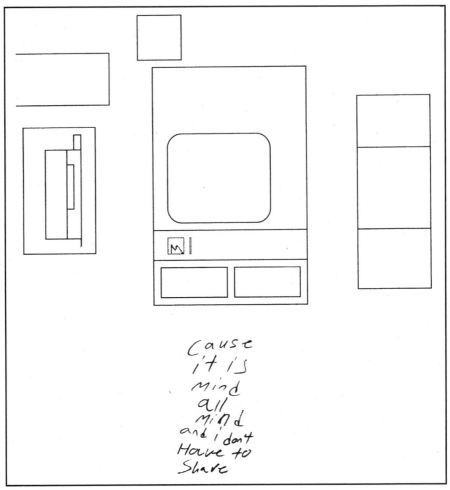

Figure 6.6 *Jermaine's response to Kyle's read-aloud of* Evan's Corner

I could'nt do my hair and my sister would'nt do my hair so I went to my mom and she did it ugly so I had to go to school with my hair like that. but every day before I go to school I go to the day care so I went their and ate Bearkfast and then went to catch the school Bus but by the time I got to the bus everyone stared skipping. all the big kids liked to fight and pick on all the little kids even my sisters . so when I went to school I went to my class room and that same day we had a test on 11 time tables and could you geast what I got? I got an D- I said in my mined I belived Mrs. B. put that D- their because she dose'nt like me. and that same day sha let the boys and girls to the bath room and me and this girl name Latoyia was pulling each other legs until I pulled her leg so hard it hit the the shalf and her leg started hurting and she went and told Mrs. B. and Mrs. B. went and told Mrs. C. then

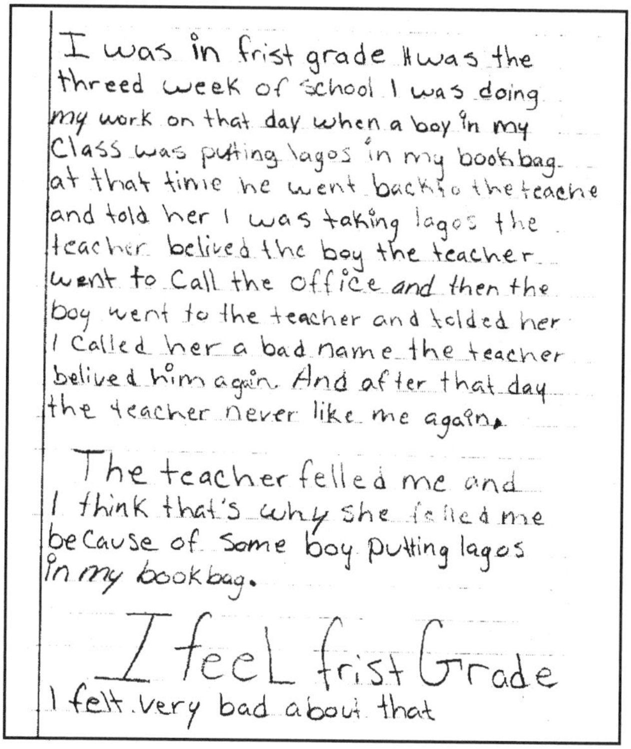

> I was in frist grade It was the
> threed week of school I was doing
> my work on that day when a boy in my
> Class was putting lagos in my book bag.
> at that time he went back to the teache
> and told her I was taking lagos the
> teacher belived the boy the teacher
> went to Call the office and then the
> boy went to the teacher and tolded her
> I Called her a bad name the teacher
> belived him again. And after that day
> the teacher never like me again.
>
> The teacher felled me and
> I think that's why she felled me
> becaue of Some boy putting lagos
> In my book bag.
>
> I feel frist Grade
> I felt very bad about that

Figure 6.7 *Corey remembers his terrible, horrible, no good, very bad day*

Mrs. C. called latoyia down to the office to tell what happend and then Mrs. C. called me down to the office and ask me what happend. I told her

For many students, this shared writing experience finally broke through the writing wall. Many of them generated pieces they wanted to revise and edit—and for the first time there was actually enough text to revise and edit! Before this their pieces had been too short to find patterns in mechanics and usage errors.

Many of our shared writing lessons were connected to the novels we read during shared reading. It is amazing to watch students find their writing voices because of the powerful response they have to a shared reading text. For Corey, it was Susan Shreve's *The Flunking of Joshua T. Bates.* Corey was open with me about his experience of "flunking first grade," but he hadn't been willing to share his feelings with the class. After I read this novel aloud, Corey spent days working on his piece about the pain he remembered from what he called "my failure."

Tabitha's writing voice came from her connection to our study of the Holocaust. During the unit, we read poetry, children's books, and excerpts from Elie Wiesel's *Night;* watched films and news clips; and listened to guest speakers. After we had read a particularly moving scene from the

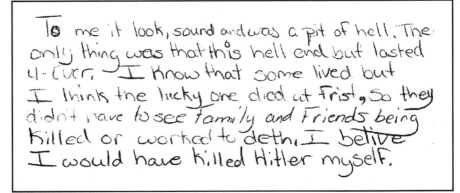

To me it look, sound and was a pit of hell. The only thing was that this hell end but lasted 4-ever. I know that some lived but I think the lucky one died at frist, So they didn't have to see family and Friends being killed or worked to deth. I belive I would have killed Hitler myself.

Figure 6.8 *Tabitha's writing about the shared reading of* Night

memoir when Wiesel is approaching Auschwitz, I asked students to think about why they had such powerful responses to it. They commented on Wiesel's descriptions of the stench of burning flesh, the painful selection process, and the dead bodies being dumped into pits. For Tabitha, the focus on sensory images unlocked her writing (see Figure 6.8).

After a shared reading we sometimes created an alternative ending to a novel as a class. My sixth graders were particularly moved as we read Lesley Conly's *Crazy Lady*. The protagonist of this story is a junior high student named Vernon, who is forced into helping Maxine and her mentally challenged son, Ronald, in exchange for some tutoring from a retired school teacher. Maxine is a colorful character whose addiction to alcohol interferes with her caring for Ronald. The friendship that develops between Vernon and Ronald led the students to anticipate an ending in total contrast to the story's actual ending. When we finished the novel, the students were furious with the author. When I suggested that they put their ideas in writing, Ashanni noted how the author could have ended the book "right" (see Figure 6.9). Jason even created his own book to help Conly along if she chose to do a rewrite for *Crazy Lady*. The personal and powerful connections students had with the book led to personal and powerful writing.

I also read a wide variety of poetry aloud. Sometimes we began or ended class with a poem; we used poems as patterns for our writing; and, I often brought in poetry to celebrate an event that was connected to a novel we were reading or a unit we were studying. As the students became more fluent in their writing, they often chose to respond to something through poetry. When we finished Cynthia DeFelice's *Weasel*, the students talked for days about the suspense and excitement in the novel. We talked about villains and how writers and directors create villains. Jason's poem captures the reading-writing connections he made through this book:

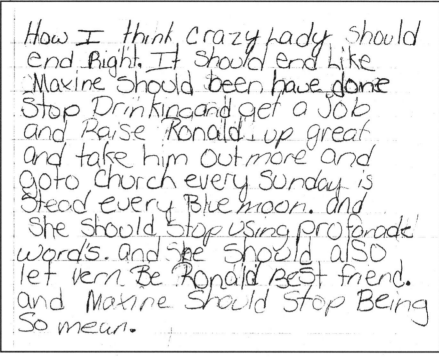

How I think crazy Lady should end Right. It should end Like Maxine Should been have done Stop Drinking and get a Job and Raise Ronald up great and take him Out more and goto Church every Sunday is Stead every Blue moon. and She should Stop using pro forade words. and She should also let vern Be Ronald Best friend. and Maxine Should Stop Being So mean.

Figure 6.9 *Ashanni's rewrite for the end of* Crazy Lady

The Weasel Poem
There was an old man that lived in a shack
and all he had was a broke back.
He didn't like kids at all.
He would catch them and hang
them on the wall.
All his heart was hate.
He would catch you before you can jump over a gate.
Now this is the end.
Don't read it again!

Shared writing helped my students become better writers. For many of them it was the impetus they needed to become independent. For others, it was a first step that needed to be followed up with assistance from me or their peers throughout the year.

Guided Writing

Guided writing gives writers the opportunity to practice a specific area of a writer's craft with the guided support of the teacher, the other students in the class, or their writing group. It's similar to a minilesson (Atwell 1987), although it can take up a full class period, during which students are introduced to and discuss certain characteristics of writing, have an opportunity to practice them, share what they have written (in pairs, small groups, and/or as a class), problem-solve the difficulties they are still encountering, and refine and revise their pieces. Guided writing can extend to independent writing as well as to responses to literature and content writing.

My students' biggest writing roadblock was that they couldn't seem to get started. Alex's attitude toward and problems with writing were characteristic of most of the writers in my classroom. He had difficulty completing any writing assignment independently. The only time he would actually write anything of substance was when I sat with him at the computer, asked him questions, and typed in the verbal responses he gave me. When left to his own devices during independent writing, he usually produced only one line. Hoping to find a way to break through this wall for all my students, I began to focus on what it would take to get Alex to write. (This was a method Janet proposed for dealing with many of my classroom problems. She would tell me to stop trying to figure out what would "fix" the whole class, choose one student who struggled with the problem, and try to implement a practice that would help that one student. Invariably, what I learned from this narrowed focus helped me rethink what I did with the entire class.)

It was a rainy Monday morning when Alex returned from ten days of suspension, and he was not particularly happy to be back. His worry about passing the seventh grade (this had not been his first suspension) seemed to give him license to stop working altogether. As soon as he entered the classroom, he began complaining about school, and his attitude was quickly picked up by others. Within minutes I became so frustrated with them I had to bring the class to a halt. "What's up with some of you today?" They were just waiting to be asked.

"School sucks."

"Why do I have to come to this stupid place, anyway?"

"Man, I wish I was at home…I hate my science teacher."

I stopped them before they could come down on the whole school and everybody in it. "Okay, I think that it's time to get some of this negativity out," I announced. "You need to get out a piece of paper and something to write with." After a great deal of shuffling around, lots of complaining, and much borrowing of paper and pens, we were finally ready to write.

"Let's take three minutes and get what we're feeling out on paper. I just want us to get our thoughts down—how we're feeling about school or what we would rather be doing right now. Remember, this is a freewrite. I don't care about spelling or punctuation at the moment. Ready? Let's write."

The students were familiar with freewrites; it's a tool I use often in class as a way to respond to something we've read or a problem we're having. I write along with the students, stopping only briefly to urge on the stragglers. After the three minutes were up, several students volunteered to share their writing, Alex among them. I was shocked. His writing was not only the longest piece he had ever completed, it also had voice and logic:

I feel board because im in hear on a Monday a rainy Monday that is it's cool that we only have 6 more week's till summer but on the other hand im scared becuse i might fail Ms. D. and Ms. C. Im going to stop hangin around the hall way an get to class to work that way i can go to 8th grade becuse it's in baressing when i see some one from when they were in 7th grade.

After class, I read through all the students' freewrites and was struck by how quickly and effectively they had begun their pieces. Wanting to celebrate all their effective writing, especially Alex's, without embarrassing them, I started identifying "great lines for guided writing." The next day I brought in overhead transparencies with effective lines from the students' freewrites to use as models for a guided writing lesson on beginnings. We looked at all of the quotes from their writing and then students brainstormed all the kinds of writing for which these lines could be beginnings. Some lines prompted ideas for short stories or novels; some seemed poetic. When we got to Alex's line, "I feel bored because I'm in here on a Monday, a rainy Monday," Tristen commented that the line sounded like the beginning of a song.

"How would it go?" I asked. He immediately stood up and improvised a quick rap using Alex's words as the first lines. Alex's look of pride taught me an important lesson about using something that is accessible to students as a model for their own writing. While the literature I usually chose was effective for some of my students, for others, it was intimidating.

As a group, we generated the characteristics of effective beginnings for stories, novels, poems, and songs. Then the students used the "great lines" of their classmates as models for their own beginnings. Here are some more "great lines" that have found their way onto overheads:

★ "She is so fat she and an elephant would be the same size."
★ "I hate some boys. They are stupid. They are such losers."
★ "I don't think that's right to kids. Kids have rights to."
★ "Why do we have to come to school at all?"
★ "I think some boys are dogs."
★ "I have this teacher who thinks she is the boss of the world."
★ "I hate some teachers because they will say something and then they will change what they said and you will get in trouble."
★ "I hate it when teachers are not right about something and when you try to help them they bite off your head."

Students need this kind of support in order to write. As they work together to find the patterns in both their own writing and that of published authors, they begin to transfer that knowledge to their independent writing.

Independent Writing

In our first months together, independent writing was difficult for my students. Few students wrote voluntarily, and those I coerced seldom wrote on topics or in genres they had chosen. When I suggested they respond to their independent reading, I got incoherent plot summaries. I noticed the glimmerings of change when several students became hooked on the books they were reading independently: they didn't leave during break, were reluctant to rejoin the whole class for direct instruction or shared reading, and were less than patient with interruptions. When I read their responses to their independent reading, I was delighted to find voice, details, and opinions:

> Dear Mars. G
> I am reading MAKE LEMONADE A novel by Virginia Euwer Wolff. It is a good book and I like better then my other book that was kind of good but I prefer this book better because it talk's about two things I like black people and children. I think that she should help clean up joll's house and clean up the kids because she have to work but she is there in the morning so she should clean them up before she comes to babysit when she get her check she should by them some clothes and she should go and wash her curtians and her clothes.

As these students became more intrigued by realistic fiction, they also became interested in nonfiction. The first nonfiction book that received widespread attention was Eve Krupinski and Dana Weikel's *Death from Child Abuse and No One Heard*. The book recounts a horrible case of child abuse that took place in the 1980s in a town near Orlando. Many of the students were particularly incensed when they discovered the convicted murderer was approaching an early release from prison. I had ordered multiple copies of the book for shared reading, then realized that I just could not read it aloud. One student read the book independently; others read it aloud in pairs during independent literacy exploration. As soon as Charlene started this reading with Shel, her writing began to reflect her engagement with the text:

> Dear Mrs. G,
> I am reading death from child abruse With Shel. We are doing good we read seven pages I don't like when Don hit her in her tummy. Just because she didn't know her abc's

This interest in nonfiction led naturally to our using newspapers and magazines as a way to find more information on the topics we were studying. In a guided reading lesson on expressing opinions through writing, I used several newspaper articles to which students could write responses. James was usually an extremely reluctant writer, but on our next independent writing day he returned to an article on child abuse in the *Bangor Daily News* (1992) to write his own opinion of the events it chronicled.

Seizing the Writing Moment

As I look at how writing instruction is conducted in our classroom, I realize that there have been two major changes: writing has become both more purposeful and more spontaneous. As a part of my ongoing assessment, I built guided writing lessons around specific inadequacies I saw in students' writing. I have continued to use shared writing to model a range of writing tasks, from increasingly more complex reading responses to five-paragraph essays.

In order to keep our literacy workshop student-centered, I have also used writing in somewhat less orthodox ways. When our time together seems out of sync somehow, I often use open-ended writing prompts as a way to check in with the students. Or again, at the end of our class, I may have students complete sentence prompts as exit slips: When I have to read, I _____. To me, books are _____. James's response, "To me, books are boring," tells me that he needs very different support from Corey, who responded, "To me, books are life."

If the students' mood seems to be one of general depression with their lives, I might change my plans so they can focus on their dreams and aspirations for a little while. Writing about a perfect day (see Figure 6.10) or their dreams for the future helps students connect the work they are doing to something meaningful in their futures.

Figure 6.10 *Todd's description of his perfect day*

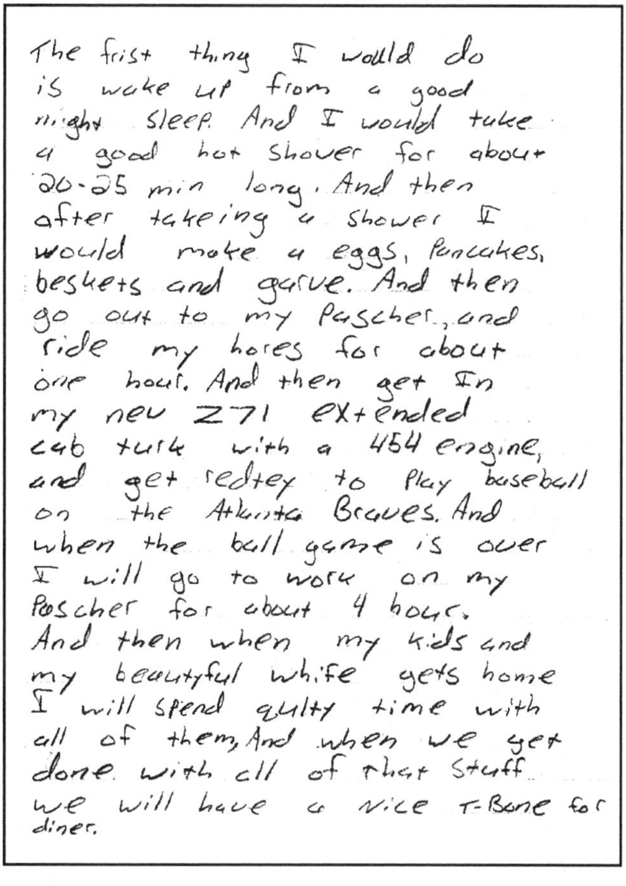

The frist thing I woлld do is wake up from a good night sleep. And I would take a good hot shower for about 20-25 min long. And then after takeing a shower I would make a eggs, Pancakes, beskets and garve. And then go out to my Pascher, and ride my hores for about one hour. And then get In my new Z71 extended cab turk with a 454 engine, and get redtey to Play baseball on the Atlanta Braves. And when the ball game is over I will go to work on my Poscher for about 4 hour. And then when my kids and my beautyful whife gets home I will spend qulty time with all of them. And when we get done with all of that stuff we will have a nice T-Bone for diner.

Some of the most effective writing, however, takes place when I simply make time in our schedule for students to write if they want or need to. Lynna wrote to express her anger at those trying to censor students' reading (see Figure 6.11). Sometimes I even receive an anonymous love letter:

Dear Mrs. G,
Hey I just wanted you to know that I love you very much. And thank you for always being there for me, and I think that you will be a very good mom. You are also a good friend 2 I hope that I can go with you 2 get my are hands don. I will always love you and when I go 2 7th and 8th will try to still came to your class. I will always think about you. You have always Ben there for me, so I will try 2 be there for you 2. well thats all for now.

Figure 6.11 *Lynna's advice letter to censors*

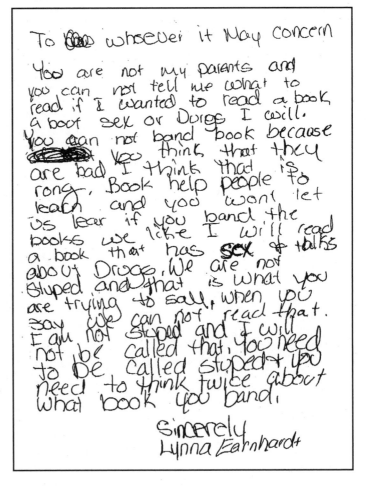

I believe that these young writers finally learned the value of putting their words on paper because they saw the value of the words in the books we read together.

Reflections by Janet

In Kyle's first year of teaching, she experienced a difficulty common to many first-year teachers—putting it all together. Beginning her teaching career by working with learners who struggled with almost everything related to literacy, her natural instinct was to fall back on things that could be easily worked into lesson plans and measured. She soon found that those things had no impact on the literacy needs of students who were one step away from the abyss. Fortunately, she was able to let go of the things her students could not do and build a foundation with those things they were able to do.

New teachers, as well as experienced ones, find it very difficult to let go of the surface features of writing for a time until students see the value of words, both their own and others'. With the increasing focus on standards and benchmarks, teachers constantly struggle between meeting students where they are and trying to get them where someone else thinks they should be. The cry "Back to basics!" is everywhere, and I agree that many of the basics have been missing in writing instruction. There are many who will disagree, but in my twenty-five years as an educator I have found that writing basics are not parts of speech, grammar, and punctuation. Those are editing basics. Listed below are some of the writing basics I have found important in order to help students, especially those who have experienced years of writing failure, become better writers:

★ Getting started
★ Finding the right word
★ Crafting effective beginnings
★ Making transitions from one idea/event to another
★ Using a variety of sentence structures
★ Using strong verbs
★ Adding effective details
★ Writing in a way that is kind to readers
★ Finding one's voice
★ Daring to take writing risks

Some might see this as a "which comes first" discussion, but I never saw changes in my students' writing when I focused on editing before they gained reading and then writing fluency. In fact, I believe that kind of teaching helped validate for students that writing was meaningless. I noticed incredible changes, however, when I found ways to help students become enthusiastic readers who read from a variety of genres and styles. Then, when I learned how to expand on that base by supporting students with shared and guided writing, I began to see even more growth.

In *Writing in the Real Classroom* (1991), Les Parsons notes: "Writing is an active, independent process in which individuals attempt to understand and cope with their world and their lives. The more dependent student writers are on teachers, the less involved they are in a true writing process" (14). Both Kyle and I have found that each year of our teaching helps move us closer to a balanced literacy program that gives students decreasing amounts of support as they are able to take on increasing amounts of independence. I know that I spent years believing that students would somehow magically become great writers because we did a lot of reading. And, for the most part, they did become better writers with very little writing support from me. I did not see myself as a writer and certainly did not have any idea how to help these students become better writers.

As I learned strategies for involving students in direct writing instruction that was meaningful, purposeful, and relevant, all of our writing improved. The balanced writing program outlined in Figure 6.12 highlights the ways I learned to accommodate writers' needs for varying levels of support through shared, guided, and independent writing. Today, I would modify Parsons's statement a little: writing can *only* be an active, independent process *if* students receive enough support along the way to be able to be successful and independent.

Figure 6.12 *Janet's guidelines for a balanced writing program*

A Balanced Writing Program			
Writing Activity	Purpose of Writing	Roles of Teacher	Preparation and Materials
Shared Writing	To engage students in writing with the teacher providing full support for the mechanics of writing while students contribute to the process of writing.	• Elicit responses from individuals and whole group as a prewriting activity. • Think aloud the process for getting started with writing tasks. • Engage students in providing text and voice. • Invite students to participate in surface-feature decisions (punctuation, usage, spelling, etc.). • Foster use of students' opinions as a way of rethinking writing tasks. • Use the whole group at all stages to complete the writing task (prewriting, drafting, revision, editing). • Take responsibility for producing a written product that can serve as an anchor for students' future writing.	• Define a writing strategy, mode of discourse, or a process of writing that you want writers to internalize. • Find literature or other materials that would provide opportunity for authentic response. • Use overheads, chart paper, or LCD panel to allow all students the opportunity to participate in the shared writing.

Writing Activity	Purpose of the Writing	Roles of Teacher	Preparation and Materials
Guided Writing	Provide writers with the opportunity to practice a specific area of a writer's craft with the guided support of the teacher, appropriate materials, and the other student writers.	• Provide multiple literary, audiovisual, or print models of the writing area (both examples and nonexamples). • Invite students to work to indentify definitional patterns or characteristics for the area of writing (effective lead, transition, strong verbs, etc). • Give students the opportunity to practice the writing task. • Bring students back together to share, problem-solve, revise, and refine craft. • Help students organize materials for easy access during independent writing.	• Find various literary, audiovisual, and print materials that make effective examples and nonexamples for the specific area of writing being guided. • Use overheads, boards, chart paper, or LCD panel for whole-class analysis of models.
Independent Writing	To allow time, choice, and opportunity for students to practice and independently solve problems encountered in real writing done for authentic purposes.	• Provide consistent time and space for independent writing. • Make yourself available as one of many writing resources in the room. • Develop a structure that allows ways for writers to share, celebrate, and publish writing.	• Classroom space conducive to independent writing: Easy access to materials. Availability of print resources. Current reference texts (dictionary, language handbooks, thesaurus, style manual, etc.). Place for writers to collaborate.

Figure 6.12 continued

Chapter 7

A Gathering of Goals

When I worked on my game, that's what I thought about. When it happened, I set another goal, a reasonable, manageable goal that I could realistically achieve if I worked hard enough. I guess I approached it with the end in mind. I knew exactly where I wanted to go, and I focused on getting there.

Michael Jordan

During Kyle's first year of teaching, although we were impressed with most of the students' consistent progress, we began to wonder whether the students saw themselves as moving toward defined literacy goals. Kyle was exhausted at the end of each day, drained by the students' seeming lack of academic focus and personal direction. I remember feeling the same way with my students: even when they began making progress, they were simply transferring control from other authority figures to me. They may have seen me as a kinder authority, but they were still leaving ownership of learning in my hands. The weight of Kyle's students' passivity, added to the incredible task of helping students become confident and competent readers and writers, was overwhelming.

We agreed that Kyle needed to find a way to help her students own their learning. Their success would be short lived if they made progress only when Kyle was part of their lives. Establishing goal setting as part of the curriculum seemed the way to do it: "Sharing this responsibility and then providing multiple opportunities for them to achieve success based on their decision moves the locus of control for their lives away from others and within themselves" (Allen 1995, 65). As we look inside Kyle's classroom, we can see the range of support it takes to help students begin to feel as though they can change their academic and their personal lives.

In the Classroom with Kyle

Purposeful Learning

After many discussions about my students' lack of motivation, I decided to use a strategy Janet had used with her ninth graders to help them begin to take control of their learning. The strategy entailed having all students set academic goals for the classroom as well as personal goals for their lives. After setting the goals, students were responsible for determining steps they would take to reach those goals. Finally, students developed markers that would indicate progress toward meeting the goals they had established. (See Figure 7.1 for an example; a blank version of this form is included as Appendix A.1.) I also added a component in which the students periodically reflected on their progress and on the challenges they were experiencing in meeting those goals.

Throughout the year I incorporated literature into the curriculum that Janet and I believed would support students in setting goals and making positive changes in their lives. Among the books I used were:

★ *The Power of Goals,* by P. Anderson (Lombard, IL: Celebrating Excellence, 1992).
★ *Nathaniel Branden's Little Blue Book of Self-Esteem,* by N. Branden (New York: Barnes & Noble, 1995).
★ *Life's Little Instruction Book,* by H. J. Brown Jr. (Nashville, TN: Rutledge, 1991).
★ *Chicken Soup for the Soul: 101 Stories to Open the Heart and Rekindle the Spirit,* by J. Canfield and M. V. Hansen (New York: Berkeley, 1993).
★ *The Aladdin Factor,* by J. Canfield and M. V. Hansen (New York: Berkeley, 1995).
★ *Reflections on a Gift of Watermelon Pickle,* edited by S. Dunning (Glenview, IL: Scott Foresman, 1995).
★ *Spin a Soft Black Song,* by N. Giovanni (Toronto: HarperCollins Canada, 1985).
★ *The Lottery Rose,* by I. Hunt (New York: Berkeley, 1976).
★ *I Can't Accept Not Trying: Michael Jordan on the Pursuit of Excellence,* by M. Jordan (New York: HarperCollins, 1994).
★ *Readings from the Hurricane Island Outward Bound School,* edited by A. M. Kuller (Hurricane Island, ME: Hurricane Island Outward Bound School, 1988).
★ *Frederick,* by L. Lionni (New York: Trumpet Club, 1967).
★ *The Flunking of Joshua T. Bates,* by S. Shreve (New York: Random House, 1984).
★ *Brian Tracy's Little Silver Book of Prosperity,* by B. Tracy (New York: Barnes & Noble, 1995).

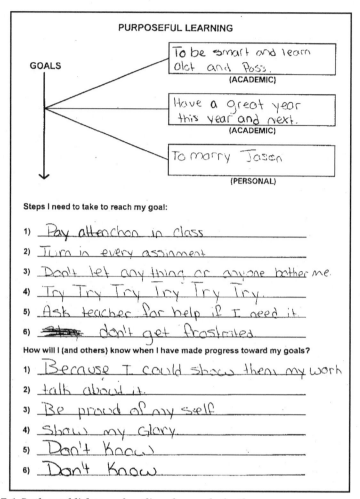

PURPOSEFUL LEARNING

GOALS

To be smart and learn alot and Poss.
(ACADEMIC)

Have a great year this year and next.
(ACADEMIC)

To marry Jason
(PERSONAL)

Steps I need to take to reach my goal:

1) Pay atteachon in class
2) Turn in every assinment
3) Don't let any thing or anyone bother me.
4) Try Try Try Try Try Try.
5) Ask teacher for help if I need it.
6) ~~Step~~ don't get frostrated

How will I (and others) know when I have made progress toward my goals?

1) Because I could show them my work
2) talk about it.
3) Be proud of my self
4) Show my Glory.
5) Don't Know
6) Don't Know.

Figure 7.1 *Ruth establishes and outlines her goals for the year*

★ *W. O. W.: Writers on Writing,* edited by J. Winokur (Philadelphia, PA: Running Press, 1986).

Finally, at the end of the grading period each student documented the steps he or she had taken toward achieving his or her goals, and I evaluated that documentation.

The two case studies that follow illustrate the journey my students and I took during our gathering-of-goals project.

Ruth. Ruth was an angry twelve-year-old when she entered our classroom in the fall. Although my teaching experiences had been limited to tutoring and internships, I had never seen a student who was as determined as Ruth to do exactly as she wanted. Unfortunately, what Ruth wanted did not fall within the parameters of success for either her academic or her personal life. She seemed intent on defying her parents and any other authority figures she encountered along the way. When she became overwhelmed by family problems during the first week of school, she escaped them by running away from home. Although we finally managed to find her and get her back to school, her poor attendance and lack of interest seemed destined to cause her to fail. Given her personal problems, I had no idea how I was going to convince her that reading was important in her life.

In spite of my efforts to help Ruth connect with literacy, her progress during the first three quarters of the school year was sporadic at best. It's impossible to document Ruth's work or progress during that period, because there was never any written evidence that she was connecting in any way with anything she encountered in shared and guided reading. The first academic ray of hope I saw occurred in late February, when Ruth began using books on tape during independent reading. Given Ruth's history, it was not surprising that Caroline Cooney's *The Face on the Milk Carton* was the book that finally reached her. I worried that perhaps I had made a mistake in giving Ruth a book that centered around a kidnapping —it was a bit too close to Ruth's fantasies of ending up in someone else's home. But Ruth stayed—both in her home and in our classroom. And she began to read.

Soon my teaching log began to fill with titles Ruth had read. When she completed her assisted reading of *The Face on the Milk Carton,* she quickly moved on to other books on tape. In a short time, Ruth had read R. L. Stine's *The Dare* and John Bellairs's *The House with a Clock in Its Walls*. After these three successes, Ruth declared that none of the other books on tape were what she wanted to read, so I needed to find someone to record her next choice, Judy Blume's *Tiger Eyes*. While she was waiting for the recording to be finished, she read shorter works such as *Disney's The Lion King* and Tim Burton's *The Nightmare Before Christmas*.

Although I was thrilled that Ruth finally seemed to be connecting with a few books, her attitude toward herself, the rest of the class, and any work we did together remained apathetic. It was frustrating to see that she still lacked any personal or academic motivation. However, as long as I could continue to get her to come to class, there was hope. That hope finally paid off during the last quarter, when Janet and I implemented the goals project. It was as if the project had been designed with Ruth in mind.

She seemed to be encouraged by the fact that she had finally found a way to get some direction in her life. More important, it was a direction she had set for herself. Ruth's goals for the last grading period were uniquely hers, and this seemed to please her. While her personal goal, "to go back out with Jason and marry him," didn't particularly please me, her academic goal, "to pass the seventh grade and to get better grades in math" gave me a glimpse of the new, healthier Ruth. Hoping to keep her on this positive track, I frequently asked her to reflect on the progress she felt she was making toward meeting her goals (see Figure 7.2). The positive effects of this focus began to carry over into her reading. She stopped using books on tape and moved on toward the unassisted reading of several novels.

When it came time for her final goal-setting evaluation, Ruth was eager to begin. I was shocked to see her come to class early, immediately sit down at the computer, and begin to write. For three days, Ruth was totally engrossed in assessing her progress; she was no longer tardy, and she didn't spend the beginning of each class trying to disrupt others. When she listed all the books she had read, it made her feel proud that she had worked hard and could see the results of that work. Here's what she wrote:

Figure 7.2 *Ruth's reflections on the progress of her personal and academic goals*

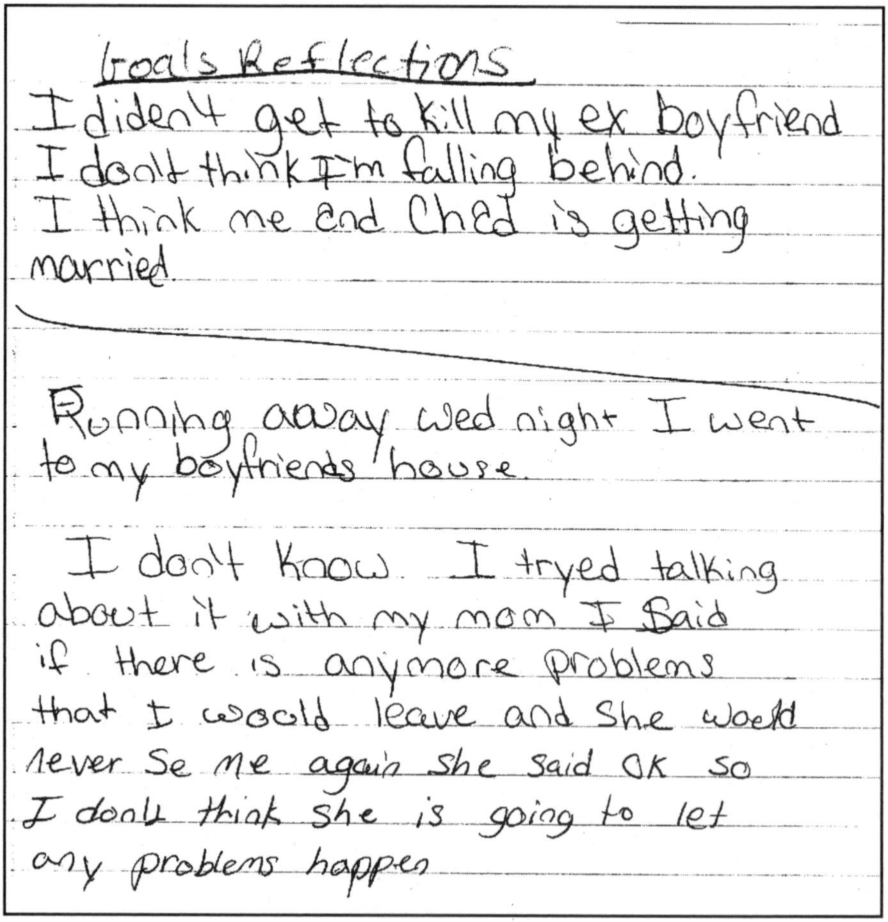

Goals Reflections

I diden't get to kill my ex boyfriend
I doalt think I'm falling behind.
I think me and Ched is getting married.

Running away wed night I went to my boyfriends house.

I don't know. I tryed talking about it with my mom I said if there is anymore problems that I woold leave and she woold never se me again she said OK so I donlt think she is going to let any problems happen

My name is Ruth Lapin, and I have achieved a lot of my goals that I have set for myself. I only wrote two of my goals that are most important to me for this nine weeks. I achieved the ones that I have been trying to work on sence the begining of this year. Those were to become a better reader I think I have acheaved those goals because I have read three books in only a couple of weeks.

One book was <u>The Face On The Milk Carton,</u> another one was <u>The Skirt,</u> and <u>The Dare.</u>

The two goals I have set for myself was to get better grades in math and to pass the seventh grade. I don't think I have improved a lot in math because it's too hard and I don't understand it.

But I believe I am doing a lot better in staying out of trouble.

But I think I have brought up my grades a lot.

My two personal goals was to go back out with Jason & marry him. But things have changed between us. We decided to just be friends I beleave I've achieved the goals Ive been working on for a long time. I think setting your goals is a good way of achieving them. I have not achieved all of my goals because I am not old enough to get married. I don't think writing down your goals and looking at them is not going to achieve anything but believing that you can achieve your goals whatever they are you can do it. I feel that you can do alot if I really put my mind to what ever it is that I want to do. I think I have changed a lot because setting goals you need to be confident in yourself and in others. Believing I could reach for my goals and acomplishing them. The biggest acomplishment that I have done is my grades.

All the books I have read 8 – 15 – through – 5 – 24 of 94 & 95.
1.) <u>More Scary Stories</u> By: Alvin Schwartz.
2.) <u>The Night Before Christmas</u> By: Tim Burton.
3.) <u>The Lion King</u> By: Don Ferguson.
4.) <u>Camp Nowhere</u> By: Cathy East DuBowski.
5.) <u>Scorpions</u> By: Walter Dean Myers.
6.) <u>The Outsiders</u> By: S. E. Hinton.
7.) <u>I Know What You Did Last Summer</u> By: Lois Duncan.
8.) <u>The Lottery Rose</u> By Irene Hunt.
9.) <u>The Face On The Milk Carton</u> By: Caroline B. Cooney.
10.) <u>The Skirt</u> By Gary Soto.
11.) <u>Ransom</u> By: Lois Duncan.
12.) <u>Tiger Eyes</u> By: Judy Blume.
13.) <u>The House With A Clock In Its Walls</u> By: John Bellairs.
14.) <u>The Dare</u> By: R. L. Stine.

I was a bit surprised that Ruth felt she had been working on her goals since the beginning of the year. Upon reflection, however, I realized that given the rapid progress she made once she began reading, she probably had begun moving toward the goal of becoming a reader long before I saw any evidence of it. It was a good reminder for me that Ruth, like most nonreaders, wanted to become a reader but lacked the motivation or strategies to overcome the stigma of early failure. The concrete nature of the goals project had brought reading into a focus where Ruth had some control—a focus that helped her see that it was within *her* power to become a reader. While Janet and I may have been responsible for finding a strategy that worked with Ruth, it was her initiative and diligence that finally made her achieve success.

Anthony. Anthony also lacked control of his academic and personal life. To classroom visitors, Anthony appeared strong and unafraid. But each time I tried to talk with him about his literacy, the only answers I got were a shy duck of his head, a shrug of his shoulders, and an occasional "I don't know." During each day of our shared reading of Irene Hunt's *The Lottery Rose,* I became more aware of how much Anthony reminded me of the shy, tormented Georgie. Like Georgie, Anthony could not read well. And, like Georgie, when asked a question, he would shrink away. Anthony hated books and would either sleep during independent reading or simply flip through the pages of the book that I had given him. Anthony, however, was not the fragile, seven-and-a-half-year-old Georgie, tormented by other students. He was a burly, thirteen-year-old with serious reading difficulties.

Like the nonreaders Janet had encountered in her teaching, Anthony hadn't been read to as a child. "It has long been my personal belief that a bond is created during a read-aloud that is unrivaled in terms of literacy. I also believe that until students experience that stage of their literacy growth, they can't move forward in their development" (Allen 1995, 45). Another obstacle for Anthony was his older brother, Corey, who was also in our class. Unlike Anthony, Corey had no problems expressing himself orally, whether during class discussions or in frequent outbursts of anger or displeasure. Both brothers ran track, but Corey was faster. Both brothers had reading difficulties, but Corey was progressing more rapidly. One of the first problems we needed to solve was finding a way to help Anthony move out of his brother's shadow, to help him speak for himself rather than allow Corey to do the talking for both of them.

After months of struggling with Anthony's apathy and frustration, I finally realized that I was definitely not meeting Anthony where he was. Anthony was at the lap-reading stage and I was trying to help him find the success I saw in fluent adolescent readers. This is a common trap teachers fall into. Jerry Johns (1993) notes: "Estimates of students who are dealing with books that are too difficult go as high as 40 percent!" (13). In my struggle to find books that might interest him, I was forgetting that these books were many years above his reading level. His years of reading frustration made it almost impossible for him to find success in chapter books written for young adults, even those on tape. For Anthony to change as a reader, he had to be able to see his role in turning "willed refusal to learn into failure to learn" (Kohl 1991, 10). The goals project helped him take on that responsibility.

I also wanted to help Anthony get past his writing fears. At Janet's suggestion, I decided to do a language experience activity (LEA) with him to show him the satisfaction that comes from seeing one's words in print. Anthony's success in reading *Disney's Beauty and the Beast* and connecting with its characters is evident in his first book response, which I typed for him as we sat together at the computer:

> The book that I'm reading is <u>Beauty and the Beast.</u> I like the pictures best in this book because they have pretty colors and not that many words.
>
> There is nothing that I do not like about this book. I like the Beast the best because he's mean. He was fighting the wolves from eating Belle and that's how the Beast and Belle met. She went to this castle and he wanted her to stay there.
>
> Belle is one of my favorite characters, too. She liked to read and about the whole book, she is reading. Everyone always looks at her because she always has her head in a book. I want to be able to read as much as Belle does.
>
> When you read it, I want you to tell me what was your best part.

Anthony moved from my transcribing for him to writing his own responses to books, but the real turning point came when he began establishing personal and academic goals. His initial attempts (Figures 7.3 and 7.4) reflect his personal quest to be an athlete and his academic goal of reading. Even in this seemingly simple exercise, Anthony shared his desire to "make his parents feel special and proud" about his reading. I

Figure 7.3 *Anthony's personal and academic goals*

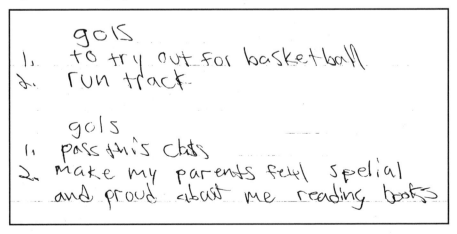

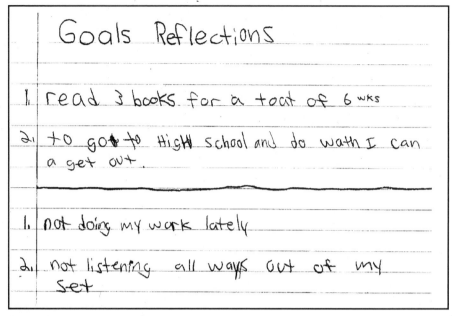

Goals Reflections

1. read 3 books. for a toat of 6 wks

2. to got to High school and do wath I can
   a get out.

1. not doing my work lately

2. not listening all ways out of my
   set

Figure 7.4 *More of Anthony's goals and what he felt kept him from achieving those goals*

can only imagine the stress that comes with feeling you have let your parents down because you can't read, but the parent connection remained a good source of motivation for Anthony's continued success.

By spring, Anthony's reading goals had become more specific (see Figure 7.5) and, as was true with Ruth, the more he focused on setting and achieving goals and then setting new ones, the more successful he became as a reader. Anthony's final reflection of the year indicated to us both that he saw the connection between his efforts and eventual success:

> 1. Beat track time. I went to practice. Every day we had track practice. We practice for 2 hr.
> 2. Making the honor roll. doing my work when I am supposed to. I have not been bad since August I have been good. I like to keep it that way.
> 3. Read one book every week for total of nine. I started reading when I set my personal goals and I have not stopped reading. I have been good for the last past weeks now I payed attention in shard reading.
> 4. Make a c or better language arts. By not getting in trouble. Just by doing my work and not talking when I am not supposed to. That just brings my grade down. I don't want that. It not good to have that happen. The books that I have read is THE FACE ON THE MILK CARTON. THE WIZARD OF OZ. ALADDIN. JIMUGLY. THE LION KING. FIND WALDO. BEAUTY AND THE BEAST. THEY WERE LONG

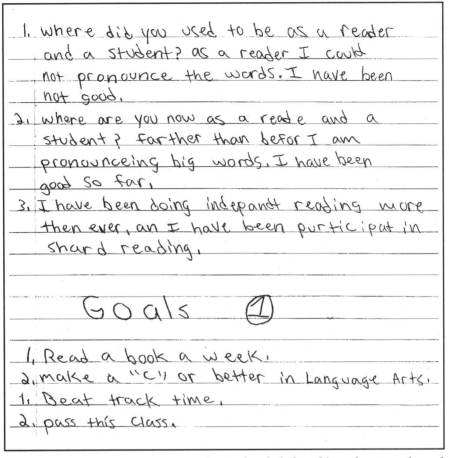

1. where did you used to be as a reader and a student? as a reader I could not pronounce the words. I have been not good.

2. where are you now as a reade and a student? farther than befor I am pronounceing big words. I have been good so far,

3. I have been doing indepandt reading more then ever, an I have been purticipat in shard reading,

Goals ①

1. Read a book a week,
2. make a "C" or better in Language Arts,
1. Beat track time,
2. pass this class,

Figure 7.5 *Anthony's response to questions Kyle asked about his goals as a reader and the new goals he set for himself*

Anthony connects his reading with his goals explicitly: "I started reading when I set my personal goals and I have not stopped reading." Anthony was on his way, and goal setting had contributed significantly to making that happen.

Impact of the Goals Project

While I had often prayed for the year to end and despaired that it ever would, by the time May came around I was sad that it had. I had concrete evidence that my students' reading and writing had significantly improved. And although Janet had told me what a difference goal setting had made with her students, I was shocked by the almost palpable connection between setting goals and increased reading and writing ability.

Several aspects of this goals project were important to the literate community I had attempted to establish. One was publication. As the students set goals, I asked them to decorate the goals and publish them on one of our many student-designed bulletin boards. When I saw the impact the goals board had on Joey, I realized how important the publication step really is.

Joey had an extremely difficult time staying on task for more than three minutes. This was especially true when the students were working independently, which they did every day. He would concentrate on his writing or reading for a brief moment and then begin his rounds, inspecting everyone else's work. Not surprisingly, this was not appreciated by most of the other students. He was screamed at, kicked, and hit, the altercations often drawing everyone's attention. As the other students became more engrossed in their independent literacy activities, Joey's behavior became even worse. His "inspections" led to many severe class disruptions.

Ironically, Joey seemed to know that he had a problem staying focused. His personal goal was "To stop wandering." Once the students' goals had been published, whenever Joey started his tour of the room either I or one of the students would point to the board where his goals were posted. Often this was enough to refocus Joey and get him back to his own reading and writing. The posted goals became a gentle reminder from himself, rather than me, about what actions he needed to take to be more successful.

Once students had internalized the significance of goal setting, it was easy for us to use their specific reading goals as part of the strategy lessons we did in class each day. The seventh and eighth graders came up with the following literacy-specific goals:

Todd—"Know all the words and how to pronounce them. Read them."
Brett—"I want to enjoy [reading]. I don't want to be bored. I want it to be very fun."
Chanelle—"To learn."
Ruth—"Understand the book and words."
Joey—"Relax and I want to be able to understand what the book is talking about."
Corey—"To enjoy and make pictures in my head."
Jeff—"Understand the words that I read."
Corian—"To be smarter and read more."
Elicia—"I want to enjoy and be able to pronounce the words."
April—"To read more books and to learn more about reading."
Carl—"To read more and learn more words."
Jen—"To enjoy it and to know that I am reading."
Tabitha—"To feel the characters' emotions."
Anthony—"I want to know the words and like the pictures."
Jermaine—"To learn new words and get smarter."
Tiffany—"To know the word when I see it."
Malcolm—"To get a book that makes me _feel_."

Each student also contributed a statement on how to become a better reader to their Super Readers bulletin board. Here are three of them:

Read at home, read at school, have reading time. Read to your sister or brother and spend time at home reading for 30 thirty minutes and write what you have read so far.
—Chanelle

Someone becomes a reader by reading every day. And studying every day how to read. Some people read to themself. Some people read in a group. When you become a super reader, you like to read every day. You love to read every day. Reading becomes fun for you.
—Tiffany

Read more often than before. You will read more than ever in your life. You won't even know that you are reading more books than you used to do. Read together, read books on tape, and read by yourself.
—Anthony

These public statements helped each student see that he or she was working toward something within reach. Before this, students seemed to believe that reading was an abstract concept; our goals project had made reading concrete *and* attainable.

As the end of the year approached, Janet felt the goals project would be an ideal way to help students reflect on their accomplishments and establish goals for summer and the following school year. She suggested that I ask students to write letters to themselves telling themselves what they had done that made them proud and what they planned to accomplish over the next few months until we were together again. Jason's letter (see Figure 7.6) may make you wonder about the "hidden" curriculum, but his pride and sense of accomplishment are certainly real. Our goals project became a beginning rather than an ending.

Reflections by Janet

As Kyle started her second year of teaching, she and I agreed that since goal setting had been instrumental in increasing students' interest and competency in literate activities, she needed to find a way to incorporate this from the beginning of the year. The year before she had been using Kirby, Liner, and Vinz's (1988) Here and Now strategy—writing a quick response to something—to help students gain writing fluency. This year, she decided to apply the strategy specifically to goals and created the writing prompts in Appendix A.18. Beginning the year with this strong connection between thinking, writing, and goal setting allows sooner and more rapid progress in reading and writing.

Kyle has learned the value of looking closely at a curricular problem, examining a number of ways the problem can be solved, and including students in the solution. The success of this project helped her realize the

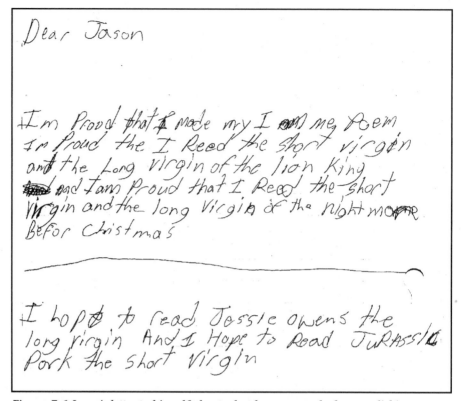

Dear Jason

I'm Proud that I made my I am me Poem
I'm Proud the I Read the short virgin
and the Long virgin of the lion King
and I am Proud that I Read the short
Virgin and the long Virgin of the night mare
Befor Christmas

I hope to read Jessie owens the
long virgin And I Hope to Read JuRASSIC
Pork the short virgin

Figure 7.6 *Jason's letter to himself about what he was proud of accomplishing throughout the year*

significance of goal setting. It had been easy to become discouraged, because her students were so far from what most would consider to be the literacy norm. Dealing with fifteen or twenty middle school students who have been pulled from their other classes because they cannot and will not read can be overwhelming. The goals project forced Kyle and her students to find ways to make learning accessible, measurable, and reproducible.

Booker T. Washington has said, "You measure the size of the accomplishment by the obstacles you had to overcome to reach your goals." For these students and Kyle, the obstacles were great. Kyle had to help her students overcome years of reading failure, years of seeing literacy as a painful experience, years of negative expectations for themselves and for school. As they worked together, they found Charles Noble's words a light along the path: "You must have long-range goals to keep you from being frustrated by short-range failures" (Anderson 1992). They would hold on to that important concept long after the goals project ended.

Chapter 8

Are You *Sure* Iced Tea Used to Be Hot?

We use what we know about the world in order to make sense of it, not blindly, but by seeking information that will answer specific questions.

Frank Smith

The Role of Background Knowledge

I believe Smith's words are never more true than as they apply to reading. Unfortunately for us and our students, we are often totally unaware of what readers bring to a text—or, more important, what they aren't bringing that is necessary for understanding. In the classroom one day I was reminded of the importance of background knowledge as I played Password with a group of boys who had all spent the morning together in an automotives class.

My student partner and I sat facing each other as he gave me clues. When Steve said, "Shoes," I replied, "Sneakers." When he said "Tires," I said, "Cars." Once again, with less patience this time, he elongated his clue "Shoes," as if saying it more slowly would help me figure out the unknown word. Steve became increasingly agitated as it became evident that we would lose this round. "Shoes!" he yelled, and I tentatively said, "Feet?" just as the buzzer rang. He jumped out of his chair and said, "What is wrong with you? Everybody in this room knows that the word that goes with shoes is brake!"

"Why would I say break if you said shoes?"

"Brake shoes, Mrs. Allen, haven't you ever heard of brake shoes?"

I lost a lot of respect when I had to admit that I had never heard of brake shoes, and I wasn't absolved of any guilt by pointing out that the actual word on the card was *break*. I had absolutely no prior knowledge of something Steve and all the other guys in the room considered necessary for basic survival. It was a good lesson for me about the assumptions we make as teachers regarding what students bring to the texts we use in class.

Prior knowledge is one of the most potent variables in overall comprehension (McKeown et al. 1992). Each time I was in Kyle's classroom, I was struck by the gap between the real-life knowledge students brought to the classroom and the curricular knowledge they lacked. In many cases Kyle's students struggled with the books they were reading because they lacked the background knowledge necessary to understand them. While using books on tape helps students decode words, it does not make up for being unfamiliar with important concepts about text, print, and subject matter.

During shared reading, since all students were reading the same book, Kyle could compensate for some lack of background knowledge by using prereading and reading strategies that allowed students to pool their knowledge: K–W–L (Ogle 1986); text highlighting (Chambers 1996); list–group–label (Taba 1967); anticipation guides (Readence, Bean, and Baldwin 1985); and PReP (Langer 1981). (See Appendix A for details about these and other strategy lessons.) Based on what she heard and saw, she pointed individual students to resources that would fill in the blanks.

Kyle also used shared reading to help students learn about text conventions: print attributes (italics and boldface), genre characteristics, support features (charts and pictures), and story grammar (Rumelhart 1977; Thorndyke 1977). As students came to understand more about the ways that words and books work, there was a positive cumulative effect on their independent reading.

But Kyle and I decided we didn't want to stop here. James Britton says that "writing floats on a sea of talk" (1970, 164). These students were in very real ways talk-deprived. Their talk was mainly the abbreviated conversation they had with friends, swapping insults or making brief utterances whose real message was conveyed by the underlying body language. (Some groups of adolescents develop an elaborate form of gestures and stances that completely take the place of talk.) For the most part, these students did not come from homes where parents talked with them about world and local events or took them to visit museums or historical sites. They were not watching news shows (as tentative a grasp as that can be on world knowledge), nor were they reading newspapers and magazines.

What if we planned an event in connection with each of the shared texts, an event whose larger goal was purposeful talk? These events could perhaps create that sea of talk whereby we could support and extend students' knowledge of the world.

In the Classroom with Kyle

The Tea Party

At the beginning of the year, I was reading Susan Shreve's *The Flunking of Joshua T. Bates* aloud to my new sixth graders, and they were loving the book. Here's the plot in brief: Two days before Joshua returns to school from his summer vacation, he discovers that he is going to have to repeat the third grade. Quite understandably, Joshua is angry. He begins the year as an outcast because he is bigger than all the other students; Tommy Wilhelm, the fourth-grade bully, torments him every day. His new teacher, Mrs. Goodwin, however, quickly discovers the knowledge that Joshua brings to the class and uses Joshua to help younger, struggling students in their third-grade classroom. Joshua and Mrs. Goodwin become a team. Joshua now also has a goal. He wants to pass the test that will qualify him to be promoted to the fourth grade before Christmas, and Mrs. Goodwin agrees to help him. Mrs. Goodwin tutors Joshua at her home after school, and during the tutoring sessions, she serves him hot tea and cookies.

When I read the part about the hot tea aloud to my students they were in shock.

"Iced tea ain't supposed to be hot. It's cold!" Ulysses proclaimed. The rest of the students agreed with him.

"Haven't you guys ever tried hot tea? I drink hot tea every morning."

"Ewwww. Gross!"

They were even more repulsed when I told them that I put honey and cream in it. My eighth graders saw me drink hot tea each day during first period and they, too, had been "grossed out."

"Wouldn't you all at least like to try hot tea?" They were hesitant, at best. These students live in Florida, where iced tea is the unofficial state drink. They couldn't fathom tea as anything other than a cold drink. By the same token they were excited about the possibility of having a party, so they decided they were willing to make the sacrifice.

On the day of the party, Janet and Philippa Stratton, our editor, came to visit the class. Students were initially shocked by Philippa's accent and privately asked Janet why that woman talked funny. Janet explained that Philippa was English, and our tea party began. I showed the kids how I made hot tea, and many of them watched in disbelief. When I finished, they enthusiastically tackled the task of making their own tea (see Figure 8.1). Some left the tea bags in too long, so to compensate for the strength of their drinks, they overflowed their cups with cream. Some added teaspoon after teaspoon of sugar. Sharone even resorted to pouring cream in a cup and sweetening it with sugar, declaring that this was much better than tea. The conversation was even richer than their sugar-and-cream-filled cups.

"Where did tea come from?"

"England, stupid. Isn't that right?" one of them asked Philippa.

As Philippa explained that tea was first known to the world as a hot drink, students stared at her in amazement.

"Hey, didn't somebody dump some tea in the water or something?"

"Dump tea in the water? You crazy—"

"Do you mean the Boston Tea Party?"

"Yeah. Why did they dump that tea? Was it hot tea?"

And so the conversation moved forward. From talk about personal tastes to China tea cups, from American history to war, students were

Figure 8.1 *The tea party celebrating Joshua's success in* The Flunking of Joshua T. Bates

engaged in productive talk with adults who could help them build and refine their knowledge of history and the world around them. This kind of talk appears to be random and unfocused and it is. It is talk that reminds us of our family dinners—each new comment takes the conversation somewhere else. I had simply set up an event that I hoped would stimulate talk and then let go so that the talk could happen.

Love Is in the Air

Any middle school teacher will tell you that love is the main concern of middle school students, especially girls. As Valentine's Day approached last year, I watched the love letters and Valentines fly and wondered how I could use my students' enthusiasm to get them involved in an academic goal.

I had been reading aloud to students both during shared reading, where students followed along in copies of the novel, and through read-alouds, where students simply listened. One of my primary sources for the read-alouds was the poetry collection I had created in one of Janet's classes at the university; using as models similar books her high school students had made, we had each compiled a book filled with poems that we liked and that we hoped to use as teachers in our classrooms. We chose poems in several categories: great read-alouds, survival, love, friendship, goals, etc.

When I asked students if they would like to celebrate Valentine's Day with love poems and cookies, they were extremely enthusiastic. They thought it was the perfect combination—food and no work. I shared my poetry notebook with them and brought in lots of poetry anthologies for them to use to find poems for their own collections. I told the students that on Valentine's Day they could each read one poem. In the process of creating their poetry resource books, students began reading their poems to me and to other students. After all my worry about ways to encourage the kids to read orally, they were doing it on their own!

Before Valentine's Day arrived, we discussed what made a good read-aloud, and students began practicing their chosen pieces. On the day of our celebration, every student read a poem to the class, and then we had a cookie-decorating party. It was obvious that for most of these students, the experience was a first. I expected the pride they would feel in finally doing an oral reading for their classmates, but I did not anticipate their excitement at decorating their cookies (see Figure 8.2). It was a positive experience that led to many other oral readings during our year together.

Figure 8.2 *Tabitha proudly displays her decorated Valentine cookie*

Ribs, Barking Dogs, and Academia

Our Valentine's Day celebration made me realize that celebrating was something these students had not done much of in their lives, especially celebrations of academic achievement. During my second year of teaching in the Literacy Project, several of my students had significantly improved their grades, some even enough to make our school's A/B honor roll. Wanting to recognize those who had achieved the academic goals they had set for themselves, I decided to host an academic dinner at my home. My husband and in-laws cooked all the food.

As the night approached, student excitement ran high. Students began arriving, whereupon my five-pound Yorkshire terrier began barking in his loudest and most protective manner. Eventually Gonzo and the students, except for Sharone, warmed up to one another. Sharone was terrified and refused to come into the house until I took her by the hand and showed her that I had put Gonzo in the back bedroom. She was embarrassed, even ashamed, of her fear, and the other students immediately began teasing her. I made them promise that the incident would not be mentioned in school on Monday, but the damage had been done. On Monday, Sharone delivered a letter (see Figure 8.3) saying she was so embarrassed that she wanted to leave my class. But the other students came through, encouraging Sharone to stay and even to come along to another party I had during the Christmas holidays.

These celebrations allowed students to enjoy my home and family. When Chanelle commented on how huge the one-bedroom apartment my husband and I lived in was and that a friend of hers had eight people living in his house, which was half as big as our apartment, I was reminded of what we take for granted. Some of these students were having their first traditional "family" meal in years.

Although having students at one's house or apartment would not be possible, or even desirable, for some teachers, it worked for us. I believe it is important to find ways to celebrate success, even if all the celebrations occur in the classroom. I learned more by watching and listening during those times than I did in conference after conference.

Recycled Art—Stealing Money and Hot-Wiring Cars

While my seventh and eighth graders were doing a shared reading of Glendon Swarthout's novel *Bless the Beasts and the Children,* Janet brought in Sue LoSasso, a volunteer at the local recycling center. The center collects industrial materials, and teachers are allowed to use spools and wires, gizmos and sprockets, for class work. Sue brought in foam sheets, computer chips, pipe cleaners, wires, metal discs, wooden spools, sample wallpaper books, etc.

Janet and I wanted this art activity to help students develop their ability to form pictures in their heads as they read. I asked the students

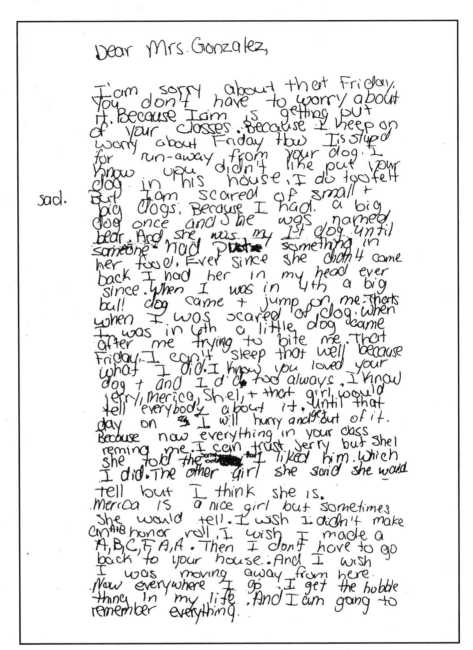

Figure 8.3 *Sharone's letter to Kyle after attending the academic dinner*

to look at their chapter maps and identify the most vivid pictures they remembered. I then asked them to close their eyes while I reread those descriptive passages and to imagine the pictures the words were painting. Finally, they sketched the pictures that had formed in their minds.

When Sue arrived, the word-artists were ready. They looked a bit skeptical, however, when they saw the bags and boxes of materials Sue had brought. Carl spoke for most of the group: "You think we're gonna make something out of that? It's just a bunch of junk!" Once they got started, however, the creative connections they made to the book exceeded anyone's expectations. For days, Jermaine and Carl constructed a scene involving a truck that Cotton and the other boys hot-wired and used for their escape. They also made a placard that proclaimed Swarthout's words:

> But they had to watch a car being bagged. Besides they wanted to believe in Teft, to be astonished by him again. Old Teft moseyed across the silent street as though he wore a Colt and a tin star. Idling around the pickup, he made certain it was unlocked and the keys gone. He kicked a couple of tires. Approaching, he stepped efficiently to the front end and raised the hood. (39)

My sixth graders, who were reading Katherine Paterson's *The Great Gilly Hopkins,* were equally adept at creating an image to illustrate the text. Charlene and Shel did an incredible depiction of the blind neighbor's living room, including the tall bookcases the book describes:

> Leaning against two walls of the crowded little room were huge antique bookcases that reached the ceiling. And stacked disorderly upside down, even put in backwards, were books—hundreds of them. They looked old and thick with dust. High on the top shelf was "Sarsaparilla to Sorcery." On tiptoe, leaning against the rickety lower shelves to keep from toppling, she could barely reach the book. She pulled at it with the tip of her fingers, catching it as it fell. Something fluttered to the floor as she did so. (33–34)

What began as junk turned into concrete reminders to students that words should form pictures in their head. We returned to those models, both the art and the words, many times throughout the year when students got bogged down in the real purposes for reading.

The Science Experiment

The second year I read Beatrice Sparks's *It Happened to Nancy,* Janet suggested that a colleague of hers would be willing to come to class to do a science experiment she had found in a science journal that would help students relate the novel to their lives. Before Dr. Johnson's visit, the students listed all the things they already knew about AIDS. This new group of students had some of the same information (and misinformation) that students in the previous class had had:

★ HIV is transmitted by kissing.
★ HIV is transmitted through mosquito bites.

★ Only faggots get it.
★ If you are scratched in a fight, you can get it.
★ A green monkey brought it here from Africa.
★ You get it from unprotected sex.

On the day Dr. Johnson came to class the students were ready with dozens of questions. The first thing Dr. Johnson did was to give each of us a small cup with clear liquid in it. As we went around the room exchanging the liquids in our cups, Dr. Johnson asked us to think of questions we might ask before exchanging liquids with someone. After several minutes, all of the cups began to turn various shades of pink, and students were ready to discuss the transmission of communicable diseases.

Reading this novel and working with Dr. Johnson not only enlightened my students about how the HIV virus can be transmitted but also helped them correct some of the misconceptions they had picked up on the streets. As they read *It Happened to Nancy* and thought about what they had learned with Dr. Johnson, they realized that this normal teenager's one act of unprotected sex led to her death. Her thoughts about love and sex were so similar to those of many of these students, they couldn't help but be affected.

When we completed the novel, I asked the students to write about what they would have done if they had been in Nancy's shoes. Nancy chose to spend the last few weeks of her teenage life preparing to publish her story; over half my class said they would have killed themselves. It was a good opportunity to talk with students about risks, challenges, and overcoming fears to make life meaningful.

Visiting the AIDS Memorial Quilt

This year Universal sponsored an exhibit in Orlando of the AIDS Memorial Quilt. I was a bit apprehensive about taking my students to see it, because our community is quite conservative. I kept expecting telephone calls from irate parents after the permission slips were sent home, but none came. I was even more apprehensive because so many of this group of middle school students were openly homophobic. I did not want them to equate AIDS with homosexuality, but I wasn't quite sure how to prepare them. I knew that we didn't have time to read *It Happened to Nancy,* and anyway, my new seventh graders probably weren't mature enough for its content, but I did want to open the door for our discussion with a piece of literature.

Finally, I found an appropriate short story in Chris Crutcher's *Athletic Shorts* (1992). The story focuses on Louie Banks, a character from another Crutcher novel, *Running Loose.* Louie lives in a small rural logging town and is spending part of his summer before leaving for college helping clean a bar a few mornings a week. The owner of the bar, Dakota, has a nephew, Darren, who comes to spend the summer with him. Darren has

AIDS and has nowhere else to go because his parents have essentially disowned him. Darren is also homosexual. When Louie discovers this, he is repulsed. He begins avoiding Darren in spite of the friendship that had been growing between them. When Louie's friend accuses him of being a "faggot" because of his friendship with Darren, Louie doesn't see Darren again until shortly before Darren's death, in the hospital. "Dakota [Darren's uncle] held him tight, and it's the only time I ever saw a tear in his eye. He told me later that it was an honor to walk to the edge with a true hero."

After we finished reading the story, I asked the students what they thought this quote meant. Charles wrote, "He meant that Darren was a hero for trying to stay alive with AIDS trying to fight for his life and when he died Dakota stayed with him until he died." The connections students made to Louie's dilemma and Darren's pain helped them become more aware of their attitudes.

The impact of our reading and discussion was obvious when we arrived at the exhibit. Neither the students nor I were prepared for how somber it was. A group of elderly ladies walking in front of us had tears streaming down their faces as they viewed the panels created in memory of children and adults who had died of AIDS. Two of the panels were for a husband and wife who had taught at a local high school. The students were quiet even when we returned to school. As students began to write about the experience, I realized anew the importance of including adolescents in the conversations we have about important life issues.

When we were ready to talk about the field trip, one of my sixth graders told us that she had lost a cousin to AIDS and wanted to know how she and her mother could make a quilt and send it to the founders of the exhibit. Several of the other sixth graders wanted to make a quilt, too, and we started talking about the heritage of quilt making. I shared with them two picture books about quilts, Patricia Polacco's *The Keeping Quilt* and Faith Ringold's *Tar Beach*. Finally the sixth graders decided to make a class quilt; every student would design a square to represent himself or herself.

We wrote letters to the faculty and staff and received donations of fabric, needles, and thread. As I write this, plans are underway for one of the secretaries and a grandmother of one of the students to come to our classroom to help us begin. This experience was a turning point for our class: students saw the value of chronicling our heritage together.

The Holocaust Museum

When one of my students said he had heard that there was no such thing as the Holocaust, I decided to make it a unit of study in both my seventh- and eighth-grade classes. There is a lot of young adult literature related to the Holocaust, but the challenge is finding a book that is appropriate for struggling readers. I read Jane Yolen's *Briar Rose,* Lois Lowry's *Number the*

Stars, and a number of other young adult or children's books. Although *Briar Rose* is one of the best books I have read about the Holocaust, it is too difficult for shared reading: it has too much flashback and is told in the second person. *The Diary of Anne Frank* seemed an obvious choice, but I knew the diary format would be difficult for my students and their interest might wane. Most of the other books I read were meant for younger children and seemed too delicate. I finally decided to use a combination of children's books, poetry, and excerpts from Elie Wiesel's *Night.*

To begin, we read two children's books: Shulamith Oppenheim's *The Lily Cupboard* and Carol Matas's *Daniel's Story. Daniel's Story* is actually a transcript of a short children's film. After I had read *Daniel's Story* aloud, I typed out the text of the story on slips of paper that I then gave to the students to illustrate. Tabitha illustrated a scene from the beginning of the story when Daniel is living in the ghetto with the other Jews and sees a dead boy lying in the street (see Figure 8.4); Jennifer illustrated the scene when Daniel and his family reach the concentration camp and have to throw their clothes away and wear uniforms (see Figure 8.5); and Jeff illustrated the scene when people are being "selected" for work or termination in the gas chamber (see Figure 8.6). As students drew their illustrations, I could sense their empathy for how the people must have felt.

Next, we read poetry together from *I Never Saw Another Butterfly.* After reading the poetry and seeing the artwork of children who died in the Holocaust, Ruth and Tabitha were inspired to write their own poetry:

Why Jews
by Ruth Lapin

What did they have that we didn't have
maybe diffrend hair color or eye colors
they were no better they had no right
or reason to kill so many people
　　Why Jews

A child can rember
by Tabitha McVay

As a tear falls down
my face I rember
the screms and crys
for help. I see in my
mind the pain. I can
almost smell the deth.
Now as many tears
fall down my face it
all comes together
as one life story.

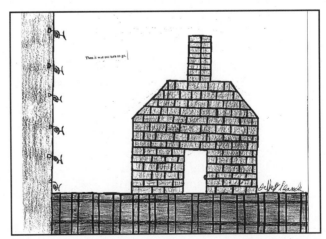

Figures 8.4, 8.5, and 8.6 *Student illustrations for passages from* Daniel's Story

I also read nonfiction to them: facts about children who perished in the Holocaust as well as articles written about survivors. I showed them a video filmed by my father-in-law when he took my husband and the rest of his family to Germany to visit the Holocaust memorials.

We culminated the unit by reading *Night*, a difficult book to read aloud because of the horrifying realities it conveys. The students were mesmerized and upset. "Why didn't they just run away?" they kept asking. I don't think they understood or could accept that escape was impossible. After I read the part where Wiesel is approaching Auschwitz after an agonizing train trip, Tabitha told me, "To me it looked and sounded like the pit of hell." I think she expressed how we all felt. Tabitha's chapter maps (one of them is shown in Figure 8.7) were representative of the intensity of the students' involvement with the text.

After we finished reading *Night*, we visited a special traveling exhibit from the Holocaust Museum, "Can You Hear Them Crying?" It featured artifacts from Auschwitz, especially those that had belonged to children. The artifacts were incredible; unfortunately, our tour guide spoke little of

Figure 8.7 *One of Tabitha's chapter maps from our shared reading of* Night

the Holocaust itself, focusing instead on World War II and the political reasons behind the Holocaust. I was amazed at how respectful the students were in spite of the difficulty they had in following what the guide was saying. I felt it was a tribute to their connection with the literature we had read and the research we had done beforehand. When we returned to class and wrote about the experience, several of the students were able to separate the boredom they felt listening to the guide from the informational and emotional impact of the trip—a remarkable distinction for these students (see Figure 8.8).

It Takes a Team

The importance of community in our classrooms can't be stressed enough. When students felt safe in the classroom, both with me and with the other students, they were more productive, took more risks with lan-

Figure 8.8 *A student's reflection on our visit to view artifacts from the Holocaust*

The field trip

I enjoyed the art work alot. It said so much and it was so deep. Almost like I was in the art work I have to say I liked the art best of all. there was one pice I fell in love with it was called "Mother" She had her son in her arms and you could see the pain in her eyes. She was trying not to cry you could tell. the painting was in black and white with a little greay. the man who was talking to us would not shut-up. But anyway when I saw the babys things I wanted to cry. All and All I liked the trip. the best part was lunch. Ha! But I think I'll rember this fild trip for along time. A very olong time. I have to see I wanted to fall asleep when that guy was talking.

guage, and allowed themselves to have deeper responses to literature. Unfortunately, a positive sense of community can be very tenuous with students who associate school with failure, who come from backgrounds where conflicts are resolved by fighting, and who daily live lives devoid of respect. Early in the year, I tried to pick books for shared reading that would help students think about issues of trust, loyalty, respect, and friendship, but students did not take what they encountered in literature and transfer it to our classroom. With middle school students, who often specialize in tormenting others because they are different or lack certain abilities or as a way to transfer anger, building trust becomes paramount. I attempted to build community every day. We had group meetings, time to share, celebrations of successes, and community-designed goals and rules. Each of these activities is highlighted in previous chapters.

During my third year of teaching in the Literacy Project, Janet and I decided to try to connect literature and trust earlier and more directly. Janet received a grant to bring a professional team builder, Troy Cunningham, to work with my classes. I had worked with Troy before, in the Central Florida Writing Project, and knew the powerful bond the trust activities he led could create. I hoped for the same results with my students. The kids immediately fell in love with Troy, who entered the classroom with hula hoops, balls, ropes, and an immense spider web he had constructed from PVC pipe and string. Troy had developed a sequence of trust activities that he connected to the shared novels I was reading in each of my classes: Rodman Philbrick's *Freak the Mighty,* in eighth grade; Jane Conly's *Crazy Lady,* in seventh grade; and, Susan Shreve's *The Flunking of Joshua T. Bates,* in sixth grade.

Each of these novels has a theme of friendship and trust between two main characters who have difficulty trusting others. Maxwell and Kevin in *Freak the Mighty* are rejected by their classmates because of the way they look. Maxwell is an enormous student who is in all the "slow" classes. His father is in prison, and he lives with his grandparents. Kevin, a genius with a dwarf body, moves in next door to Maxwell, and the two begin a friendship unlike any other seen at school. In *Crazy Lady,* Vernon is failing the eighth grade. His mom died a few years before and he is struggling to make it with his dad and numerous brothers and sisters. In return for being tutored by a retired teacher in his neighborhood, he helps out Maxine and her retarded son, Ronald. Vernon and his friends have been making fun of Maxine for years as the neighborhood drunk; now Vernon is faced with having to spend considerable time with her. Joshua in *The Flunking of Joshua T. Bates* is a boy who has failed the third grade and must put up with his tormentors. He and his teacher, Mrs. Goodman, strike up a friendship in which they both learn to trust others.

The trust activities Troy led allowed us to connect with the main characters of the books and then with the other inhabitants of our classroom. The activities required students to analyze a problem, brainstorm possible solutions, and figure out ways to keep everyone safe and involved; students began to think about new ways to use each other as resources. As the students became more involved in meeting the ever-greater challenges Troy put before them, they encouraged each other, cheered, and shouted advice and encouragement. All their differences were forgotten. If a student was afraid to try the trust fall, Troy asked for volunteer "encouragers"; when someone was too small to attempt a particular exercise safely, Troy gave him or her a unique ancillary role; every student was always involved. Troy would frequently stop and say, "What would it take for everyone to feel safe? Are there ways we can encourage each other more?" I participated in all of the activities with the students, even trusting them to lift me through the spider web.

As Troy asked the students to reflect on their learning at the end of their day together, he once again took them back to the books they were reading. Was trust needed between any of the characters? Did the characters help each other out and support one another? He then transferred that behavior to their school and their classroom. What did it take to build trust in friendships? Was that different from trust that could be built between classmates? After Troy left that day, my students, especially those who were new to the school and the Literacy Project, saw our classroom as a safe haven in which to work and learn together.

We were fortunate to have been given funds to bring in a team builder, but any teacher can adapt these trust initiatives and activities, connecting them directly with the unique curriculum and dynamic of his or her classroom.

Reflections by Janet

Brazilian educator and philosopher Paulo Freire talked about the importance of teaching people to "read their world." The activities that Kyle designed for her students did just that. There are hundreds and thousands of critics of public education who will point to students' lack of knowledge of facts, names, events, and the common rules of etiquette, yet few who will take the time to stop and teach those things to just one child. Children need the same kind of support in learning to "read their world" as they need in learning to read words.

For each area of knowledge we want students to explore, we need to have in place the conditions that will support them in that learning. Brian Cambourne, in *The Whole Story* (1988), enumerates these conditions of engagement: immersion, demonstration, expectation, responsibility, approximation, use, and response. These were the conditions we looked at as we tried to build support for students to expand their world knowledge.

What did students learn through these activities? I believe they learned much. They learned that someone cared enough about their learning to go the extra step. They learned that learning is a lifelong activity that can begin even at their age. They learned how to be responsible for their own behavior and learning as well as how to support peers who have the same goals. In the end, of course, there are no real guarantees about what students will learn. I agree with Susan Ohanian (1994):

> But, I guess if I have one tenet in teaching it is that no one can *make* a resistant high school student—or a third grader, for that matter—learn anything. You can't threaten or cajole anybody into learning. You can't collaborate them into learning either. You can only provide an environment for possibilities—and hope. (28)

If Kyle and the thousands of teachers like her can look back on their teaching and feel that they have provided their students with possibilities and hope, their work has been meaningful indeed.

Chapter 9

It Makes a Difference to This One

Reading was the ticket that entitled me to my place in the world. Because I read when I could still believe in magic, reading was magical, not merely breaking a code or translating one set of symbols into another.

Lynne Sharon Schwartz, *Ruined by Reading*

A Reminder of What Is Important

When I work with teachers across the country, one thing is common. Whether they work in urban or rural schools, whether they have large classes or are responsible for small pullout programs, teachers have many days when they feel that what they do does not make a difference. I can remember days that turned into weeks when I felt the same way. In a climate where education bashing is not only acceptable but almost a sign of social awareness, teachers and students suffer from feelings of inadequacy.

One thing that helped me gain a healthier perspective in my own classroom was becoming an active teacher-researcher. In Gay Su Pinnell and Myna L. Matlin's edited collection, *Teachers and Research: Language Learning in the Classroom* (1989), Marie Clay states: "I believe that teachers are masters of the complexity of their tasks; they have a good, if intuitive, grasp of the changes that occur in pupils over time" (30). For me, documenting my practice and my students' responses helped me translate the intuitive into something that could be transferred to other learning moments or shared with others. Research also helped me shift my perspective from the general picture, which most often focused on what teachers and students were *not* doing, to single individuals or classes, where I could focus on what was working. As I look back on my teaching career, I can honestly say that I have seldom changed my classroom practice based on any national or international statistics. I have, however, often changed my practice based on what I learned from close observations of individual learners.

Such close observation of students' learning also helped me change my understanding of the significance of the time I spent with these students. As a secondary English teacher, I was involved in many discussions about content standards and any number of large-scale assessment meetings. These general discussions of what every student should know and be able to do often turned into diatribes about students' lack of basic skills and knowledge. I would return to my classroom discouraged and convinced that nothing I was doing in the classroom mattered.

During my last three years of public school teaching, I learned to anticipate this discouragement and found a way to counteract it. Each year I chose four students whose learning I documented. If students stayed with me for more than one year, I continued to track their progress, still adding four new students each year. This record not only helped me identify areas in my teaching that needed to be changed, it also helped me see that students really were learning. If we focus on our students as a class, there is always someone who is failing. If, however, we focus on students as individuals, there is always a glimmer of hope that our work together will have lasting results.

I knew that Kyle often became discouraged as she worked in the Literacy Project classroom, because her students seemed so far from being able to meet any of the standards established by the county and state. One of the first things I asked her to do was choose a few students and document the time they spent with her. This focus helped her maintain a sense of the importance of her work in spite of the difficulties she encountered every day. Kyle's stories of her work with Chanelle, Charlene, and Tiffany speak for themselves.

In the Classroom with Kyle

Chanelle

What I remember most about my first meetings with Chanelle was how incredibly quiet she was and how she towered over the other sixth graders. While she differed from the others in appearance and demeanor, she shared with them a long history of academic challenge and failure. Her elementary school records showed she had been reading below grade level since the first grade. She had been tested for language impairment, recommended for remedial reading programs, and considered twice for retention but then given social promotions. She had received Ds and Fs in reading and Cs and Ds in language arts throughout her school career. However, in our time together, I was to learn much from this young woman.

The first of those learning moments happened in the computer lab in the fall of her first year in the Literacy Project. Nineteen at-risk sixth graders and I were trying to master the new computers. The tutorial software that was supposed to teach the students how to operate the computers was far too difficult for them to understand, so I was trying to interpret. I thought I could just help them with the instructions and they would eventually catch on. I read aloud the directions on page one of the tutorial and said, "Okay, the directions on the screen will tell you where to go next." Chaos quickly erupted as nineteen hands and voices frantically called for my help. I learned a valuable lesson that day: I had not really grasped nor respected the real difficulties struggling readers face each day in school.

In the midst of the confusion and frustration, I glanced over at Chanelle. I worried about her because she was one of the quiet ones. As Michael Dorris reminds us in *Sees Behind Trees* (1996), "When all is in movement, you eventually notice the thing that is still" (80). Had her quiet demeanor helped her fall through the educational cracks? She was easy to leave alone, not only because she was not disruptive but also because she was so committed to completing each task. In my short time teaching, I had already noticed how easy it is to ignore the quiet students when so many others clamor for attention.

I am ashamed to admit that as I approached Chanelle in the computer lab that day, the things flashing through my mind were the labels I had read in her cumulative records. While the other students had charged recklessly into the computer program, Chanelle had not gotten past the first screen. She had abandoned her chair and was kneeling in front of the computer, desperately trying to decipher the home keys.

"How are you doing?" I asked.

"What buttons am I supposed to mash?" Her eyes betrayed her quiet anger at not being able to master the computer. For a minute, I did not understand what she was asking; I asked her to repeat her question.

"On this thing. What buttons am I supposed to mash?"

"Oh, do you mean press?"

"Press? What? No, mash," she insisted. "What buttons am I supposed to mash to make this stupid thing work?"

I felt a wave of shame wash over me. How could I have put her, and the rest of the students, through this? Their feelings of failure were mounting as the minutes passed. I paused a moment, then put my hands over hers and together we "mashed the right buttons."

From that day on, Chanelle had a special place in my heart. She reminded me of myself in sixth grade: extremely quiet, eager to please, afraid to ask questions, but silently determined to succeed. But Chanelle faced a great obstacle that I did not have as a sixth grader: she was a struggling reader.

During the three years Chanelle was in the literacy workshop, her days were filled with shared and independent reading. Like the other students, she faced initial obstacles because of her struggles with reading and writing. She was unique in that she did not succumb to the overwhelming negativity that so many of the students had already developed toward school. Her goals reflected her determination. Her academic goals were to "get a's, b's, and c's on my report card" and "to be organized." Her personal goals were to "try hard, do all of my work and don't be scared to ask questions." Early in the year, I asked the students to complete a Here and Now (Kirby, Liner, and Vinz 1988) on what they wanted from reading. Chanelle's response made it clear that motivation was not going to be the problem:

> The things I want from reading is to learn, have fun by reading, laugh, care, wonder and think. I want from reading is to learn and when Mrs. Gonzalez say Independent reading I am going to get out a book and read it and read far as I can.

She possessed a quiet inner resolve to be a lifelong reader and writer. She had a passion for words that I did not see in any of the other sixth graders. My first step was to find books that she could read, that would interest her, and that would help her feel successful as a reader. She started with picture books—Disney's *The Lion King*, *Disney' Beauty and the Beast*, *Garfield at Large*, *The Great Waldo Search*—and short books on tape—Jack Prelutsky's *The Dragons Are Singing Tonight*, Gary Paulsen's *Nightjohn*. She also fell in love with poetry, choosing to read independently from some of the collections that I read aloud to the class. She repeatedly read her three favorites: Kali Dakos's *If You're Not Here, Please Raise Your Hand;* Stephen Dunning's *Reflections on a Gift of Watermelon Pickle;* and Eloise Greenfield's *Honey, I Love.*

Chanelle was one of the first students in my sixth-grade class to make the transition from assisted to independent reading. After Christmas, she started reading novels that were relatively long, had smaller type, and contained fewer illustrations. She was attracted to books that were humorous: in another Here and Now she wrote, "When I have to read sometimes I am mad but when I get the story that makes me laugh out loud because it be funny and that what makes me read all the time." Following her lead, I found three books for her that were a great success: Johanna Hurwitz's *Class Clown;* Debbie Dadey and Marcia Jones's *Vampires Don't Wear Polka Dots;* and Catherine Morrow's *The Jellybean Principal*. In my anecdotal records, I noted that Chanelle's choices for independent reading followed the pattern I was using for shared reading. We had begun with short, humorous books with illustrations and moved to longer shared novels: Jon Scieszka's *The Good, the Bad, and the Goofy* and *Knights of the Kitchen Table* and Katherine Paterson's *The Great Gilly Hopkins*. I saw the importance of building classroom collections that supported and extended the books we read in shared reading.

At the beginning of her seventh-grade year, Chanelle was ready for novels that were longer. We started the year with a suspense novel in shared reading, Cynthia DeFelice's *Weasel*, which Chanelle thoroughly enjoyed. True to the pattern she'd established the previous year, she now wanted to read suspense novels. She found several and quickly became addicted to the genre: Alan Simmons's *Smoke*, Jeannette Sanderson's *Buying Trouble*, Alvin Schwartz's *Scary Stories to Tell in the Dark*, and Robert Sansouci's *Short and Shivery*. She then tried full-length novels, such as R. L. Stine's *Bad Dreams* and *The New Boy*, which she read with the assistance of recordings.

When I moved the seventh graders from suspense to realistic fiction by reading Walter Dean Myers's *Scorpions*, Glendon Swarthout's *Bless the Beasts and the Children*, and Beatrice Sparks's *It Happened to Nancy* with them, Chanelle began experimenting with this new genre. She overheard me giving a book talk about Sparks's *Go Ask Alice* to an eighth grader and was immediately interested in reading the novel. I was concerned because the book was not only long but also written as a diary. Not wanting her to lose the momentum of her success, I did guided reading sessions with her for the first few chapters in order to ground her in the diary format and other challenging aspects of the text. With that help, she was able to get started and continue, albeit slowly.

With her typical commitment, Chanelle was determined to read this book. She plowed along for several weeks, leaning back against the wall or hunched over at her seat, her brow furrowed in concentration, lips silently mouthing the words. I was afraid it was taking her so long to finish she might get discouraged with reading in general. I asked Janet what she thought. She said, "Ask her if she needs your help. If not, isn't she doing what we all do when we move on to more challenging books than we're used to reading?" Chanelle assured me that she was just fine but would let me know if she needed anything. And she finished it without any further assistance from me. Then she asked for other books "just like it," and I did my best to accommodate. She read Anne Snyder's *My Name Is Davy and I'm an Alcoholic;* John Durham's *A New Life for Sarita;* Judy Blume's *Just as Long as We're Together;* Eve Krupinski and Dana Weikel's *Death from Child Abuse and No One Heard;* and Jacqueline Woodson's *I Hadn't Meant to Tell You This.*

What affected me most about Chanelle's journey into literacy was the deep connection she made with literature—a connection that many of the students in "regular" classes during my internship had not made. She was hesitant to respond verbally to what she read, but when it came to writing, emotion flowed through her words. In her last year in my class, Chanelle read Alice Childress's *Rainbow Jordan*, a story about a teenage black girl who is in and out of foster care because her mother periodically leaves for weeks at a time. Chanelle summarized her reading soon after she began the book:

I am reading <u>Rainbow Jordan</u>. It is about this girl name rainbow she 13 and she's beging [beginning] to become a woman and her mother leaves her at home by herself like for weeks and the home caught on fire and then the HRS took her and she had to go through court and she keep going to the HRS shelter and her mother hits her for nothing and I think that she need to go and stay with Mrs. Jones because I think she great for rainbow they talk about things rainbow could not talk to her mother about and the book is great.

Later in the story, Rainbow struggles with yet another serious issue in her life. She has to decide whether or not to have sex with her boyfriend. Chanelle's response indicates the level of connection she has with Rainbow:

Rainbow Jordan boyfriend say he is in love with her and he wants to have sex with her, but, she don't want to have sex with him not until she's ready and her boyfriend get all mad and then one day she tell him she's ready but she's not she tells him that because she don't want him to get mad at her and go find another girl so she told him to come over on sat. so he said O.k. and started smiling but rainbow don't know that he already got a girlfriend so he come over and he just happens to bring his girlfriend and Rainbow was mad that they could not do nothing and she was mad that he got a girlfriend already. But I thought that it was great that they could not do nothing because she was not ready to have sex with him.

I think that Rainbow Jordan boyfriend need to back off and stop rushing things.

Chanelle's writing engagement paralleled her reading progress. While the majority of the sixth graders in her class groaned at the mere mention of writing, Chanelle quietly went off on her own and wrote. I had been reading poetry aloud to the students several days a week, so I was not surprised to find that Chanelle's first piece of independent writing was a poem.

I Woke up early one morning
I woke up early one morning
the light was shining in My eyes.

Then I walked over by the table
    and said, "Oh, My, My."

My head was hurting and
My throat was dry.

So I went to the refrigerator and
    cried, "I, I, I."

Then My stomach started to ache.
Then My body started shaking.

Then I cried, "Oh, My, My, My."

This from a child whose file had read, "did not perform to standards of her grade level" and "language impaired" because she rarely spoke and was difficult to understand. When I asked her what had inspired the poem, she simply shrugged her shoulders and said, "I don't know."

When I suggested that we submit it to *Merlyn's Pen* for possible publication, she excitedly filled out the form. A few months later she received a rejection letter, but I could see the difference just receiving the response to her poem had made. Our media specialist heard about Chanelle's poem and posted both the poem and the letter in the main display case for our new media center's grand opening.

Chanelle wrote often during sixth grade. She wrote a short story retelling *The Good, the Bad, and the Goofy* in her own words. She also wrote a short story featuring our class after she had read the picture book *The Teacher from the Black Lagoon* by Mike Thaler. But her writing genre of choice continued to be poetry. When we studied the Holocaust during her seventh-grade year and read Elie Wiesel's *Night*, Chanelle's response was once again a poem.

Never Again
Dying, frying, were all used
in the Holocaust
but Never Again

Killing, thrilling, stealing were all used
in the Holocaust
but Never Again

Starvation, concentration, and hatred
were all used in the Holocaust
but Never Again,
    Never Again,
        Never Again.

One day during a conference, Chanelle and I were talking about her progress as a writer. I mentioned some of the famous female black authors I had read: Zora Neale Hurston, Toni Morrison, and Alice Walker. "Will you remember me when you're a famous author?" I asked her. She ducked her head down so I couldn't see her eyes and nodded. The connection she made during that conference with black female writers made her eager to begin our next shared reading, *Warriors Don't Cry* by Melba Pattillo Beals. Sadly, Chanelle was to be reminded that the segregation we were reading about in Beals's account of being one of the Little Rock Nine was still alive and ugly in some parts of our country today.

She and her oldest brother were driving to Kentucky to visit family. He was driving a fairly nice rental car and, for no apparent reason, they were pulled over by the police.

"They pulled us over for nothin'. I was scared."

"Nothing? Was your brother speeding or anything?" I asked.

"Nah, man, they just pulled us over, talking junk. My brother, ooh, he was so mad 'cause they checked the trunk and he asked if he could stand outside of the car when they checked. He wanted to make sure that they didn't put no drugs or nothin' in there. They told him to stay in the car."

"What was in the trunk?" I asked.

"Nothin' but my book bag from school."

"Well," I began hesitantly, "why do you think you got pulled over if your brother wasn't speeding?"

"It was 'cause we was black and they probably figured that black people can't drive nice cars."

The books we were reading, the writing she was doing, and the life she was living were all connected for Chanelle. As many others before her have done, she was learning that literature is a reflection of life and that the words we write can affect our life. Throughout her three years in middle school, Chanelle struggled patiently to achieve in all her classes, often missing the honor roll by just one or two grades. She finally made the honor roll her last semester. As I watched Chanelle continue to grow stronger in her literacy journey, I could see it reflected in her demeanor and her writing. The words in this poem of hers resonate with confidence and poise:

"I Am"

I am somebody,
I am smart,
I am sweet but not always neat,
I am somebody trying to
make a good education in
this crazy world today.
I am a great sports athlete,
I am the fourth child out of eight kids.
I am the future that begins
and ends with me.
I am a beautiful black
African American woman.
So do you get what I mean?
I mean that I am *everything*.

Charlene

I met Charlene first when I took her older brothers, Corey and Anthony, to their home one day after school. She was incredibly shy. By the time she entered middle school and became a student in the Literacy Project classroom, she was not so shy and quiet. I wouldn't describe our first year together as particularly pleasant. She thought I picked on her and was mean and bossy. I thought she was loud, stubborn, and rude.

Charlene was large for her age, and I guessed that part of her hostile attitude was a defense mechanism. She was a paradox: shy, but also over-bearing; a little girl in her emotions and behavior, but physically large; soft-spoken one minute and hollering the next. On top of all that, frequent ear infections had caused a partial hearing loss.

I occasionally saw Charlene's older sister, Lavaunya, in the hallway outside my room. She was usually intimidating someone with her booming voice and profanity. When students harassed Lavaunya for being overweight, they were likely to suffer the consequences. Charlene appeared to be following in Lavaunya's footsteps.

Charlene and I butted heads numerous times during her sixth-grade year. Whenever we had a problem, I would confer with her in the hallway, trying to figure out how I could help, how we could live with each other, how I could get her to trust me. These conferences would often end with my apologizing for yelling at her or hurting her feelings. She would simply lean against the lockers, her head down, refusing to look at or speak to me. Sometimes tears streamed down her face, but no words came out. When she cried, I felt like a monster, but I also felt extremely frustrated. I didn't see how I was ever going to be able to reach her—as a person or as a reader.

She was frequently absent that first year. She would be in school for a day or two, then out for several days with an ear infection. Her education was at a standstill, but I was determined to get Charlene reading. She was fascinated by the Walkmans and books on tape. In fact, that was pretty much the only thing that interested her.

The books I initially offered her were hit-and-miss. She tried to read Mildred Taylor's *Roll of Thunder, Hear My Cry,* but it was "too long." Then she tried Zilpha Snyder's *Witches of Worm,* but it was "too boring." When she started R. L. Stine's *Bad Dreams,* I thought she'd finally found a book she liked, but she missed so many days of school she couldn't remember what she'd read from one time to the next. I began to feel that Goldilocks (me) was never going to find a book that was "just right" for Charlene.

I finally decided that if she was ever going to complete any books, they had to be ones she could read in a day. So we switched to picture books. Some of her favorites were the *Disney's The Little Mermaid,* Audrey Wood's *King Bidgood's in the Bathtub,* Linda Williams's *The Little Old Lady Who Wasn't Afraid of Anything,* and Anne Isaac's *Swamp Angel.* She was able to read most picture books independently, but the books that I had on tape were too long or too difficult. I had only one collection of short stories on tape, Alvin Schwartz's *Scary Stories to Tell in the Dark,* but I gave it a try. She loved it! But my relief was short-lived, since I had nothing similar with which to follow it. My search began again.

One day, Charlene picked up the book and tape of Beatrix Potter's *The Tale of Squirrel Nutkin,* which I had found on sale at a local book store. Since she liked this book, I thought she might also like Kenneth

Grahame's *Wind in the Willows,* which I happened to have on tape as well. She struggled through it for a few independent reading sessions, but then told me she didn't like it because "the words are too small."

I had just about lost patience. My time and resources were running out. Charlene had started several novels, but had actually only finished various picture books and the recorded collection of short stories. When I asked Janet for advice, she said, "Keep inviting her with other books...keep talking with her. Be patient. You'll find something that she connects with if you keep trying."

Janet was right. After Christmas, some funds from a minigrant came through and we were able to order a few more books on tape. As Charlene was helping me unpack them, she pulled out Roald Dahl's *The Witches,* which has a wonderful cover. She said, "Mrs. G., what's this?" I gave a little book talk and encouraged her to at least try it. I expected to hear, "Are you crazy? This book is too thick!" What I heard instead was, "Okay. It looks good." She read it during our independent reading session the next day, through the next period, and all of the next day. For the rest of the week, she did nothing during our class time except read *The Witches.* At last, the hook!

After this book, I showed her a beautifully illustrated collection of fairy tales (some with witch characters) that I had read on tape for Jason the year before. Next, she chose to read Laurence Yep's *The Rainbow People,* another collection of short folktales. She then picked out Robert Newton Peck's *Soup in Love,* which she enjoyed so much she asked if she could take it home. When she brought the book back, she announced, "I want something scary." Her older brother Corey had told her about R. L. Stine's *Double Date,* so I found the book and tape for her and she became immediately engrossed.

From then on, even though Charlene was still absent at least one day a week, she read far longer than the required time in class; she read during independent literacy exploration and often took books and tapes home. During the rest of the year, she completed Stine's *The Thrill Club* and *The New Boy,* as well as Avi's *Wolf Rider.*

One day as Charlene and I were discussing one of the books she had recently finished, she said, "Yeah, my daddy really liked it, too." Then she told me that her older sister and her father had read it with the help of the tapes she had taken home. I was thrilled, and told her that any time she wanted to check books or tapes out for her dad or sister, I'd be happy to let her take them home. After that, if Charlene happened to be absent, Corey or Anthony would breeze in with remarks such as, "Mrs. G., Lavaunya wants to know if she can read *The New Boy.* Is Tiffany done with it yet?" Just when I felt like giving up with Charlene, I had found the book that was right for her, and her reading enthusiasm had infected the lives of her father and her sister, who had never been in our class.

Charlene made the switch from assisted to independent reading soon after she started seventh grade. During that year, she read E. B. White's

Charlotte's Web and R. L. Stine's *The Dead Girlfriend, Beach Party,* and *Blind Date* (as well as his *The New Boy,* which she had previously read with the assistance of a tape). Between each of the novels, she would take a break to enjoy short story collections such as Schwartz's *Scary Stories III* and Allan Zullo's *Haunted Schools.* She also took breaks from these more difficult books by reading picture books and revisiting books such as Irene Hunt's *The Lottery Rose,* a book we had read during shared reading when she was in the sixth grade.

Once Charlene became a reader, she began to set high standards for herself in the goals she established each quarter. Her academic goals included "to read for 2–3 periods," while her personal goal was "not [to] run around the classroom." She decided she needed to take the following steps to accomplish her goals:

1. Pick out a book to read.
2. Listen to the words I hear.
3. Get comfortable.
4. Stay in my seat.
5. Listen to my mind read.
6. Follow along in the book.
7. To read more.
8. Read night & day.
9. To get a short book then read another.
10. Start long books after the short ones.

Charlene and I discussed how we would recognize that she was making progress toward these goals, and she listed these signs:

1. I will start reading faster.
2. I will read faster and get done and be on another book.
3. By how many books I read.
4. How I find new words.
5. How I am sitting.
6. How I don't move around.
7. How I read faster.
8. How I learn bigger words.

As Charlene's reading ability changed and progressed, so did her ability to connect with the books she read. Samples of her responses to books she read during the fall of sixth grade and the spring of seventh grade (see Figures 9.1 and 9.2) demonstrate her progress with language arts. There are physical changes in her handwriting, as well as improved spelling, emergence of voice, references to previously read texts, and experimentation with mechanics (underlining book titles, using apostrophes, and indenting paragraphs).

I am happy to say that as Charlene's interest in reading grew, so did our mutual respect. She appreciated the good things I found for her to read, and I was in constant awe of her progress. When she started seventh

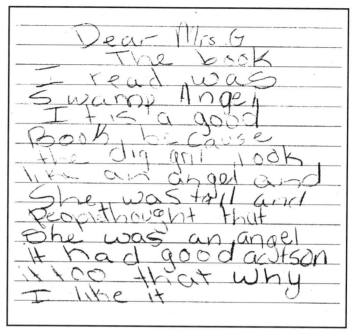

Dear Mrs G
The book
I read was
Swamp Angel
It is a good
Book be-cause
the dig gril look
like an angel and
She was tall and
People thought that
She was an angel
It had good actson
tioo that why
I like it

Figure 9.1 *A book response Charlene wrote in sixth grade*

grade, she became my ally instead of my enemy. It was not uncommon for her to holler, "Ya'll better *shut up* and listen to Mrs. G!" if other students were being noisy. Her favorite place to sit was at or beside my desk, and she even got permission from her science teacher to come to my class to read when she had completed her science work.

Charlene also began to take some risks with her writing that year. She wrote a wonderful short story in which she even used ellipses correctly. When I asked her where she had learned to use them, she replied, "They were in some books I read." She felt confident enough to experiment with new words and literary devices that she picked up from our shared reading lessons as well as her independent reading.

One day Charlene came into my classroom while the sixth graders were reading. She made obvious efforts to enter the classroom quietly so as not to disturb the "gits," as the older students call the new ones. When she approached my desk, I took her hand and said, "Do you know how happy I am that you're my student? Do you know how proud I am of you?" I saw the smile before she ducked her head in embarrassment and then I saw her nod.

Tiffany

I thought Tiffany was one of the most boy-crazy middle school girls I had ever met. She had a seemingly uncontrollable urge to flirt with any boy

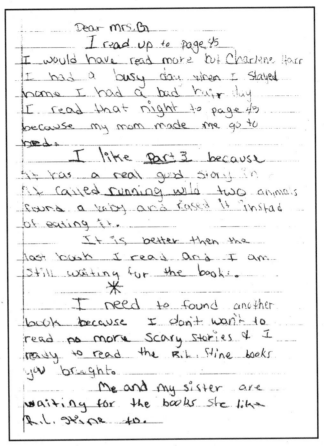

Dear mrs. G.
I read up to page 45
I would have read more but Charlene Harr
I had a busy day when I stayed
home I had a bad hair day
I read that night to page 45
because my mom made me go to
bed.
I like Part 3 because
it has a real good story in
it called running wild two animals
found a baby and raised it instead
of eating it.
It is better then the
last book I read and I am
still waiting for the book.
*
I need to found another
book because I don't want to
read no more scary stories & I
ready to read the R.L. Stine books
you brought.
Me and my sister are
waiting for the books she like
R.L. Stine to.

Figure 9.2 *A book response Charlene wrote in seventh grade*

in her vicinity. Her portfolio had hearts drawn all over it, with the accompanying words "Nothing but love for you, baby." Many of the middle school boys were scared of her. If anyone wanted information about a middle school romance that was blossoming, dying, or terminated, Tiffany was the one to ask.

Despite her loud voice and antics, Tiffany had a tender soul. At the end of her sixth-grade year, I told my students that I would be getting married the week after school was out. On the day of my wedding, as I was rushing around frantically, I stopped to listen to the messages on my answering machine. I heard Tiffany's voice telling me that she wanted to read a poem to me on my wedding day. After she finished, she said, "I know that I'm supposed to credit the author with his work because of that copyright thing you taught us, but the author's name isn't here." What a gift!

Tiffany, like the rest of my students, was a challenge. She came to middle school ranked in the third stanine. She had an overall average of D/F in her reading and language arts classes and had been recommended for reme-dial reading in the third grade. Like Chanelle, she had been considered for retention twice in elementary school, but was promoted both times. Tiffany was different from many of the other students, however, in that despite her academic records, she could tell me about many of her favorite books. Her love of story was apparent in our first one-on-one conferences.

As with so many of my students, picture books were among Tiffany's first reading efforts. She read Maurice Sendak's *Where the Wild Things Are*, Norman Bridwell's *Clifford's Happy Day*, Shulamith Oppenheim's *The Lily Cupboard*, and the *Disney's Beauty and the Beast*. After a few weeks of pic-ture books, I decided to try assisted reading. I offered her recorded books that had short chapters and some illustrations. She completed Johanna Hurwitz's *Class Clown* and Avi's *S.O.R. Losers*. As I suspected, she responded positively to the recorded books, avidly following the text and eagerly retelling the stories to me.

When she finished those two books, I talked with her about what she should read next. I used my typical opening lines: "What are you in the mood for today? Long? Short? Funny? Scary? On tape? Not on tape?"

"Don't you have any books about black people?" she asked me. I immediately thought that Gary Paulsen's *Nightjohn*, the story of a young slave girl who learns to read, might appeal to her.

"Okay, Mrs. G., I want more books like this," she told me when she completed *Nightjohn*. Her next book was Julius Lester's *To Be a Slave*, fol-lowed by *Roll of Thunder, Hear My Cry*. She fell in love with *Roll of Thunder* because "it seemed like a real family and a real story. Can you get me more books by this lady?" Since I didn't have any other Mildred Taylor books on tape, I thought this might be a good time to begin the transition from assisted to independent reading. Tiffany had been doing more indepen-dent reading than I required (two periods per week), and her comprehen-sion and the connections she made to other books were both improving.

I read the first few chapters of Taylor's *Song of the Trees* on tape for her. The book still had illustrations, wasn't terribly long, and hadn't been set in tiny type. Tiffany was able to finish the book independently. From there, she went on to read Taylor's *The Road to Memphis* and *The Friendship and the Gold Cadillac*, which were similar in format to *Song of the Trees*. She then read *Mississippi Bridge*, also by Taylor. When she began *Let the Circle Be Unbroken*, I suggested that she write a letter to Mildred Taylor telling her how much she was enjoying her books. She immediately began working on the letter, wanting to make sure that she got it "just right":

Dear Ms. Taylor,

My name is Tiffany Latrice Collins and I am in the sixth grade. I am writing you because I have just got done with Roll Of Thunder Hear My Cry. I am reading a new book called Let The Circle Be Unbroken, the sequel to Roll of Thunder Hear My Cry. I really like all of your books because they explain how I feel sometimes. Sometimes I'm sad. Sometimes I'm happy. Sometimes I'm cheerful and the Logan family is a great way to tell me that I am not alone.

I like to read your books because mostly they are about black people and I am interested in mostly black books. You bring me joy when you write all of these good books. It seems that you are a very beautiful person of the heart. You know very much about how people felt while they were in slavery and how people felt about the hatred between whites and blacks. I love your writing and I think that you are a very talented person.

I want you to write me back and tell me when you were born and is the Logan family a real family? Please respond quickly. Your picture on the back of the book <u>Let the Circle be Unbroken</u> shows that you are a very beautiful person. It looks like you are eighteen years old in the picture.

Tiffany continued to flourish in independent reading during seventh grade, drawn to suspense books that were lengthier than any novels she had read before. She loved Caroline Cooney's *The Face on the Milk Carton,* which she read with the help of a tape. Like so many other students, Tiffany devoured the R. L. Stine books we had on tape: *Bad Dreams, The Dare, The Thrill Club,* and *Double Date.* By the time she had finished them, I had purchased the sequel to *The Face on the Milk Carton.* Unfortunately, I didn't have the tape, so Tiffany had to try unassisted reading with a much longer book than she was used to. Because her motivation was strong, I felt she would be successful if I gave her enough support. I read the first few chapters on tape for her and did several guided reading lessons, and she was able to complete the book on her own.

When I read Jacqueline Woodson's *I Hadn't Meant to Tell You This,* I immediately thought of Tiffany. While I was pretty sure she would like the main character, a young black girl in middle school who befriends a "white trash" girl, I knew it would be rather difficult going. The book was a new genre for Tiffany, is told in second person, and opens with a lengthy prologue. In addition, the author uses flashback and lots of metaphors. Trying to figure out how to support Tiffany's reading of this book, I decided to buy another copy so that Tiffany and Chanelle could read it together. I also created the guided reading sheet below to help them through it:

Guided Reading
I Hadn't Meant to Tell You This

1. Please look at the cover of this book and make a prediction. Notice the illustration and the title. What do you think this book may be about?
2. Read the very first page, starting with the sentence, "'What does it feel like, Lena?' I asked, wanting to know what a father's

touch was like." Now what do you think the book may be about?

3. Read pages 1–5. Do they confirm or reject your earlier predictions?
4. Read Chapter 1. Does it have anything to do with the introductory pages that you read prior to Chapter 1? Does it give you any clues about the narrator's (the person who is telling the story) mother? Point out text that backs up your predictions.
5. Read Chapter 2. Who is Lena? What do you think happens to her? Refer to clues from the text.
6. Now, confirm or revise your earlier predictions about this book from what you have read thus far.
7. Read Chapter 3.
8. Read Chapter 4. Does it tell more about who Lena is and the background of the narrator? Refer to clues in the text.
9. Read Chapter 5. Confirm or reject predictions. Point out hints in the text that Lena and the narrator are becoming friends.
10. Read Chapter 6, which focuses on the narrator's mother's leaving.
11. Read Chapter 7. Confirm or reject predictions. How does the narrator's father feel about white people? Does the narrator listen to her father or to her heart about Lena?
12. Read Chapter 8, which deals with little girls' becoming young women and fathers' becoming uncomfortable with hugs, touching, etc. Are there hints that Lena is being abused?
13. Read Chapter 9. Are there hints that the narrator's mother had been depressed before she left? Back up your opinion by referring to the text.

The novel was difficult for them at first, but after they became caught up in the characters and the plot, Chanelle and Tiffany both loved it. They also liked being able to read and talk about a novel together.

Tiffany's response to Rita Williams-Garcia's *Like Sisters on the Homefront* shows that she has made a solid connection to reading:

The book that I'm reading is <u>Like Sisters on the Homefront</u>. It is a great book she is not scared to talk about what she has done in the 14 years of her life. She was pregnant and she had her baby it was by a married man named Jose. She named her baby after his father. Then she got pregnant by a boy or man named Troy. She did not want to get an abortion but her mom made her get one. Her mom sent her away to Georgia to live with her aunt and uncle and her cousin, Cookie. Her uncle was a preacher.

I thought it was a good book the way it started off. I thought it was bad for her to do that because she was so young. I think it was good that her mother sent her away because she changed. She started acting better and stuff and she started going to church and she got saved.

Tiffany's comprehension, her writing, and language all showed incredible improvement. Unfortunately, this success did not carry over into her other classes. Personality clashes with several teachers, rather than her ability, seemed to be the cause for her lack of success.

Tiffany was very skillful in helping her peers, however. I told her she was so good at helping others work out their romantic conflicts, I wondered if she had considered being a peer mediator at our school. She applied, was one of twenty students accepted, and excelled in the program. She registered for the high school peer mediation program, as well as the child-care class.

When I was nominated for teacher of the year in my county, Tiffany wrote this letter of recommendation on my behalf:

To Whom It May Concern:

Hello. My name is Tiffany Collins and I am a student in Mrs. Gonzalez's class. When she asked me to write this letter I was very excited and VERY proud that she asked ME to write this letter of recommendation. She told me that you, who ever it may concern, wanted to hear why she should be teacher of the year. Now I am going to tell you why. The reason I think that she should be the teacher of the year is that she is the nicest teacher that I ever had in Middle School. She is a great teacher and before I got in her class I never used to read. When the teachers used to call on me I used to read but I never wanted to and did not do it well but now I volunteer to read and I do it very well!!

And another reason that Mrs. Gonzalez should get teacher of the year is because she understands how others feel and she is the only teacher that I would go to for help. I would go to Mrs. Gonzalez before I would go to the Guidance Counselor. That's how much I admire her. I have been in her class for three years and she has been the kindest person I know. When I used to go home I used to talk about her all the time in a good way and my sisters used to pick on me. They used to say all you do is talk about Mrs. Gonzalez. And that was true. All I used to do is talk abut Mrs. Gonzalez because she changed my life. I started to try harder and did better on my work. I always try even if I know that I can't do it. She taught me to try. She taught me if I don't try, how do I know I can't do it?

I know that she's just starting teaching but she is good at it. She may not feel that she is great but she is. She has changed more lives than she knows about. I can't put all that I like about her down on a piece of paper because it is too large. It would take me almost 9 or 10 pages to talk about why I like her and how much I like her.

But I can tell you why she should be teacher of the year because she is the best teacher that any one that has had her for a teacher has EVER had. I can't speak for others but all I can say is, "YOU CHANGED MY LIFE."

Sincerely,

Tiffany Latrice Collins

Students like Tiffany remind me, even on the desperate days, of the meaningful work I do. I miss her and the notes she used to leave on my desk: "Dear Mrs. G, How are you? I love to read!" It makes me proud that she took with her not only the literacy skills but also the compassion she learned from the books she read during our time together.

Reflections by Janet

What can we learn from Kyle's focus on these three students? One thing I hear as I read through these case studies is the way Kyle follows her students' leads. When she needs to know something, she asks them. When she reflects on how to help them next, she thinks back to what worked before. Kyle has begun to fine-tune her intuitive sense of when to trust her students' judgments about their next learning steps.

Even as a new teacher, Kyle is developing some very successful scaffolds to help her students learn. Taping the beginnings of books, finding a reading partner for a student who is attempting a difficult text, taking time to guide readers through challenging books, are all things she does to help her students become successful readers and writers.

These case studies also demonstrate that Kyle is learning to let go of the curriculum. It's not that she doesn't balance direct and indirect instruction, very carefully planning the next steps for the class and for individuals within the class. But she is willing to let go of her planned curriculum when it gets in the way of a student who is experiencing the excitement of her first connection to books. When Charlene discovered Dahl's *The Witches,* Kyle allowed Charlene to stay with the book rather than participate in whole-group activities. That decision is a hard one to make.

Kyle is also comfortable with teaching as a matter of the heart. She has learned (and relearned on the days when she has forgotten) that there is value in spending her time helping children become literate. She has learned to listen to her students and to respond in ways that help them become progressively more successful. Teachers in traditional classrooms often say, "Well, sure, if I had only fifteen or twenty kids in each class, I could save them all, too." But anyone who has taught classes of nonreaders with a long history of school failure knows the story is not in the numbers. It is easy to lose one's sense of purpose with these children. Kyle and I have often felt as though we are taking on the negative attitudes of our students instead of their learning positive ones from us.

Finding a way to remind ourselves of what matters is one of the most important things we can do regardless of our student population. We share inspirational writing, new books, and stories about students as a way to validate the work and the love that goes into that work. The following anecdote, author unknown, has had a significant impact on many a teaching life:

> The Starfish Flinger
> As an old woman walked the beach at dawn, she noticed a young girl ahead of her picking up starfish and flinging them into the sea. Finally catching up with the girl, she asked her why she was doing this. The girl answered that the stranded starfish would die in the morning sun if they remained on the beach.
>
> "But the beach goes on and on for miles and there are millions of starfish," countered the woman. "How can your effort make any difference?"
>
> The young girl looked at the starfish in her hand and then threw it to the safety of the waves. "It makes a difference to this one," she said.

Focusing on the individual successes we see each day is one way to make sure we don't lose sight of the significance of connecting books and children—particularly those adolescents who seem otherwise certain to be lost.

Chapter 10

Assessment and Record Keeping

All that counts cannot be counted and all that can be counted doesn't count.

Albert Einstein

Knowing Our Learners and Their Learning

Assessment and evaluation are two of the most challenging issues teachers face. Each day we find themselves embroiled in an assessment tug of war: the professional literature is filled with research and strategies supporting authentic assessment, but some parents still want twenty-five spelling words sent home for weekly tests or nightly grammar worksheets and quizzes; administrators send us to assessment workshops to learn about portfolios and then demand that we spend weeks preparing students for state-mandated multiple-choice tests.

As I watch teachers and students try to find their way through the maze of conflicting demands and research, I'm reminded of one of the pieces in Pleasant de Spain's *Thirty-Three Multicultural Tales to Tell*. In a tale entitled "Grandfather Spider's Feast," Grandfather Spider is excited because he has heard that there are going to be four feasts in the same week but wonders how he can manage to get to all of them. Calling his four spider children to him, he asks them to help carry out the clever plan he has devised. He ties four strings around his waist and then ties the strings around each of his four children's waists and sends them on their way: one to the north, one to the east, one to the south, and one to the west. Each is instructed to tug on the string when the feast begins. Unfortunately for Grandfather, all the feasts begin at the same time, with predictable consequences. Teachers are experiencing the same unrealistic tugs today, with the same unfortunate results. Everything in education is a trade-off, and assessment is no exception. We can't get to every feast; it can't be both quick and meaningful, both easy to score and authentic. We have to choose our feast and then move patiently in a consistent direction to reach it.

In *Assessing Student Performance* (1993), Grant Wiggins asserts that educators have made conscious choices that have brought about some of the assessment/testing dilemmas we see in American classrooms. "The stubborn problems in assessment reform have to do with a pervasive thoughtlessness about testing and a failure to understand the relationship between assessment and learning. We have the tests we deserve because we are wont to reduce 'assessment' to 'testing' and to see testing as *separate* from learning" (3). When we instituted the Literacy Project classrooms, we wanted to look at ways that we could support teachers in moving from traditional ways of knowing to ways that would better inform students, parents, administrators, and instruction.

Traditionally, language arts classroom assessments consisted of worksheets; true/false, matching, or multiple-choice tests; short-answer responses to teacher-written essays; and projects. Most produced easily quantifiable results, yet many teachers questioned the depth of response measured by these means. In the past decade, teachers and researchers have actively pursued alternatives to those assessments and have found many effective ways to reflect more appropriately the diverse learning that is happening in classrooms. Yet these new tools are still missing in many classrooms as teachers cling to the comfort of tried (if not true) methods.

Robert Rothman, in his book *Measuring Up* (1995), cites teacher discomfort as one of the reasons that classroom assessment practices remain relatively unchanged in many schools and classrooms. "The idea of giving children responsibility for their learning may be daunting for those teachers who are accustomed to staying in control of their classrooms, as well as for students used to following rules" (15). As Kyle and I planned assessments for students in her literacy workshop, we knew that these practices would not be what the students expected nor would they be ones with which Kyle had experience. We also knew that we would have to trust the students, as well as Kyle's ability to teach responsively. We learned that giving up some of the control did not mean giving up the planning: Kyle's middle school students did not respond any better to such statements as Why don't you each come up with a way to show me that you've learned something? than my university students did.

When Kyle began teaching, she found herself using the same type of formal tests she had taken during her own schooling. Even though her instruction was very different from traditional language arts instruction, when it came "time" to assess, her methods reverted to the traditional. As Kyle began to experience some disequilibrium with this, we generated lists of possible types of assessment which might work in her classroom and with which she might experiment:

read and retell	self-evaluations
essays	presentations
discussions	conference notes
computer projects	meetings with parents/guardians
checklists	information from content teachers
interest inventories	learning logs
personal journals	interviews
academic journals	portfolios
recordings of oral reading	open-ended problem solving
running records	use of strategies
writing samples	observations
anecdotal records	independent literacy activities

Ultimately we wanted to make sure that whatever assessment practices Kyle developed would be grounded in the underlying principles that Lois Bridges outlines on page 8 of *Assessment: Continuous Learning* (1995). The assessment had to be continuous, be an integral part of the curriculum, be developmentally appropriate, focus and build on students' strengths, build on self-assessment, reflect individuals working together, and inform instruction.

Realistically, it was impossible for Kyle to implement every innovative assessment practice we listed—certainly not in her first year of teaching! As we watch Kyle grapple with assessment in her classroom, we see how she slowly built an assessment foundation and then worked with students to make assessment increasingly more meaningful. Mary Henning-Stout (1994) points out that "actively enlisting the student in assessment and intervention planning emerges as this framework's most unique feature" (28). The assessment in Kyle's classroom is unique for the same reason: at each step, she attempts to find ways to include students in the process. Her classroom is a living reflection of Sheila Valencia's words in *Authentic Reading Assessment: Practices and Possibilities* (1994): "Classroom assessment places both teachers and students in positions of power: they are responsible for evaluation, and they are considered the primary consumers as well as producers of information that can be used for decision making, self-reflection, and goal setting" (23). The students in this classroom had experienced limited voice during their previous schooling, but their voices ring true as they experience the power of assessment as another tool for learning.

In the Classroom with Kyle

From Theory to Practice

One of the most difficult tasks I have faced in my classroom is how to assess and evaluate student progress fairly. When I interned, I followed the standard procedure of giving a test at the end of the unit but instead of using the test in the teacher's guide, I prepared the questions myself. I felt I was being rather creative. It didn't matter that out of a hundred and fifty students, only a third received above a C. The rest did badly because they hadn't paid attention, hadn't done the reading, hadn't studied. Then I moved on to teach and assess the next unit as if everyone had negotiated the previous one successfully.

When I began teaching in the Literacy Project, assessment was the first thing on my mind. With so many people attuned to the success or failure of this project, I knew that I wanted grades in the grade book that I could show to parents, administrators, and students. I assigned homework but assured visitors that this homework was different because I had allowed students to vote on which nights they wanted to do it. And I was quite resentful when my students didn't do the homework even though I had given them this "choice." I told myself that they just needed some additional reminding. After all, these were at-risk students. When a month passed and no one had turned in any homework, I began worrying. Still it couldn't be my fault. The students were just being irresponsible and lazy. When I assigned grades at the end of the quarter, homework was the biggest detriment, even though I only counted it as 10 percent of the total. Then I panicked. After all, this classroom was supposed to build on success, not failure.

In a 1992 address at a Phi Delta Kappan conference in Orlando, Howard Johnston reminded his audience that homework was the single most significant indicator of failure in the middle school and asked his listeners to think about who traditionally does most of the homework assigned in middle school—parents. It finally occurred to me that for the most part, these students did not come from homes in which homework was a priority. Further, I began to understand that my harassment of the students for not turning in their homework was making them lose respect for me and lose enthusiasm for the work we were doing together. I stopped giving homework. With homework suddenly a nonissue, I had the energy and the students' cooperation (sometimes) to make our assessment more meaningful and useful. We began rethinking assessment in the areas in which we spent most of our time and moved outward from there. In each case, I had to look at what I believed, what we were doing, and what needed to change to make my beliefs consistent with my practice.

Observations, Anecdotal Records, and Independent Reading

I firmly believe reading is a meaning-making process that is highly dependent on readers' individual interactions with the text. I know that traditional reading assessment has focused on the subskills of reading rather than assessing the meaning-making process of individual readers. Nevertheless, while we concentrated on making meaning during independent reading, my assessments of independent reading still concentrated on reading subskills. The book *Best Practice* (Zemelman, Daniels, and Hyde 1993) recommends Yetta Goodman's "kidwatching" as one of the best forms of assessment: "The best possible assessment would occur when teachers observe and interact with students as they read authentic texts for genuine purposes, and then keep anecdotal records of students' developing skills, problems, changes, and goals in reading" (29). During independent reading, my students read authentic texts for genuine purposes. During independent reading, I can help students individualize their reading goals, because students are choosing their own books. It makes sense that independent reading assessment also be individualized.

Independent reading occurs at least biweekly in our literacy workshop. At the beginning of the year I keep the sessions short, usually fifteen minutes. As students get hooked on what they're reading, we are gradually able to increase the sessions to forty-five minutes of uninterrupted silent reading.

To assess students during independent reading, I kidwatch. I designed a Weekly Independent Reading Chart (see Figure 10.1 and Appendix A.3)

Figure 10.1 *The chart Kyle uses to assess her students' progress during independent reading*

Weekly Independent Reading Chart

Period: 2&3

Student Name	Title of Book	Session I	Session II	Session III	Comments
Merica Beverly	Outsiders (A)	161? 116-	Finished!	Driver's Ed (A) 1-19	Loves it. 19-
Tasha Sattell (~~Noel Brown~~)	Two Under Par (A)	1-14	14-22	Absent	Wow! went from reading w/tape to independent. Awesome! Motivated--read yesterday too.
Tricia Fischer	The Wager (I)	126-142	272-Finished	Reviews (A) 1-	
Shelmetris Harp	Chocolate Fever (I)	1-17	Absent	17- (I)	
Charlene Harris	~~Scary Stories~~ The Littles (A)	29-	Haunted Schools 14-5 → Chap. 5 Chapter		
James Parish	Stonefox	37-55 (1/2)	55-Finished!	Death from Child Abuse (I) 1- Picked own book!	Very reluctant to get ready for reading today. Did extremely well today though reluctant to get started.

to help organize my anecdotal records. Each Monday I print out a new chart and record the reading progress of my students. The first thing I look at is whether students are reading independently or with the assistance of a recorded book. The goal is to create independent, lifelong readers through various forms of support and teaching. Recorded unabridged books are one of the strategies I employ to assist students who are not quite ready to read independently. That goal, therefore, needs to be reflected in the assessment I use.

If students are reading with the assistance of a recorded book, I note that with the letter *A*; if they are reading independently, I note that with an *I*. I also write down the title of the book students are reading for that session as well as their beginning page numbers. For students who have trouble keeping their place on a tape, I also write down the side of the tape they are on and the last sentence they read.

I read along with the students during independent reading, because they need to see that their teacher values reading so much that nothing else—conferences, working on the computer, grading papers—interferes. Nevertheless, I occasionally glance up and check their progress and behavior. If a student is engrossed in what he or she is reading, I jot down some sort of descriptor: engrossed, very interested, involved, following along diligently with the tape. If I see this behavior several times during the reading session, I know the student is probably not going to need much, if any, support or assistance. If the behavior continues, I leave the comment area blank so in future I can spend my note-taking time on students who are still struggling.

Behavior that indicates a struggling reader includes not following along with the recorded book text, talking or whispering to another student, repeatedly rewinding and fast-forwarding a tape, asking to use the rest room or get a drink, sleeping, and moving around the classroom. As I look for patterns in my anecdotal records, I often find that this kind of behavior means that a book is too difficult for the student or one the student sees as boring. I then help that student choose a book that is a better match with his ability and interest.

Observations and assessment obviously influence what is traditionally called classroom management. For example, if a behavior threatens the concentration of other members of the class, I immediately intervene. I try to be as nonconfrontational and supportive as I can; it doesn't take much for a student who is struggling with reading to become agitated. I quietly crouch down next to the student and ask, "How are you feeling about your book? Is it interesting or boring to you?" If the student feels the book is unappealing, I ask what he is in the mood to read: funny? scary? long? short? on tape? We then decide where to go from there.

I also note significant changes—when students move from assisted to independent reading, for example. At the beginning of the school year, Tasha (see Figure 10.1) had been struggling with keeping her place in the book while following along as she listened to the recorded version. We tried recorded books that were shorter, had larger print, and contained illustrations, and she found those much easier to follow along in. Then, in the first week of October, she started a new recorded book, *Two Under Par* by Kevin Henkes, that was a bit longer. During the first two sessions she used the tapes and then during the third session, I observed her reading independently.

When independent reading is over, I use the remainder of the class to speak with each student about what she or he did that day. I offer positive comments and suggestions, and we discuss any trouble that might have been encountered. In our classroom, each forty-five minute session is worth one hundred points. At the beginning of the year, students and I discuss what quality work will look like during independent reading: reading silently for the entire session, following along with the tape if participating in shared reading, and making efforts to reach individual goals. If a student reads for the entire time, she gets the full number of points. If a student is reading with the assistance of the tape, he gets full points only if he follows along in the text. If someone repeatedly doesn't follow along in the text, even after we've talked about how necessary it is, I often suggest switching to a book that isn't as lengthy or that is a better match with her ability and interests.

Assessing reading with my students has been a powerful tool in our classroom. In an article in *Voices in the Middle,* Judith Wright states, "For some time, I have been hooked on the notion that students must evaluate their own learning in order to grow" (1995, 21), and I have found this to be true. While this may sound too individualized for a classroom of forty students, rather than fifteen, it isn't. In a large class of students with varied reading attitudes and abilities, kidwatching can be done with all students, with the anecdotal records focusing on those students who most need support. Kidwatching does not require an extensive amount of effort once you establish a routine. At first our miniconferences at the end of class took about fifteen minutes. Now we do them in five. Also, it's unlikely that a class of forty students would include forty nonreaders. Students who are successful readers can track their own reading progress, just as my students eventually do. For example, I have an elective class, Adolescent Literature, for students who are reading at or above grade level. For part of their grade, they assess their own reading progress, and I designed an Independent Reading Log (see Appendix A.2) as a tool to help them. Students note pages read and jot down a brief response at the end of class.

Assessment and Shared Reading

During shared reading all the students are reading the same book at the same time, so I use a modified form of kidwatching as I read aloud, making mental notes about who is struggling with the text. I don't stop to write these notes down because I don't want to interrupt the flow of the text. During breaks in the reading, I briefly check in with students who seem to be struggling or need support. The number one sign that a student is struggling is not following along as I read. If several students are not following along, I look at my reading, the level of difficulty of the book, and the content.

I introduce students to the guidelines for shared reading at the beginning of the year. They can earn the full amount of possible points—usually one hundred for a thirty- to forty-minute reading session, simply by following along in the book. If they listen to the story and do not follow along, they earn half the points. As with independent reading, we start with short sessions, usually ten or fifteen minutes, and lengthen them as the year progresses. We also set aside time at the end of the class for students to confer briefly with me as a whole group about how they did in that session of shared reading.

Chapter mapping and book logs work well as a means for students to self-assess their comprehension during shared reading and for me to see what they are getting and not getting. When I do the first shared reading with a class, we stop at the end of each chapter and students write about or draw what they see as the significant events or people in the chapter (see Appendix A.4). I walk around the room, checking to see which students are comprehending the chapter and which students may need extra guidance. As students retitle each chapter, I can assess how well they are able to find the main ideas and synthesize what we are reading together. When students become more comfortable with shared reading, we move on to the Independent Reading Log (see Appendix A.2), which accomplishes the same thing but isn't as time-consuming: students go back to the text and pick out a sentence or paragraph they found interesting, funny, hard to understand, etc.

One of the most important assessment tools for shared reading is discussion. Students need to talk about the stories we read together and relate the stories to their own lives. Jane Hansen (1981) has noted that while some children do not relate what they read to their background knowledge, they can be taught to do so. The general questions in Aidan Chambers's *Tell Me* (1996) are excellent prompts to get students to dig beneath the surface.

Projects

My students really enjoyed the projects they completed as shared-reading assessments. Each student was free to create his or her individual response to a particular novel we had read together. With so many gifted artists, creativity and sharing took center stage. Students were able to look at such benchmarks as commitment, quality, connection, and composition without the fear that usually accompanies more word-driven responses.

Portfolios

When I first started teaching, my friend Becky conducted a workshop for interns and beginning teachers. Speaking about her experience with portfolios in her classroom, she said they had turned into "glorified note-books" rather than authentic assessment tools. I was determined to create a portfolio that would effectively assess student progress in our class. Together the students and I revised the structure and criteria for two years, driving ourselves crazy in the process. But we finally arrived at something I consider an assessment rather than an organizational tool.

I modeled parts of the portfolio on the academic notebooks Janet had used in her ninth-grade classroom. The sections in my students' portfolios are Class Business; Things I Am Learning How to Do; Things I Know How to Do; Words; Writing; and My Stuff.

Class Business. This is where class rules go after they have been voted on and word-processed by the students. We also put here any other classroom business/management that is important, like field trip etiquette (see Figure 10.2), comfy chair seating charts, and rules for more effective classroom discussions.

Figure 10.2 *Tricia's field trip etiquette suggestions that then went into the Class Business section of her portfolio*

Things I Am Learning How to Do. This section contains exactly that—things students are learning how to do in reading and writing. Students record what they are learning and include work samples that show what they are learning. For example, at the beginning of one year, my sixth graders were learning how to make a prediction about a book before we read it together. They put their illustrated predictions in this section and then wrote down how to make a prediction.

Or again, my eighth graders this past year were learning how to appreciate written language. As I read aloud Walter Dean Myers's *Scorpions,* they kept a book log in which they copied down sentences or paragraphs that struck them in some way—funny, poignant, personally meaningful—and wrote about why they chose them. In doing so, they were also learning how to use quotation marks correctly. These book logs are kept in this section of the portfolio.

Things I Know How to Do. This section in the students' portfolios contains what they know how to do in reading and writing—things they could teach someone else. Again, work samples are included. For example, the sixth graders learned about predictions in August. In October several of them automatically made predictions prior to and during reading. When I saw students successfully making predictions on their own, I asked them to note their "know how" in this section of the portfolio and include samples that demonstrated their knowledge of this strategy.

Recently Charlene, one of my seventh graders, was writing a short story for Halloween. In her draft, she had used dialogue very effectively. We discussed dialogue and how she had learned to use it correctly. Charlene then recorded this "know how" in her portfolio, documented her knowledge with her story, and then noted her process for learning it (from shared and independent reading).

Words. It seems to me that in my few years of teaching I've tried every vocabulary activity known to humanity to get my students interested in new words. One of the characteristics of mature readers is that they are conscious of learning new words. When students first enter the literacy workshop, they have not had enough experience with books and reading to find delight in words. In fact, new words are the enemy for many of these students, especially if oral correctness has been valued over meaning.

When I read a book Janet recommended, Monalisa DeGross's *Donovan's Word Jar,* I recognized a way for students to delight in new words. In this book, Donovan is a collector of words, which he saves in a word jar. I decided to follow Donovan's example and get word jars for each of my classes. I went to our cafeteria manager and explained what I was attempting to do. She immediately went to the back of the kitchen and returned with four large pickle jars—perfect receptacles for our word collections!

After the students had decorated and labeled the jars, I announced that I wanted them to become connoisseurs of words. I asked them to find a new word anywhere they could, write down the word and its source, include what they thought the word meant, and then add the slip of paper to the word jar. Students began collecting words from their independent reading, our shared reading, television and videos, and eaves-dropped conversations. Each day, I pulled at least one slip of paper from the word jar and we discussed the word and its context. Students then added these new words to the Words section of their portfolio. One of the funniest examples follows:

Word:	comacorten
Definition:	"pick u up"
Source:	Little Rascls

Fortunately, the word made sense to me when I read it aloud. Jamie had certainly hit the definition: come a courtin' means to pick you up! (Blank word slips are provided in Appendix A.5.)

Writing. This section of the portfolios celebrates the students' favorite pieces of writing, whether rough drafts or final versions. As they begin to get more stories in their heads, students are less afraid to write. The seventh graders celebrated Halloween with read-alouds of several scary short stories. We examined some of the devices used by the authors, the most popular being using clues to lead the reader on, flashback, and suspense. I put samples of these writing devices on the overhead, things the students could record in section 2 of their portfolios (Things I Am Learning How To Do). As students began including these devices in their writing, those writing pieces were included in the Writing section.

Students are free to put any writing in this section—responses to independent reading, poetry, quickwrites, and personal pieces; in fact, students sometimes include the writing of others they admire.

My Stuff. The items in this section are those important to the students: tests on which they have felt successful, drawings they have completed, pictures from magazines. It's a catchall in a way, but very revealing.

Still Other Forms of Assessment

When I first started teaching in the literacy workshop, I had days where I felt the students were leaving with absolutely no idea or recollection of what we had done in our two periods together. I would ask myself, Are they connecting to what we've read? Will they remember the strategy we did today? To ease my concern, I started making them check out with me before they left: I asked each student to tell me something new he or she had learned that day. When the oral telling proved too frustrating for some students, I created the Daily Activity Log (see Figure 10.3), which I used for only a few weeks. I didn't want students to get bogged down

Daily Activity Log

****

Date: 8-21-95

Today I did... Worked on goals, address card, read a fable

Today I learned... About academic and personal goals so we can ac ~~~~~ So I can see what I can insted of can't do!

****

Date: 8-22-95

Today I did... Read Jashua T. Bates... and talked about hole in are life bbad habits

Today I learned...

****

Date: 8-23-95

Today I did...(continue writing on the back of this paper)
Read together, did a grade contract, discussed substitute. Chapter map. looked at new words.

Figure 10.3 *Daily activity logs were one way for Kyle to assess what her students had learned each day*

with paperwork, but I did want them consciously to think about and assess their activities and their learning. After completing this log for a short time, students began to realize the connection between their work and their progress in learning. It seemed to help them internalize the locus of control. Ownership of the assessment led to ownership of learning.

In her ninth-grade classroom, Janet had asked her students to evaluate their work at the end of each week. I followed her example and began asking my students what they had learned each week. It was a way to give closure to the week just past and suggest things we might do during our next week together. A typical week in the literacy workshop included shared reading, independent reading, writing, work on individual academic and personal goals, and research. In his Looking at Our Practice form (see Appendix A.16), Corey listed independent reading, shared reading, writing, and goals as things he had done. In independent reading he learned to read better and to read more. He also learned that reading can take you to a different place, "escape to another world." In shared reading, he learned about making predictions and how to differentiate characters in a book. His goals project helped him learn about what he wants to do in his future and what he needs to do to get there. Looking at Our Practice is another example of an assessment my students and I shared. Completing my own Looking at Our Practice form helped me refine our classroom learning; completing theirs helped students begin to own their learning in a way they never had before.

Test Taking and Formal Tests

Our school, like most, requires a formal exam at the end of each grading period. When I first began teaching, the school had nine-week grading periods, which meant I had to give a nine-week exam and a semester exam each semester. While I was required to give the tests, parameters for the test were not specified. Following Zemelman, Daniels, and Hyde's advice (1993) that reading assessment should match classroom practice, I attempted to make my exams match what we did every day in the classroom.

I wanted even our formal tests to be continuous, informative, appropriate, collaborative, and built on students' strengths. So the students and I designed the formal test together; students were allowed to use classroom resources (dictionaries, our literacy banner, their portfolios, the books we had read) while taking the test; and several days of class time were devoted to completing the test, the students working for short periods of time and then taking a break during which they could read or write independently. I included some questions on the test just as the students had generated them; others I reworded to assess areas the students had not considered.

Before we could design the exam, however, we had to address test-taking strategies. These students had experienced very little school success, so anything related to a test was a low priority. I began our strategy session by asking students to brainstorm a list of problems they had previously encountered with test taking. My exact words were, "Okay, you guys, let's talk abut tests." I had no idea the word *tests* would stir them up so much.

"Man, teachers always be tryin' them things. I hate tests."

"I agree with you."

"Okay, then just don't give us no tests!" Corian yelled.

"I am required to give you an exam at the end of each grading period. Let's figure out how you can perform better on them."

The amazing thing was that my students were all convinced that the only students who did well on tests were the rich kids (the "preps"); teachers' pets; and those who were just born smart. They had no idea that lots of students had to study and prepare for exams and were as afraid of failing as they were.

We brainstormed some of the problems that people face when they take tests and then discussed ways these test-taking problems could be solved or at least lessened. Their problems included:

Going blank.
Worrying about getting a bad grade.
Having to go to the bathroom.
Breaking the lead in the pencil.
Copying and cheating.
Getting a stomachache.

They then suggested mature solutions for the problems they had articulated:

Study.
Get between seven and eight hours of sleep the night before.
Eat a good breakfast.
Reread, reread, reread the questions.
Think positively.
Bring a sweater in case the room you take a test in is cold.
Go to the bathroom before the test.
Take deep breaths when you start to get nervous.
Don't spend too long on questions that you're not sure about.

After our test-taking discussion, we began designing the test together. We agreed that the most important requirement was that students had to *explain* their answers. The sixth-grade exam consisted mostly of short-answer questions about the shared reading novel, their independent reading, and their responses and reactions to our class activities. The seventh- and eighth-grade students tended to ask more in-depth questions (see Figure 10.4) but still focused on shared reading and goals as the main way to demonstrate their learning. (Tabitha's answers to the final exam are shown in Figure 10.5. Although she skipped question 6, she had plenty to say in response to question 7!)

This process was a living example of what Paul Crowley (1995) says about bringing students into the assessment process: "Middle school kids are trying to figure out who they want to be. They need to feel comfortable with their success and their errors, to know what they know and use it" (11).

Standardized Tests

While it was exciting to be involved in something as big as the Literacy Project, it also meant being involved in a great deal of standardized testing. In the first year of the project, our students were given five stan-

Directions: Please answer the following questions, making sure to EXPLAIN your answers. This means to give reasons, back up what you say, tell me your thoughts, etc. You may use your portfolios for this exam. PLEASE WRITE ALL ANSWERS ON A SEPARATE SHEET OF PAPER. YOU WILL NEED AT LEAST TWO PIECES OF PAPER FOR THIS EXAM.

Goals

1. List your personal goal for the year. Tell me every step you have taken toward achieving this goal. For example, if your goal was to read more, tell me how often you read, what you read, etc. BE SPECIFIC!
2. List your academic goal for this nine week period. Tell me EVERY STEP you have taken toward achieving this goal.
3. Did you run into any obstacles while attempting to reach your goals? Explain.
4. Please list ONE goal that you have for yourself this summer.
5. What grade do you feel you have earned in working toward achieving your goals for the year?

Shared Reading

6. Essay question. Please write at least TWENTY sentences about *It Happened to Nancy.* Please address (which means talk about) the following points in your essay:
   **Collin/Throw Up—what you think about him and what he did
   **Nancy—what you think about her having AIDS
   **One FACT that you know about AIDS
   **What you learned about AIDS that you didn't know before (DO NOT ANSWER NOTHING)
   **What you would do if you were in Nancy's shoes
   **What you think about the entire book
7. Please write another essay about the things that you as a seventh or eight grader worry about in your life. World peace? Grades? Friends? Parents? Relationships? EXPLAIN YOUR ANSWER!!
8. Please write on a separate sheet of paper a letter to yourself, telling yourself all of the things you are proud of accomplishing this year and what you hope to accomplish in the future.

Figure 10.4 *Seventh- and eighth-grade final exam*

dardized tests at the beginning and end of the school year. These tests were in addition to the interviews, surveys, and reviews of discipline and attendance records. Given the angst these students had about tests, the fact that they had so many tests and were under such time constraints to complete the tests made them even more agitated. The majority of my students could not even read the tests, so they certainly entered the test arena with negative feelings. In the face of research showing that reading instruction and assessment should focus on constructing meaning from print, these tests seemed to contradict the instructional program they were ostensibly meant to assess. The county has now modified the assess-

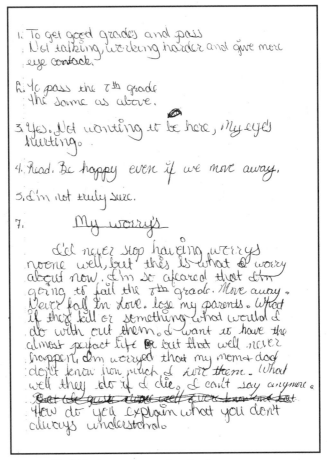

Figure 10.5 *Some of Tabitha's answers on her final exam*

ment of the Literacy Project and uses only the Degrees of Reading Power (DRP) instrument. If a test has to be given, this does seem to match instruction more closely, since it consists entirely of cloze passages of meaningful information.

Reflections by Janet

Kyle and her students are learning firsthand how difficult authentic assessment is. They are constantly struggling with how to assess meaning making rather than an easily graded subskill. *Assessment Alternatives for Diverse Classrooms* (Farr and Trumbull 1997) reminds readers, "Just as instructional techniques need to be varied and diversified in order to match the learning styles of students from different cultural groups, assessment techniques must be similarly varied to match the communication, presentation, and performance styles of diverse students" (xvi). Everyone in the literacy workshop is a learner, especially when it comes to assessment. For students it is the first time they have been asked to participate in assessment; for Kyle, it is a constant struggle to align assessment with her beliefs about the integrated nature of assessment and instruction.

Teachers often say to me, "This stuff sounds great, but the bottom line in my classroom is putting a grade on a report card." Kyle has the same bottom line: each of the assessment techniques she and her students try must be translated into grades. For two years, Kyle has used the Organizer for Language Arts (see Appendix A.6) as a way to translate the class's assessments into grades. Using it is sometimes cumbersome and time-consuming, but it works better than anything else Kyle has tried because students can keep track of their accomplishments in a concrete way.

Howard Gardner and Tom Hatch (1989) state: "A consideration of a broader range of talents brings to the fore individuals who previously had been considered unexceptional or even at risk for school failure" (4). Inviting students to participate in assessment and then supporting them during this process brings out the talents many students have kept hidden—talents that make them less at risk and more with promise.

Chapter 11

But What About...

It is better to ask some of the questions than know all of the answers.

James Thurber

Whenever Kyle and I speak at conferences or work with classroom teachers, we are asked questions about literacy workshops. These questions come from teachers of students in grades four through twelve, from teachers in rural and urban settings, from teachers who work with small numbers of students in pullout programs, from teachers with forty students per class. Our answers vary, depending on the context. Here, we attempt to answer them within the context of the literacy workshop—which includes shared, guided, and independent reading and writing—regardless of class size or grade level. While the responses overlap somewhat, we have grouped the questions by category: writing, reading, classroom environment, classroom management, evaluation, and beginning/continuing.

Writing

1. How important are peer conference groups in writing workshop and how do you manage them?
While we both believe in the value of peer conference groups, neither of us has been successful in implementing them. We quickly discovered that students who are nonreaders are also nonwriters and that lack of background knowledge relative to reading and writing makes it difficult for them to help one another as writers. We haven't given up; when Kyle has had the same students over a number of years, some of them have developed the ability to confer with each about their pieces. One of the most helpful books we have found for giving us support as we try to implement peer conferences is Karen Spear's *Sharing Writing: Peer Response Groups in English Classes* (1988).

2. What things do you do to prepare students for state writing tests?
Both Kyle and I have taught in states with mandated writing tests. These
tests consist of writing prompts that are responded to in a timed, con-
trolled environment. For two years I worked with the Department of
Education in Maine as one of a group of people who designed and scored
the writing assessment. As I worked with teachers who were attempting
to help students improve their writing scores, I always gave them the same
advice: hook students as readers and their writing will improve. I still
believe that today. Wide and varied reading gives students the opportunity to see thousands of new words in a variety of contexts, to experience a
range of writing styles, and to see the impact of writing on readers.

Today, however, I would add that this reading must be tied to direct
and explicit instruction in writing. This occurs in the literacy workshop
in many ways, but most explicitly in the three situations described in
Chapter 6: shared writing, guided writing, and individual conferences.
During shared writing, the teacher holds the lion's share of responsibility for constructing the writing. As students dictate their ideas and explo-
rations, the teacher transcribes them, stopping at critical stages to explore
options for communicating both the purpose and the spirit of the writing. This modified LEA (language experience activity) helps students
explore the choices we can make as writers to communicate effectively.
In guided writing, the teacher demonstrates a type of writing or a writing
issue, students practice the writing individually, and the group then
comes back together to share these purposeful pieces. For example, if I
notice that my students are all struggling with writing leads, we would
look at effective leads in several pieces of fiction and nonfiction: perhaps
John Steinbeck's short story "The Origin of Tularecito," Robert Cormier's
We All Fall Down, a Nikki Giovanni essay from her collection *Sacred Cows
and Other Edibles,* and a Time-Life article on the Sunday school bombing
in Birmingham, Alabama. We would analyze the techniques these writers
used to lead readers into their writing and discuss the characteristics of
effective leads. For contrast, we would then look at some pieces with inef-
fective leads. Finally, the students would take a piece of their own writing
(one in process or a new piece) and attempt to craft an effective lead.
Depending on the students' ability and sophistication, they can share
their efforts first in pairs and small groups and then bring particularly
effective examples to the whole class as models.

In my classroom, students kept these guided writing characteristics,
examples, and attempts in their academic notebooks in a section entitled
Things I Am Learning How to Do. As the year progressed, they had developed their own language resource books. In addition, if editing skills are
taught in small groups or individual conferences as necessary, students
develop excellent resources for improving their writing.

During Kyle's first year of teaching, she felt she spent too much time
trying to prepare her students for the writing test. As she continued to

work with some of the same students for the next two years, she was able to integrate writing instruction during shared reading and writing in ways that helped the students more successfully complete the state assessment. This year, just before the test, she zeroed in on test-taking strategies in general and on analyzing and practicing expository and persuasive writing. She used prompts and samples sent by the state department of education so students would have specific examples of what was expected of them. This helped students feel prepared for the test without taking valuable time away from reading.

3. How do you manage editing and publishing with students whose skills are so limited?

This is discussed in more detail in Chapter 6. What I find most effective is to ask students to document editing mechanics in their academic notebooks. For example, if students are struggling with how to punctuate dialogue, I ask them to take the book they are currently reading independently and find a place where a character is speaking. We put a few examples on the board or the overhead and analyze the punctuation and capitalization patterns. Students then copy their individual passage into their academic notebook in the Things I Am Learning How to Do section, highlighting quotation marks, capital letters, and internal/end-quote punctuation. This becomes an individual, authentic reference.

Kyle and I both find that poetry is one of the least threatening types of writing for reluctant writers to publish—students sense that there is a freedom in punctuation and capitalization in poetry that they haven't experienced with prose. When we edit our pieces for classroom publishing, we focus on one element at a time (students can learn only one truly new thing at a time); the work is not perfect, it is correct in the one element on which we are focusing. If work is being published for a larger audience and surface-level correctness is required, students edit for the elements they know and we edit the rest of the piece together. (The editing we do tells us how and when to set up small groups for editing instruction.)

Kyle has often pointed out that when students first come into the literacy workshop, editing focuses mainly on surface features (spelling, capitalization, punctuation); they are not ready for more sophisticated writing lessons on style and voice. These occur later in the year as students get more reading history behind them. As they become more adept and thoughtful readers, they begin to incorporate the writing strategies of the authors they read into their own writing: flashback, dialogue, sensory description, suspense.

4. What about students who don't/won't write?

Kyle and I both use the LEA (language experience activity) as a starting place with reluctant writers. We first connect writing and whole-group responses to shared reading and then apply the same techniques individually. During ILE (independent literacy exploration) we sit one-on-one with students and let them dictate their stories, responses, even lists, to us. Copies are placed in their academic journals as a reference for their future writing.

We also let students dictate into a tape recorder, and then either the student or we transcribe what was said. In large groups, students can dictate to another student. These scaffolding activities help reluctant writers move gradually toward independent writing.

5. How do you find time to edit one-on-one with students?

Certainly, finding time to edit one-on-one with a large class is almost impossible unless the class is set up as a workshop that meets several times a week. In small classes, such as Kyle's Literacy Project classes, it is easier to meet with individual students during independent literacy exploration. During editing meetings, I try to help the student work on one new area in his or her writing. I connect the topic to the book the student is currently reading, and it is logged into the student's academic notebook in the Things I Am Learning How to Do section.

In some classes, students can share the editing responsibility. One student can be responsible for commas in a series; another can be the expert on *their, there,* and *they're.* This takes incredible planning, however. Quite honestly, it was beyond my organizational ability to keep it all working. I did find that the more time we devoted to ILE, the more time I had to meet with individual students for editing and other conferences.

6. Should most writing that students do be on self-selected topics?

During the first ten years I taught, I believed the only real writing was that done when students had chosen their own topics. However, while I was working with the Maine State Department of Education, we discovered that the students who scored the highest on our state-mandated writing test wrote on self-selected topics in school only about half the time. In the other half of their school writing program, the teacher demonstrated writing patterns, techniques, and forms and supported students while they practiced these patterns, techniques, and forms. The opportunity for self-selected topics was often embedded in this guided writing, but the teacher was still actively involved. In my last three years of high school teaching, I used this effectively and found that students were able to transfer the modeled writing we did together to the writing they did independently.

For reluctant readers and writers, the writing task is often overwhelming if left too open-ended. Both Kyle and I find that students of this type initially do best with writing that is prompted by their reading or events in their lives.

7. What is interactive writing and how can it be used effectively?

Teachers and students share responsibility for both the surface and the deeper structure of interactive writing. For example, after our initial reading of S. E. Hinton's *Taming the Star Runner,* I might stand at the overhead and begin a response log entry by writing, "Travis should have known he was in trouble when _____." Then I would ask the students how I might end the sentence. After several options have been suggested, I would choose one and then perhaps ask a student to suggest a follow-up sentence. I believe this is an effective way to scaffold writing for students. As you work through both the meaning and the mechanics of the writing, students internalize the process of construction as well as the way you revise and edit.

8. How do you convince students to add more descriptive details?

An activity Kyle uses is to pull out descriptive passages from the books she chooses for shared reading. Students then compare these descriptions and decide which ones they think are most effective.

One of my favorite activities is to show the students in the front of the room a line drawing. Each person looks at the picture for several seconds and then whispers a description of the picture to the person behind him or her. This person repeats the description to the next person, and so on. The last person in each row draws the picture, as it has been described, on an overhead transparency. After the transparency drawings have been compared with the original, everyone identifies one or two specific descriptive words or phrases that could have been used to communicate the picture more effectively.

9. How do you motivate students who will only write two or three sentences?

I think the strategies we have already discussed motivate students to expand their writing and support them in doing so. For many students, literacy workshop is one of the first times they have had models from which to work. While we don't want to introduce students to patterned writing and then abandon them, for some it is the first step toward finding their voice and their confidence.

10. How does lack of motor skills affect a child's desire to write?

Kyle says that as a student she remembers the pain and humiliation of having poor penmanship equated with an inability to write. A lack of motor skills and the attendant criticism take away any writing initiative a student like this might have. It makes a tremendous difference when students are able to use the computer. The amount of text they generate on a word processor is incredible.

11. What about spelling?

Spelling continues to be a struggle for most students in the Literacy Project classes. For visual learners, the more they read and see words repeated, the more accurate their spelling becomes. Most students, however, need more formal and direct instruction in the patterns that words follow. Neither Kyle nor I use spelling tests. In fact, we both essentially ignore spelling for the first few weeks of school in order to gain the students' trust while we try to hook them as readers and writers. We have, however, developed several strategies that help students focus on spelling patterns and recognize the playfulness with which language can be approached.

An excellent book entitled *Ideas for Spelling* (Bolton and Snowball 1993) discusses developmental issues related to spelling and presents a number of effective spelling strategies: the word jar; an alphabetic word wall of words related to specific shared texts; charts of words fitting/not fitting spelling patterns; and individual spelling texts are helpful ways to get students to focus on correct spelling.

12. How do you keep journals from becoming boring and monotonous?
Neither Kyle nor I use personal journals for long periods of time. We use them for specific purposes (beginning-of-the-year get-to-know-you tools) and then let students choose whether or not to continue them. Many do use them to carry on a dialogue with us. Others find them a waste of time.

I learned a valuable lesson from a German exchange student at our high school. She came to me from journal writing in another English class one day and said, "Mrs. Allen, what is this lima bean," pronouncing lima with a short *i*. When I finally discovered what she talking about, I drew one for her and asked her why she wanted to know. "What do you do with them?" she asked. When I told her that some people eat them, she really looked puzzled. "If people eat them, why would I want to pretend to be one for ten minutes?" A good question and one that reminded me of the ludicrous writing prompts we give to students in the name of writing fluency. From that day on, I became much more aware of asking students to write in authentic ways.

Journals can be incredible tools for students who see them as a way to keep track of ideas and issues. I find writer's notebooks of more value than journals but they are harder for students who struggle as readers and writers, because they have so few literacy habits.

Reading

13. How do you model reading and still make sure that the kids are reading?
This question usually relates to how we get students to follow along during shared reading. The first thing we do to make sure that students are reading is choose books that are interesting to them. Then we explain how following along will help them become better readers, writers, and spellers: by seeing and hearing the same words repeated often, they will internalize the words and own them for life.

As we read aloud during shared reading, we stop fairly often (every few pages) to ask a question or *briefly* discuss a word or an idea. Then we remind everyone where we are in the book so that those who have gotten lost because they can't or won't keep up can find the appropriate spot. Typically, as students become more fluent readers, this becomes less of an issue.

14. What strategies do you use to teach vocabulary?

We use a variety of activities to teach vocabulary. Clearly, we believe a wide and diverse reading curriculum is the single most significant contributor to an enhanced vocabulary. In addition, we use specific vocabulary strategies from NCTE's *Ideas Plus,* content-area textbooks, and journal articles. The vocabulary activity Kyle's students seem to enjoy most is the word jar described in Chapter 10.

15. What kind of follow-up activities should there be for students using recorded books?

Students can follow their encounter with a recorded book with the same responses they use when they read a book independently: they can write log entries, poetry, and letters; they can discuss the book during a conference; they can advertise the book on a classroom bulletin board; they can track their progress on their personal reading chart.

16. What if I have to teach the classics? Do you have any shortcuts for teaching *Great Expectations?*

If your school curriculum requires you to teach the classics or if there are certain classics you think your students should read, then I suggest the following:

   a. Find a way to help students develop some background knowledge: show the film (or excerpts from it), read relevant poems or short stories, play music from the period, or have the students look at art from the period.
   b. Find a way to connect the book to students' lives. Without that, it will be difficult to get them interested.
   c. Think about why you are teaching this classic. What do you want students to take from the work? See whether reading parts of the book rather than the whole thing will accomplish this. For example, when I asked English teachers why they read *Great Expectations,* they told me they wanted students to experience Dickens's writing, learn about the class system in England, encounter characters such as Pip and Miss Havisham, and understand the theme of the novel. I reread *Great Expectations* and found that all these things could be accomplished by seven chapters. A positive encounter with seven chapters of Great Expectations may bring students back to the book later in their lives. A negative experience with the entire book will ensure they never return.

  d. Always read *at least* the first chapter together so that you can help students work through the characters, setting, and literary devices.

17. Is it enough just to get kids to love reading? What about comprehension tests?

This question implies that comprehension can only be measured through tests. There are many other ways to ascertain whether students are comprehending what they read: conferences, "I Am" poems, reading responses, plot games, characterization charts, comparisons with other works, discussions. My students often *demanded* tests so they could prove they had read the book. In an attempt to thwart their notion that there are single right answers, I always included open-ended questions.

18. What do you do about students who are too shy to read aloud?

Students should not be forced to read aloud to the entire group. In my classroom, I asked shy students to record themselves reading aloud. I also asked them to read a book with a partner and read aloud to just each other. We read plays in which the reluctant readers were assigned only a line or two. We shared poetry and short stories that the students practiced ahead of time. And the thrill of sharing a slightly off-color limerick sometimes overcomes even the strongest reticence!

Shared reading is *not* the time for round-robin reading, in which each student reads a few lines or paragraphs. The purpose of shared reading is for students to follow along with consistent, fluent reading. Each time a round-robin reader changes, many students lose track of where they are.

19. How much time is enough time for SSR?

If you have five fifty-minute class periods a week, then fifty minutes is probably all the time you can find for SSR, and even that may take a lot of juggling. As I've said in earlier chapters, I advocate offering silent reading as an option during independent literacy exploration (ILE).

20. Where can I find lists of books related to topics I'm teaching in history or social studies?

Professional articles in subject-area journals (or journals for specific grade levels, such as *Voices in the Middle*) often include bibliographies. In addition, NCTE's *High Interest—Easy Reading* volumes are annotated bibliographies for a particular subject: science, history, etc. Social studies books such as *If This Is Social Studies, Why Isn't It Boring?* (Steffey and Hood 1994), *Connecting with the Past* (Brown 1994), and *The Story of Ourselves* (Tunnell and Ammon 1993) all have extensive bibliographies that support shared, guided, and independent reading in social studies classes.

21. Should I decide what follow-up activity students should do after they read a novel, or should I let students decide?

A balance between the two works best. Sometimes we ask all students to do the same response activity after a shared reading: seeing how others construct meaning and demonstrate understanding enlarges one's repertoire for doing the same. For independent reading, however, all students always choose the way they will respond to the books they read. We pull entries from individual response charts and reading logs to use as examples in whole-class discussions of literary elements and vocabulary.

22. How can I find age-appropriate books that older struggling readers can manage independently?

The resource section of this book lists several high-interest–low-skill options. More and more companies are creating materials appropriate for struggling readers, but these materials need to be screened carefully to make sure the format and language are not demeaning.

Classroom Environment

23. How do you select books for the classroom?

We choose books for our classrooms somewhat haphazardly; they are primarily books and articles we ourselves have read. Sometimes we choose read-alouds that reinforce content or concepts we are studying. Sometimes we choose them just because they are engaging. For shared reading, we look for different things at different points in the year. At the beginning of the year when we are just hooking students as readers, we pick books that are engaging, have relatively short chapters and larger print, and contain enough substance to support strategy lessons. I often joke that just as realtors know that "location, location, location" sells homes, middle school teachers know that "plot, plot, plot" sells their students on books. For independent reading, "more is more." Since we never know which books will grab readers, we try to have a variety of readability levels, genres, styles, and subjects available all the time.

24. Should the room be quiet?

In the literacy workshop, there should be at least one period of time when the room is totally quiet, with all students and the teacher engaged in sustained silent reading (SSR) of novels, short story and poetry collections, picture books, or nonfiction (with or without the assistance of recorded books). (We don't allow our students to read magazines or newspapers during this time, because they can't seem to do so in either a sustained or a silent manner.) There should be at least one more period each week for individual literacy exploration, when students can choose to read silently or work on a variety of literacy activities or projects. (This is when our students may choose to read newspapers and magazines.)

25. Do you have any creative ideas for getting books for our classrooms?

Here's my potato-barrel story. During my first year of teaching, I had no books in my classroom. One day, a student came in with a bag of books and asked if I wanted them. Since this was a student I had assumed lived in a home where there were no books, it occurred to me that probably all my students had books at home that weren't wanted any longer. I went to the principal and asked him whether I could have a contest to see which of my five classes could bring in the most books for our class library. At the end of three weeks, I had over three thousand books. About half of them were appropriate for our classroom. The others I returned to their rightful places (books "borrowed" from other classrooms or public libraries) or traded at two-for-one bookstores. I recently shared this idea with teachers at West High School in Anchorage, Alaska. Just yesterday a teacher there faxed me that they had tried it as a schoolwide project and received over ten thousand books.

Kyle has applied for grants from her PTSO as well as the local reading councils. This past year, we applied for an AT&T grant through the university at which I teach. Other teachers have solicited local businesses to provide a different book for each child in the class, a class set of a novel, a set of science-related books, etc. Service organizations are often willing to collect books from their members and donate them to a classroom.

26. How important is it to preselect a theme?

A shared book should address the needs and interests of the students in the class. Any theme should emerge from that context. Themes should always be secondary to the students. There is an interesting study of student interest in concepts in *Young Adult Literature: The Heart of the Middle School Curriculum* (Stover 1996). The author found students were least interested in balance, immigration, boundaries, sources, and patterns—all concepts that often are the focus of middle school units that last from four to nine weeks. Middle school should be a time to expose students to the widest possible variety of books that have the greatest potential for engaging them as readers.

27. I have two distinct groups in my classroom: the doers and the watchers. How can I get the watchers to become doers?

One of the fastest ways to move a student from the watcher to the doer category is to make the curriculum so engaging that students want to participate in the activities. When we were doing team-building activities in Kyle's classroom, the students literally could not keep their hands off the materials. If a student was hesitant, the team builder found a job that only that student could do. I've watched boxes of new books, new recorded-book cassettes, science experiments related to *It Happened to Nancy,* and shared reading novels that no one wanted to end trigger the same excitement.

28. How would you respond to this question from a sixth grader: Why do I need to learn to read or write better?

Reading is the place where I am never alone. No matter how bad my life is, I can always escape in a book. When I felt like committing suicide, I read a book that changed my thinking. In books, I can always find someone who has fought the same battles I am fighting. Books have helped me find friends. In a speech Maya Angelou gave at our university, she quoted her mama: "Sister, Mama loves to see you reading that poetry. It puts starch in your backbone. It shows you that someone before you went through this and survived." Honestly talking with students about the incredible difference books have made in your life really does have an impact on students. Of course, one has to have that passion for books in order to express it.

Classroom Management

29. How do you keep students on task?

The best remedy for keeping students on task is making the task something worth doing. I recently saw an interesting takeoff on a familiar adage: "Anything not worth doing is not worth doing well." Many of the assignments I used to give students were just not worth doing. They were the equivalent of pretending to be a lima bean for ten minutes.

On the other hand, many students find *anything* we ask them to do not worth doing. Again, the right book can engage a student in ways that we could not have imagined. All of this takes time. I smile when I hear teachers in the Literacy Project say, "I told those students that they better straighten up or we would put students in this class who would appreciate it." Those motivated, appreciative students probably don't need the class. For students who over years have established a pattern of not doing as a way of not failing, it will take time, patience, respect, caring, and an engaging curriculum to get them anywhere near the task.

30. How do you maintain student interest in long-term projects?

Other than shared reading and portfolios, most of the projects in our classrooms are relatively short-term. High absenteeism makes long-term projects very difficult. However, the Organizer for Language Arts (see Appendix A.6) can help students keep track of what is happening, what they've missed, and how they can get back on track.

31. How can I help students quickly find their place on a tape?

This has been a difficult problem in our classes. The first thing we do is allow only one student at a time to use a tape. (If a book requires more than one tape, however, someone else can use tape 1 after the first person has moved on to tape 2.) Kyle has also had students write down the tape number, side, and last line they heard as a way to help them find that spot again.

32. Are there effective strategies for making the transition from one literacy task to another without losing the students' motivation and enthusiasm?
Whether or not one uses something like the Organizer for Language Arts, any written agenda helps students keep track of their time and make more efficient transitions. If an agenda or organizer is displayed on the overhead at the beginning of the period, students can see the plan for the day and pick up the tools they need to complete the tasks. Let's not forget that they are adolescents, however. I'm not sure anything will prevent the occasional bump or backfire.

33. What about homework?
When I was teaching in high school, I gave students homework twice a week. One night it would be something I assigned (directly related to work we were doing or books we were reading but able to be done without their parents' help); one other night of their choice they read at home. When they came in the next day, they reported and recorded their homework on a form. All students had the opportunity to do homework but many opted not to work outside the classroom. Homework should not be the significant piece in any grading plan.

Evaluation

34. How do you grade seeing the light finally come on in a student's eyes? Is that an A? a B?
It's a shame standardized tests don't measure that light. If they did, perhaps more teachers would be interested in seeing that light come on. Obviously, that kind of response to books can't be measured numerically, but students' grades do improve once that light has come on. However, in some cases students must first go through a period when everything other than the book is irrelevant, so they still don't do well. Part of our job as teachers is to help students find a level of success in required as well as free-choice activities.

35. How do you grade when all kids aren't doing the same thing?
Students are graded on completing the work as well as on the quality of the work. If students are actively engaged during independent literacy exploration, they receive the full number of points for that activity. Individual assignments are grouped together for students' portfolios; students choose one or more from each group to demonstrate quality work related to preestablished criteria.

36. By what criteria do students qualify for the Literacy Project?
Students are chosen for the Literacy Project based on many factors: input from teachers, counselors, and administrators; standardized test

scores; at-risk characteristics; and a history of failing grades in reading/ language arts.

Beginning/Continuing

37. What advice would you give new teachers who are trying to implement this kind of teaching?
Here are Allen and Gonzalez's Top Ten Ways to Keep Your Sanity (the order varies with the day):

> 10. Find a friend who doesn't mind listening to you cry.
> 9. Find a way to relax.
> 8. Make sure you have the support of an administrator.
> 7. Remind yourself that you wanted this job.
> 6. Laugh *at* yourself and *with* your students.
> 5. Con everyone you know to get lots of books for your room.
> 4. Reflect and write.
> 3. Read.
> 2. Know *how* to adapt your teaching strategies.
> 1. Know *why* you are teaching this way.

38. What's the average preparation time I can expect for a day in a classroom like yours?
The preparation time varies in the extreme. On the one hand, you are always preparing. You should always be reading new children's and young adult books. You should always have a professional book at least haunting you from your nightstand. Specific preparation time changes with the day. For a day devoted to sustained silent reading and individual literacy exploration, your preparation time is not great. You will look at your anecdotal records from the last ILE to identify students with whom you want to confer individually or a group of students who need a guided reading lesson. For days when you are doing shared reading or writing, you will need to photocopy organizers, plan strategy lessons, and choose literature that supports those lessons.

39. How do I deal with colleagues who think the literacy workshop is a waste of time?
Oh, I don't know—tell them they could have these students back in their classes? Seriously, I'm aware that this is a significant problem for many teachers. Both Kyle and I have been recipients of this negative attitude. At one point in my teaching, I had a colleague complain to the principal that I couldn't possibly be teaching these kids anything because they were enjoying the class. We'll never convince everyone. The best cure is successful students.

A positive aspect of the Literacy Project is that other teachers have begun to see the Literacy Project teachers as resources for materials and new books. This has helped deflect some of the resentment triggered because the classes are smaller.

40. What aspects of this program would have to be changed for bilingual students?

Everything we have outlined in this book can and is being used with bilingual students. However, teachers of bilingual students have to do additional work with decoding strategies, vocabulary, and background knowledge.

41. What aspects of this program would have to change for classes with more than twenty students?

The same components can still be used: read-alouds; shared, guided, and independent reading and writing; authentic assessment; and goal setting. What does have to change is the handling of conferences and editing and the use of physical space. In classes with thirty-five to forty students, it is just not possible to have conferences with every student as often as you do in classes with twenty students. You can steal additional time during individual literacy exploration or independent writing, but even then it will take careful grouping and planning to make sure students receive individual attention.

42. How do you teach kids to care about literacy when everything else in their lives is horrible and destructive?

The first thing we need to do is make sure their lives are not horrible and destructive while they are with us or in other classrooms in our school. We can teach students the possibility of living a different life only if they see examples of those possibilities while they are with us. Sometimes people ask me whether Kyle really talks to her students the way I say she does. Believe me, she does. She treats them and their words with incredible respect. Those students know that she cares about them and their learning. She believes these students can change their lives, and many of them do *because* she believes they will.

The horror stories surrounding some of these children are incredibly depressing. Drugs, abuse, violence, murder, all find their way into their lives. Their time in school should be a reprieve. Books need to be shared that have hopeful messages; time needs to be allotted for listening; words need to be carefully chosen to give students healthy messages about who they are and who they are becoming. Most important, students like this need to be surrounded by people who truly care about children.

Chapter 12

Finding the Keys, Opening the Locks

"Is that how all your magic's done?"
"Most all. You just give folks a key, and they can rightly open their own locks."

Robert McCammon, *Boy's Life*

It's hard to imagine that three years have passed since Kyle Gonzalez was hired as one of the first three teachers in the Orange County Literacy Project. Today, Kyle's is one of many literacy workshop classrooms throughout the country. This year, Kyle traveled with me to Los Angeles, where we worked for a week with middle school teachers who shared our hopefulness that it is not too late for middle school struggling readers. The past three years have been a time of learning, refinement, adaptation, reflection, and planning. While we have learned much professionally from working together, our roles in the project have allowed us to grow personally as well. Kyle's journey as a new teacher has a great deal to teach us as we create preservice and inservice education that will give new teachers both the preparation they need to enter today's diverse classrooms ready to teach and the support they need to stay there.

Looking Back with Kyle

I can definitely say that I would be a completely different kind of teacher today had I not begun my career in the Literacy Project. Often when people ask me what I do for a living and I tell them that I teach, they say, "Wow. I could never do that." When they ask the grade I teach and I tell them middle school, I see them cringe. The brave ones continue by asking what subject. I tell them I work with struggling readers, and most of them wince and mutter their sympathies. Had I not taken this job, I would have been one of the wincers and mutterers.

Although I have had and will continue to have many difficult days, I know that if I hadn't had the opportunity to focus all of my energy on at-risk students, I would have brushed them off. In a traditional classroom, I would have felt relief on the days when the most troublesome students were absent or suspended. The at-risk students would have remained fairly anonymous because of the large numbers of students and the content that needed to be covered. The Literacy Project did not allow that anonymity. In order to make any progress with my students, I was forced to get to know them personally. I had to see where they lived and examine their lives. I had to get to know all of them, empathize with their personal struggles, and use that knowledge to help them down a literacy path. This kind of attention is not possible with large classes. For those students who have experienced six or more years of school failure, however, it may be the only hope we have of keeping them in school.

I will not always teach in a Literacy Project classroom. I may leave teaching for a time to start a family or continue my education, and when I return it may be to a high school rather than a middle school. So, what will I take with me from this experience? There are physical things, of course: a collection of young adult and children's books, comfy chairs, and art materials. As for my method of teaching, one thing will remain unchanged for me regardless of class size or grade level: the focus on reading. I would not teach without incorporating shared and independent reading in all of my classes. I have seen the positive results that come from teaching not only the love and value of story, but also the mechanics of reading when engaging texts are at the center. Shared reading has been the core of my curriculum out of which all the other language arts emerged. Each novel I read with my students became our textbook, and most of the direct teaching that I did was related to these shared reading texts. The reading and writing lessons my students learned within this meaningful context have formed the foundation of their literacy success. Many of these students made connections between reading, writing, listening, and speaking for the first time. These texts became the vehicle for reading strategy lessons, shared and guided writing lessons, grammar and usage study, and vocabulary enrichment.

Many teachers face the difficulties of heterogeneous abilities and learning styles in traditional classes of thirty or forty students. I did my internships in classes like this, and I can appreciate the difficulty of assigning a single novel to students whose reading levels might range from primary school through college. Janet stresses that shared reading allows all readers to be on the same page at the same time, and that is how I would accommodate that range of reading abilities. After the luxury of being able to choose materials based solely on the needs and interests of my students, it would be difficult for me to "follow a curriculum" the way many teachers are expected to do. Using shared reading as the core would be a way for me to help students gain a love for language regardless of class size, ability range, or curricular restraints.

My Literacy Project classes have taught me to be a better person, to count the blessings in my life, to know my limits, and to accept that I can't save, control, or even reach every student. I've also learned that there is no way to know which ones won't be reached until I've tried everything believing they all will be. I've learned that I can provide a safe classroom environment for kids to come to and explore the world of literacy and education. I've learned how to be a better teacher, how to listen to students, how not always to have to be right, to have all the answers, just because I'm the teacher.

Above all, I've learned to respect students who struggle. Some might question what there is to respect in students who are behavior problems in the classroom, who don't pay attention, who don't turn in work, who earn poor marks, and who do not seem to care about school. I respect these students for their perseverance. They continue to make the effort to come to school, a place where they have met personal and academic failure for years, a place where they are often openly disliked by their teachers. I'm shocked by the comments that some teachers make ("He's just too lazy" "She is just so bad in class" "I hate to say this, but he is headed straight for jail" "Culture doesn't have anything to do with reading and standardized test scores; some cultures just don't make their kids sit down and study, that's all" "She's suspended, thank God" "Where are these kids' parents?"), and I'm angered when students tell me teachers say these things to them. I am in no way a perfect teacher, and in desperate moments, many of these same thoughts jump into my mind. When they do, I remind myself that I've been to these students' homes; I don't have to wonder where their parents are.

I have to respect Jennifer, who comes to class with holes in her clothing and pretends that she doesn't hear the other students' comments. When her father was in jail, her grades dropped but she continued to come to school. I have to respect Charles for coming to school every day even though he rotates between his mother's, his grandmother's, and his older brother's houses. I admire him for continuing to come to school when his brother's friends stay up all night partying and he has had no sleep. I admire him for continuing to go to a class he gets kicked out of every day and to another class whose teacher tells him that he is a loser who will be taking his order at McDonald's one day.

Despite their outward apathy and anger, there is a fragility about these students. They are desperately clinging to that small part of hopefulness left inside them. With each passing day of stunted literacy and failure in school, the hopeful part of these kids gets harder and harder to hold on to, until, for many, it disappears. These children are at-risk for many reasons. It is terribly unfair to deny them the literacy that may be the key to the only door that leads out.

⋆ ⋆ ⋆ Looking Ahead with Janet

The three years of research that has gone into writing this book has been an incredible learning experience for me. The days I have spent with Kyle in her classroom have kept me in touch with students during what could have been the "theory years" of my career in education. Instead of spending my time in a university office, I have been able to be with students and teachers, to continue the learning that started in my own high school classroom in 1972.

From a teacher educator's point of view, this time in Kyle's and the other Literacy Project teachers' classrooms has been an eye opener. I came to the university after twenty years in the classroom, but it was not until I started going back into classrooms that I realized how much I was leaving out of the preservice classes I taught at the university. In these undergraduate classes, I found myself ignoring so many of the specifics of the struggle it took to achieve a balance in my high school classroom. We talked about large concepts such as authentic assessment, reader response, and multiple intelligences, but we virtually ignored areas such as fights over seating arrangements, children who tell you they are sexually active, and classroom management.

As I sat in Kyle's classroom one day, I noted in my journal that I had never known a teacher who had quit teaching because she couldn't get reader response to work, but that each year we lose hundreds of teachers because they cannot find a way to get the students engaged enough not to wreck the room. Kyle was well prepared in her knowledge of young adult literature, alternative assessment, and thematic units, but she didn't know what to do when a brawl started over the comfy chairs and she had no idea how to turn all of her ongoing assessment into a numerical grade. This time has been a healthy reminder to me that we have an awesome responsibility at the university level to maintain contact with the dilemmas that teachers face every day. We need to help them find ways to accommodate the best practices research has shown us in a classroom that is organized and logical enough to allow them to teach.

As I have worked with hundreds of teachers trying to implement variations of literacy workshops in their classrooms, one common denominator indicates the relative success of their attempts. If teachers are readers and willing to read a wide variety of children's and young adult literature, their chances of success are greatly increased. Those with little background in young adult literature have great difficulty choosing novels for shared reading that match the needs and interests of their students; often they rely on the suggestions of others. An effective shared reading is only as effective as the connection an individual teacher's students make with the characters and events in any novel. Supporting students for independent reading and using literature models for reading and writing strategy lessons are even more difficult than shared reading for the teacher who is not a reader.

This research has once again validated for me the importance of reflection for our teaching and continued learning. I experienced dramatic changes as a teacher the moment I began documenting my questions and taking the time to honestly reflect on what I was seeing and hearing. For the first time in my life, I came to see writing as a way to think instead of just as a way to record thoughts. That distinction highlights the difference I began to see in my teaching. As I was teaching, I not only captured *what* happened, but constantly questioned what was happening *while* it happened. It was exciting to watch this same reflective process take hold in Kyle's teaching life.

Finally, our collaborative work has reminded me of the value of mentorship. Kyle has said many times that she would have quit teaching had it not been for our work together. Several of Kyle's classmates did, in fact, leave the classroom either after their internships or after their first year of teaching. These were talented students, great readers and writers, and teachers who wanted to make a difference. Yet we lost them.

Responsive teaching has ever been easy. In classrooms where teachers repeat lesson plans year after year regardless of changing student populations and new materials, teaching is no doubt much less difficult. In classrooms where teachers constantly question their practices, it is hard to find and maintain a sense of balance. Teachers like this often find themselves without a personal life. Or they work nonstop for weeks and then crash because they are overwhelmed. New teachers are especially susceptible to this kind of struggle. In times of frustration, many decide there must be an easier way. They give up their dreams of helping children become lifelong readers and writers and opt for jobs that have balance, financial rewards, or respect.

All teachers need mentors, but new teachers and those who are trying to completely change their classroom practice need them especially. They need someone who has experience but is willing not to let that experience get in the way of listening to the new teacher's experiences. They need someone who has expertise rather than right answers. They need someone who is willing to help them take risks, to support new ideas, and to remind them of why they are teaching on the days when they forget. I am honored that Kyle sees me as her mentor. It makes me proud to see her passing that time and encouragement along to others. We can't lose sight of the fact that teaching is a helping profession—helping our teaching peers as well as the students.

There are many reasons why Kyle and I have been able to pursue hopefulness together in the five years we have known each other. We have shared common philosophies, common practice, and common values. However, the most critical reason we have been able to work so closely is that we each believe that literacy truly transforms lives. Whether we are working with teachers in workshops, with students in university classes, or with students in public school classrooms, our purpose is to help people find and read the book that will make a difference.

In our own lives, we have experienced the ways in which books have taken us out of ourselves and helped us become people we might never have imagined. Like Sheila, the battered and bruised child in Torey Hayden's *One Child,* who becomes a strong and confident adolescent in *The Tiger's Child,* we have discovered for ourselves and helped our students discover that books can tell us "there's something bigger than myself." In this passage from *The Tiger's Child,* Sheila is telling her teacher, Torey, what happens when she reads.

> "God...when I read this, it makes me...how does one describe it? Expand? No. No, that's not it." She paused, pensive. "It's like I'm in this little attic room—that's my normal life—and there's this skylight above me that I can see, but I can never reach. Then when I read this, something inside me grows. Pushes me up, and for just a moment, I can lift the skylight and see out. Just glimpse the world beyond, know what I mean? But I can glimpse it. For just a moment I can tell there's something bigger than myself." (183–84)

Books are the one indispensable gift we can give each of our students— the place where there will always be room for them.

Forms

A.1 Purposeful Learning

A chart students can use to set and track their academic and personal goals.

A.2 Independent Reading Log

A chart on which students can keep track of and remember the books they read. The response can be either a comment about the book or a quotation from the book.

A.3 Weekly Independent Reading Chart

A chart on which the teacher can record students' weekly progress in reading.

A.4 Chapter Map

A form on which students can draw the most significant ideas or events in a chapter or section of a book.

A.5 Word Jar Slips

Slips on which students can record the new words they've discovered and learned.

A.6 Organizer for Language Arts

A form on which students can keep track of their assignments and grades.

A.7 Compare and Contrast

A chart on which to identify elements in two shared reading texts as a basis for a comparison/contrast discussion.

A.8 Stickman Characterization Organizer

A graphic organizer for character information.

A.9 K–W–L

A chart for finding out what students already know about a subject, what they want to know, and what they have learned after research or study. This particular chart was used in connection with *I Know What You Did Last Summer*, a book in which drinking and driving figures prominently.

A.10 Reading Attitude Survey

An instrument with which to assess student attitudes toward literacy.

A.11 Anticipation Guides

An Anticipation Guide is used to prepare students for an upcoming shared reading selection. It helps students think about ideas, themes, and concepts that are prominent in the book. It can be presented in any format the teacher finds appropriate. Six examples are included here:

Anticipation Guide for *The Lottery Rose*

Anticipation Guide for *The Good, the Bad, and the Goofy*

Anticipation Guide for *The Flunking of Joshua T. Bates*

Anticipation Guide for *The Great Gilly Hopkins*

Anticipation Guide for *From the Mixed-Up Files of Mrs. Basil E. Frankweiler*

Anticipation Guide for *Daydreamers*

A.12 Highlighting Strategy

Students can use this form to focus their responses for the text highlighting strategy (Chambers 1996).

A.13 Writing to Learn

This graphic organizer can be used by students to focus their responses to three pieces of writing that deal with the same topic but that are written from different perspectives.

A.14 List–Group–Label

A strategy, adapted from Taba 1967, for building vocabulary. It's based on activating and categorizing prior knowledge.

A.15 Pre-Reading Plan (PReP)

A strategy, taken from Langer 1981, to document students' prior knowledge of a topic.

A.16 Looking at Our Practice

A tool to assist students in recording their activities and reflecting on what they have learned from those activities.

A.17 Test Taking

A form used to help students brainstorm problems they experienced with taking tests and solutions for those problems.

A.18 Here and Now, Goals (Versions 1, 2, and 3)

These brief writing prompts are used to assist students in setting and examining personal and academic goals.

A.19 Literacy Project Form Letter and Survey

Form letter and survey sent to the feeder elementary schools in order to identify candidates for the Literacy Project classroom each year.

A.1 *Purposeful Learning*

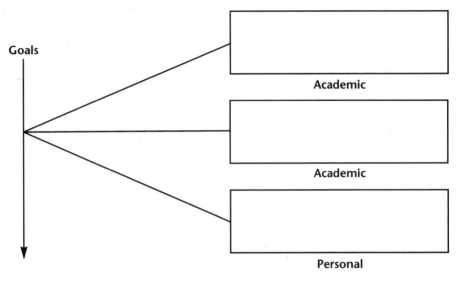

Goals

Academic

Academic

Personal

Steps I need to take to reach my goal:

1. _____

2. _____

3. _____

4. _____

5. _____

6. _____

How will I (and others) know when I have made progress toward my goals?

1. _____

2. _____

3. _____

4. _____

5. _____

6. _____

A.2 *Independent Reading Log*

Book Title:

Date	Author's Name	Page Number(s)	Response

A.3 *Weekly Independent Reading Chart*

Period: **Week of:**

Student Name	Title of Book	Session I	Session II	Session III	Comments

A.4 *Chapter Map*

After reading each chapter, please create your own title and then illustrate what you feel were the most important things that happened in the chapter.

Your Title for the Chapter	Your Title for the Chapter
Your Title for the Chapter	Your Title for the Chapter

A.5 *Word Jar Slips*

Your Name: Word: Definition: Book Word Came From:	Your Name: Word: Definition: Book Word Came From:
Your Name: Word: Definition: Book Word Came From:	Your Name: Word: Definition: Book Word Came From:
Your Name: Word: Definition: Book Word Came From:	Your Name: Word: Definition: Book Word Came From:
Your Name: Word: Definition: Book Word Came From:	Your Name: Word: Definition: Book Word Came From:

A.6 *Organizer for Language Arts*

Date	Assignment Number	Assignment	Category	Points Possible	Points Earned	My Grade So Far

Key for Category

Category	Abbreviation
Shared Reading	SR
Independent Reading	IR
Peabody	P
Test	T
Special Project	SP
Literacy Explorations	LE
Homework	HW
Miscellaneous	M

Grading Scale

90 – 100	= A
80 – 89	= B
70 – 79	= C
60 – 69	= D
59 – below	= Failing

A.7 *Compare and Contrast*

Title: _____	Title: _____
Setting	Setting
Time Period	Time Period
Conflicts	Conflicts
Resolution	Resolution
Development of Main Character	Development of Main Character
Challenges	Challenges

A.8 *Stickman Characterization Organizer (for describing people or a group)*

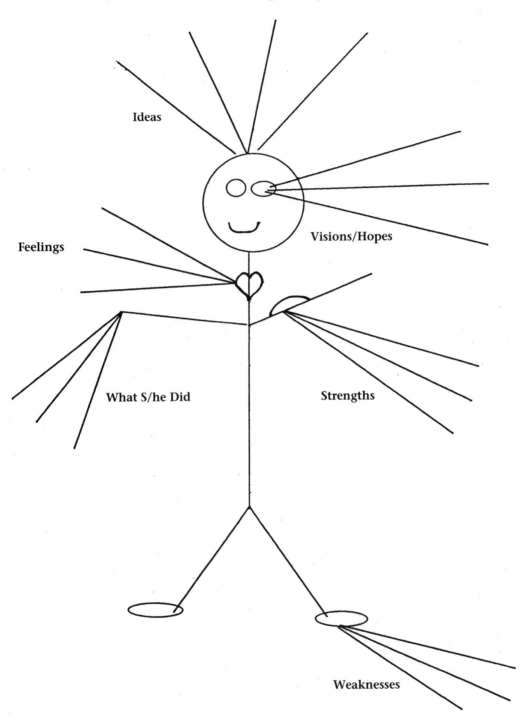

Ideas

Visions/Hopes

Feelings

What S/he Did

Strengths

Weaknesses

A.9 *K–W–L for* I Know What You Did Last Summer

Before Reading: As a group, please discuss any information that you know about drinking and driving. Please write this under the "Know" column. After you have discussed everything that your group knows about drinking and driving, please think of everything that you want to know about it. Write these questions under the "Want to Know" column. Don't worry about the "Learned" column just yet.

K (Know)	W (Want to Know)	L (Learned)

After Reading: Now that you have finished reading *I Know What You Did Last Summer,* please take time within your group to look over what you knew about drinking and driving before you read the book, what you wanted to know about it, and what you know now about it. Please be prepared to discuss your findings.

A.10 *Reading Attitude Survey*

N = No, almost never

S = Sometimes

A = Almost always

Do you like to hear and use new words?	N	S	A
Do you enjoy making up new words or playing games with words you already know?	N	S	A
Do you enjoy listening to stories or poems that are read to you?	N	S	A
When you start a book, do you expect the book to be fun and/or exciting?	N	S	A
Do you enjoy books that you have read before?	N	S	A
Do you want to read?	N	S	A
Do you enjoy responding in some way to your reading?	N	S	A
Do you expect the reading to make sense to you?	N	S	A
Do you see yourself as a reader?	N	S	A
Do you feel comfortable attempting to pronounce a word even if you are unsure of the word?	N	S	A
Does it bother you to receive feedback from other people about the way you read?	N	S	A
Are you eager to read increasingly longer stories/books?	N	S	A
Do you expect to get meaning from the texts (books) that you read?	N	S	A
Are you willing to work at getting the meaning?	N	S	A
Do you see reading as more than just being able to say the words on the page?	N	S	A
Are you confident in taking risks because you see this as a way to learn?	N	S	A

A.10 *Reading Attitute Survey* (continued)

N = No, almost never

S = Sometimes

A = Almost always

Do you feel comfortable sharing your ideas, thoughts, and feelings about what you read?	N	S	A
Are you eager to build on reading success by reading a new book?	N	S	A
Are you eager to read aloud to others?	N	S	A
Do you ask for feedback (help) with your reading?	N	S	A
Do you expect to take an active part in your reading by trying to understand and add your own meaning to the author's message?	N	S	A
Do you expect reading to be challenging but you're confident that you can overcome the challenges?	N	S	A
Do you expect to get something out of a book each time you read it?	N	S	A
Are you eager to choose books on your own, perhaps choosing books on new subjects or by new authors?	N	S	A
Do you respond to books, either by writing or talking about the books, without someone asking you to do so?	N	S	A
Do you expect to agree with everything you read?	N	S	A
Do you see books as a way of finding answers to some of your questions?	N	S	A
Do you expect books to be part of your daily life?	N	S	A
Do you try to find some time or make time to read?	N	S	A

A.11 *Anticipation Guides*

Anticipation Guide for *The Lottery Rose,* by Irene Hunt

Please read the following sentences. After *carefully* reading each sentence and thinking about it, please tell me whether or not you **Agree = A, Disagree = D,** or if you are **Unsure = U.**

Key Agree = A Disagree = D Unsure = U	Before Reading	After Reading	Observations/Comparisons After you have finished reading, please take time to look at your responses in the Before Reading and After Reading columns. Do you notice any differences? In this column, please write down what is different and WHY. What made you change your mind or not change your mind?
Children or young adults who cannot read are stupid.			
Children or young adults who cannot read can never learn to read.			
People who are mentally disabled do not have feelings.			
Children or young adults who are abused are weak if they don't fight back.			
Children or young adults who are abused should tell someone else.			
Being afraid makes a person a wimp.			
Everyone needs to be loved and cared for.			
Every child and young adult deserves to be loved, regardless of how smart or dumb they are.			
Children and young adults are capable of learning how to read.			

A.11 *Anticipation Guides* (continued)

Anticipation Guide for *The Good, the Bad, and the Goofy,* by Jon Scieszka

Below is the classified section from Joe, Fred, and Sam's hometown newspaper. Please read through the ads and write down the character that you feel best fits the ad. Be ready to come up with a few ads of your own.

Now Hiring: A young man who fears nothing. Must be able to ride horses well, protect family and friends from enemies. Painting skills would be a help.	Looking For: A piece of literature that will take you places that you had never dreamed of visiting before.	Help! Someone who can teach a good friend when he should and should not be sarcastic.
Yuck! Needed: A relative who will give me something besides a dumb old book for my birthday.	Searching for a friend who loves adventure, no matter what the cost!	Be on the lookout for a brave who sees with anger. His lands have been attacked. He is not happy to let three young boys who come from the race that has killed and lied to his people live.
Replacement needed for a cooking position. Must know how to spit tobacco juice far distances and cook something besides beans and bacon.	An assertive, strong person with experience driving cattle over long distances needed. A friendly personality is not required.	Writer wanted: Someone who is creative at writing spells. Experience with magic is a must!

A.11 *Anticipation Guides* (continued)

Anticipation Guide for *The Flunking of Joshua T. Bates,* by Susan Shreve

Before we read *The Flunking of Joshua T. Bates,* please take the time to read over the following statements. If you agree, please respond by writing "Yes" under the Before Reading column. If you disagree, please respond by writing "No" under the Before Reading column. Don't worry about the After Reading column yet. Remember, there are no right or wrong answers. Your *thoughts* are what I am looking for.

Statements	Before Reading	After Reading
1. Students who are retained (flunk a grade) are stupid.	_____	_____
2. Students who have failed a grade are often tormented (cruelly made fun of).	_____	_____
3. Testing scores or grades are the only thing that show what someone knows or has learned.	_____	_____
4. Students who have flunked a grade will never learn to read.	_____	_____
5. Students who do not pass should feel ashamed.	_____	_____
6. Students who stay back a grade may learn differently than most other students.	_____	_____
7. If someone learns differently than other students, they should fail anyway.	_____	_____
8. Students who learn differently than most other students should be taught more than one way of learning in school.	_____	_____

Now that you have finished reading *The Flunking of Joshua T. Bates,* please read through the statements that you answered earlier. Did any of your responses change? Why did they change? Please write below or on the back of this page and explain why your responses changed. Be ready to discuss them.

A.11 *Anticipation Guides* (continued)

Anticipation Guide for *The Great Gilly Hopkins,* by Katherine Paterson

Before reading *The Great Gilly Hopkins,* please look over the five statements below. Read each statement and decide whether or not you agree with it. Write "Yes" or "No" next to the sentence, depending how you feel about it. There is no right or wrong to these statements; just give what you feel is the best answer.

Statements

_____ 1. Children who are given up for adoption are "bad."

_____ 2. All children should live with their parents.

_____ 3. Running away will solve any problem.

_____ 4. Children who misbehave in school are stupid.

_____ 5. It is hard for children who have been moved from home to home to trust other people.

_____ 6. People who are different from you and your friends cannot be trusted.

Now that you have finished reading *The Great Gilly Hopkins,* please read over the five statements above. Respond to each statement from three points of view: yours, Gilly's, and Trotter's.

1. _____ You _____ Gilly _____ Trotter

2. _____ You _____ Gilly _____ Trotter

3. _____ You _____ Gilly _____ Trotter

4. _____ You _____ Gilly _____ Trotter

5. _____ You _____ Gilly _____ Trotter

6. _____ You _____ Gilly _____ Trotter

A.11 *Anticipation Guides* (continued)

Anticipation Guide for *From the Mixed-Up Files of Mrs. Basil E. Frankweiler,* by E. L. Koningsburg

Read each statement below. (A statement is a sentence that declares a fact.) If you believe that the statement is true, please place a check under **Agree**. If you think that the statement is not true, please place a check under **Disagree**. Please be ready to explain your answers.

Statements	**Agree**	**Disagree**
1. Children or young adults whose parents make them empty the garbage in the house should run away from home.	_____	_____
2. If a child or young adult is having a problem at home, he or she should keep it to him/herself and not tell anyone.	_____	_____
3. Big cities, like Miami or New York, are safe places for children or young adults to go to if they are having problems at home.	_____	_____
4. Most young adults who run away from home are safe on the streets.	_____	_____
5. Young adults who run away from home easily find safe places to live and have money for food.	_____	_____
6. All young adults who run away from home graduate from high school.	_____	_____

Now that you have finished reading *From the Mixed-Up Files of Mrs. Basil E. Frankweiler* (fiction) and the article about teenage runaways (nonfiction), take some time to reflect over the statements listed above. Have your opinions about the statements changed at all? In a few sentences below, please tell me which piece that you read affected your thoughts. Please tell me WHY. Explain your thoughts to me.

A.11 *Anticipation Guides* (continued)

Anticipation Guide for *Daydreamers,* by Tom Feelings and Eloise Greenfield

Please write down below in one or two sentences what you think a daydreamer is.

Before reading the poem "Daydreamers," please respond under the Before column to what you think about the following statements below. Please write "Yes" if you agree, "No" if you disagree.

Before		After	Author
_____	1. Daydreamers do not do well in school.	_____	_____
_____	2. People who get good grades do not daydream.	_____	_____
_____	3. Dreams are what help people achieve things in life.	_____	_____
_____	4. Adults do not daydream.	_____	_____
_____	5. Daydreams are a waste of time.	_____	_____

Now that you have finished reading the poem, please reread the statements listed above. Please react to the statements again by writing "Yes" or "No" in the After column. Do you notice any changes? What are they? Be ready to talk about them.

After you have reacted to these statements, please react from the author's point of view with "Yes" or "No." Are the author's reactions different from your own? Please be ready to talk about these differences.

A.12 *Highlighting Strategy*

Likes	Dislikes	Puzzles "I wonder if... "	Patterns

Adapted from *Tell Me: Children, Reading, and Talk* by A. Chambers (1996), pp. 69–75.

A.13 *Writing to Learn*

Source:	Source:	Source:
Facts:	Facts:	Facts:
Response:	Response:	Response:
	Connection:	Connection:
	I wonder_____	Now that I know... _____
	_____	_____
	_____	_____
	_____	_____
	I want to know_____	I'm interested in knowing... ____
	_____	_____
	_____	_____
	_____	_____

A.14 *List–Group–Label*

1. *List:* Ask students to list all of the words they can think of related to the concept/ word we will be studying. For example, if we were about to begin reading *Roll of Thunder, Hear My Cry,* I would ask students to list all of the words they could think of related to prejudice.

2. *Group:* Divide students into three- to five-member groups, and ask them to combine their words into one large list, grouping the words by category. Coming to a consensus on which group a word should be placed in is stressful, so I often let them put some words in more than one group.

3. *Label:* Ask students to create a label for each category. As students create labels for the categories, they usually eliminate some words and create new categories.

A.15 *Pre-Reading Plan (PReP)*

In this strategy the teacher asks students to document their prior knowledge related to a topic. For example, if we were about to begin reading Conly's *Crazy Lady,* I would ask students to begin by telling me anything they know about alcoholism.

1. *Initial Association with the Concept:* Ask students to "tell me anything that comes to mind when I say the word *alcoholism.*" As students respond, record their responses.

2. *Reflections on Initial Associations:* Ask students to reflect on what made them think of the word(s) they wrote down or said. "What made you think of _____ when I said the word *alcoholism*?" This can be done orally or in writing.

3. *Reformulation of Knowledge:* Ask students to decide whether or not they have any new ideas after hearing their classmates' words and discussions.

A.16 *Looking at Our Practice*

What Do We Do?	What Is Learned?

A.17 *Test Taking*

Problems	Strategies

A.18 *Here and Now, Goals (Version 1)*

"Goals are like automobiles, they won't run by themselves except downhill."

The Power of Goals

Please read the quote above and answer the following questions:

1. Please list all of your goals.

2. Please tell me what this quote means to you.

3. Why do you think that I wrote this quote down?

4. What does this quote have to do with you and your goals? BE SPECIFIC! (Use the back of this paper to answer.)

5. What have you done this week to make your goals happen?

A.18 *Here and Now, Goals (Version 2)*

"What would you try to accomplish if you believed it was impossible to fail?"

The Power of Goals

Please read the quote above AT LEAST three times and answer the following questions:

1. What does this quote mean?

2. List at least TEN things that you would try to accomplish if you believed that it was impossible to fail. Yes, TEN!

3. How would your life be different if you accomplished these ten things?

4. What is holding you back from accomplishing what you really want with your life?

A.18 *Here and Now, Goals (Version 3)*

Goals! Goals! Goals! Please take a few moments to reflect on the academic and personal goals that you have set. Answer the questions below:

1. What is your academic goal?

2. Why is this goal important to you?

3. What steps have you taken toward this goal?

4. What, if anything, has held you back from achieving this goal?

5. Do you think that you will achieve your academic goal?

   Why or why not?

6. What is your personal goal?

7. Why did you choose this goal for yourself?

8. What steps have you taken toward achieving this goal?

9. What, if anything, has held you back from achieving your personal goal?

A.19 *Literacy Project Form Letter and Survey*

Dear 5th Grade Teachers,

We are in our third year of offering a special reading project here at [Lakeview Middle School, now titled the Orange County Literacy Project]. Students who are reading below grade level (third-grade level or below) and *are not being serviced by any other exceptional program* (such as SLD, EMH, EH, or ESOL) are eligible to be considered for the Literacy Project.

The Literacy Project is a small class (roughly fifteen students) that meets for a double-block period each day, taking the place of the language arts and one elective credit. Components of the class include shared/guided reading, independent reading, and a multimedia program. The successes of the program have been significant, both in terms of improved literacy and improved discipline and attendance.

Since each class consists of a small number of students, we are only able to accept a total of fifteen sixth graders from all of our feeder elementary schools. Enclosed are surveys that will help us assess the needs of your at-risk readers, so please be specific in your comments and evaluations. Please fill out the enclosed surveys and return to [Lakeview]. We thank you for your assistance and wish you an enjoyable completion of the school year.

Sincerely,

[Kyle E. Gonzalez, Literacy Instructor]

A.19 *Literacy Project Form Letter and Survey* (continued)

Prospective Students for 1995–1996 Reading Pilot Program

Please rate the student on the criteria listed below. Please circle the appropriate description.

Instructor's Name: _____ School Name: _____

Student's Name: _____ Student's Age: _____

1. This student has difficulty pronouncing words:	rarely often always
2. This student has difficulty with sustained silent reading:	rarely often always
3. This student has difficulty reading a textbook:	rarely often always
4. This student has difficulty comprehending what he or she reads:	rarely often always
5. This student has difficulty comprehending what someone else reads to him or her:	rarely often always
6. This student enjoys being read aloud to:	rarely often always
7. This student shows an interest in reading but lacks ability:	rarely often always
8. This student's reading ability affects his/her overall learning process:	rarely often always
9. This student's reading ability affects the learning process of others:	rarely often always
10. This student reads independently:	rarely often always

11. Your overall rating of this student's reading ability: moderately low   low   extremely low

12. Please comment on any behavioral problems that you feel this student might have:

If you have any of the following information, we would greatly appreciate it if you could provide it for us:

Student's S9_____ Overall Language Arts Grade History_____
Has this student ever been retained?_____ If so, from which grade level?_____

Please feel free to add any additional comments:

Resources

ALAN (Assembly on Literature for Adolescents
of the National Council of Teachers of English)
1111 W. Kenyon Road
Urbana, IL 61801-1096
The *ALAN Review,* published three times a year,
includes articles related to the reading and teaching of young adult literature and pullout
booknotes for newly published young adult
titles. The is an excellent resource for keeping up
with what's new in young adult literature.

Bantam Doubleday Dell Books for Young Readers
School and Library Marketing Department
1540 Broadway
New York, NY 10036
This company publishes a great selection of
young adult literature and offers discounts for
volume purchases.

Capstone Press
818 North Willow Street
Mankato, MN 56001
This company publishes high-interest nonfiction
written at readability levels appropriate for reluctant and struggling readers. They cover subjects
ranging from science to roller coasters to low riders.

Christopher-Gordon Publishers, Inc.
480 Washington Street
Norwood, MA 02062
617-762-5577
FAX 617-762-2110
This company publishes a series that helps teach-
ers connect young adult literature to the classics
—*Adolescent Literature as a Complement to the
Classics,* vols. 1, 2, & 3, edited by Joan Kaywell.

Curriculum Associates, Inc.
P.O. Box 2001
North Billerica, MA 01862-0901
1-800-225-0248
FAX 800-366-1158
Two excellent resources from this company
include their collection of Nonfiction Hi-Lo
Readers (from skateboarding to sports around the
world) and their books and videos related to sto-
rytelling.

Discovery Enterprises, Ltd.
31 Laurelwood Drive
Carlisle, MA 01741
508-287-5401
FAX 508-287-5407
1-800-729-1720
Educational materials related to history and
social studies. Historical plays and collections of
primary source materials related to specific time
periods: Salem witch trials, the Underground
Railroad, the Great Depression.

Essential Learning Products Company (ELP)
2300 West Fifth Avenue
P.O. Box 2590
Columbus, OH 43216-2590
614-486-0633
FAX 614-487-2272
This company offers a variety of instructional
materials, but the one that helps at-risk readers
the most is the *PrimeTime Library.* The is a
book/cassette collection of titles that support science and health, social studies, art, sports, and
reading and literature. Each tape follows the text
word for word.

Kids In Between
P.O. Box 1037
Ballwin, MO 63021
1-800-481-2799
FAX 314-230-3708
This company produces soft-covered texts (30 to 80 pages long) for students who are reading at the lowest levels. These books are high-interest books with readability as low as 1.0.

Labtec Enterprises
3801 NE 109th Avenue, Suite J
Vancouver, WA 98682
This company offers a durable headphone that can be used with both computers and Walkmans. Model #LT-820 has good sound quality and is comfortable to wear.

National Council of Teachers of English (NCTE)
1111 W. Kenyon Road
Urbana, IL 61801-6283
NCTE offers a wide range of support for beginning as well as experienced teachers. The journals it publishes include *Language Arts* (K–8) , *English Journal* (secondary), *Voices from the Middle* (middle school), and *The Bulletin* (Children's Literature Assembly). It also publishes a wide range of professional books, including annotated bibliographies such as *High Interest—Easy Reading*.

National Middle School Association
2600 Corporate Exchange Drive, Suite 370
Columbus, OH 43231-1672
1-800-528-NMSA
www.nmsa.org
NMSA offers a variety of professional materials for middle-level teachers. There are many books addressing issues specific to middle-level schools and teachers, such as tracking, integration, and teaming.

Recorded Books, Inc.
270 Skipjack Road
Prince Frederick, MD 20678
1-800-638-1304
This company provides various children's, young adult, and adult titles of unabridged, recorded books.

The Reusable Resources Adventure Center
P.O. Box 360507
Melbourne, FL 32936
This group provides resources that have been recycled from business and industry. Teachers can pick up crates of specific materials or packages that contain a variety of materials.

Scholastic Book Clubs, Inc.
2931 East McCarty Street
P.O. Box 7503
Jefferson City, MO 65102-7503
1-800-724-2424
This company offers books at discounted prices and has clubs for specific grade levels: Firefly (preschool), Seesaw (K–1), Lucky (2–3), Arrow (4–6), and Tab (7–9). All purchases accrue bonus points that can be used toward free books.

Steck-Vaughn Company
P.O. Box 26105
Austin, TX 78755
1-800-531-5015
http://www.steck-vaughn.com
This company has a wide variety of resources for readers who are reading below grade level as well as high-interest, content-specific materials. Materials that are very appropriate for middle-level learners include the *Stories of America* series, *Contemporary Biographies and World Myths, The American History* and *The World History Heralds* (newspapers specific to certain time periods), and the *Mystery, Adventure, and Science Fiction Collections*.

Team Esteem
Troy Cunningham
P.O. Box 588
Presque Isle, ME 04769
207-762-6060
Provides team-building and creative problem-solving activities for students and teachers.

Touchstone Applied Science Associates, Inc. (TASA)
Fields Lane, P.O. Box 382
Brewster, NY 10509-0382
914-277-4900
FAX: 914-277-3548

TASA publishes the test used as a pretest and posttest measure not only for the Literacy Project classes, but also for other screenings in Orange County. The test consists of cloze passages that students complete. The passages have enough context for students to practice the reading strategies taught in a literacy classroom. The test yields a DRP score and these scores can be matched to DRPs for specific titles.

Time for Kids
Time & Life Building
1271 Avenue of the Americas
New York, NY 10020-1393
1-800-777-8600
Time for Kids is not only an excellent publication to help students connect with national and world events and people, but a great way to help students make the transition to news magazines. Each news article is written with an adolescent in mind. History-related spots such as "Mystery Person of the Week" catch readers' attention.

Troll Book Clubs
2 Lethbridge Plaza
Mahwah, NJ 07430
1-800-541-1097
This company offers books at discounted book club prices. Troll titles often have book versions of current movies—a popular commodity for struggling readers.

The Trumpet Club
P.O. Box 6003
Columbia, MO 63205-6003
This company offers books at discounted prices for various grade levels. All purchases accrue bonus points that can be used for future books. Trumpet often offers a wide selection of Newbery and Caldecott books.

Weekly Reader Corporation
P.O. Box 2791
Middletown, CT 06457-9291
Weekly Reader's *Read* magazine offers a wealth of short stories marked for guided reading, content-specific plays for students, and high-interest language activities.

Suggested Titles for Shared Reading

Author's Name	Book Title	Comments
Angelou, Maya	*Maya Angelou Poems*	Varied collection of poetry; enjoyed by older middle school students
Beals, Melba Pattillo	*Warriors Don't Cry*	An incredible account of one of the nine students who integrated at Central High School in Little Rock, Arkansas in 1957; diary format in parts; advanced read-aloud; excellent history connections
Bennet, Jill	*Noisy Poems*	Poetry collection; fun language
Coerr, Eleanor	*Sadako and the Thousand Paper Cranes*	Short story about a young girl who is suffering from radiation sickness due to the bombing of Hiroshima; short chapters; illustrations; beginning read-aloud; good history connections
Conly, Leslie	*Crazy Lady*	Very humorous story about a twelve-year-old boy coming to terms with his mother's death and striking an odd friendship with the neighborhood drunk and her mentally handicapped son; beginning to intermediate read-aloud; realistic fiction
Dahl, Roald	*Revolting Rhymes*	Poetry collection; extremely humorous
Dakos, Kali	*If You're Not Here, Please Raise Your Hand*	Hilarious collection of poems about the ills of school; great for reading aloud
DeFelice, Cynthia	*Lostman's River*	Tale of a boy living in Florida during its early settlement; deals with the dangers of poaching; short chapters; suspenseful; good history/geography connections; adventure
DeFelice, Cynthia	*Weasel*	Tale of a young boy, Nathan, living in the West during its early settlement; as he and his younger sister are getting over their mother's death they must also face their father's mysterious disappearance connected to the infamous Weasel, a wild man who was once contracted to kill Indians; short chapters; very suspenseful; adventure
DeGross, Monalisa	*Donovan's Word Jar*	Children's story about a young boy who collects words; great read-aloud for introduction of vocabulary
Draper, Sharon	*Tears of a Tiger*	Story of Andy, a high school boy, whose best friend, the captain of the basketball team, is killed in a car accident

		resulting from Andy drinking and driving; Andy completely isolates himself from his friends and family as he attempts to deal with the incident; very mature content; advanced read-aloud; point of view and format of chapters vary
Duncan, Lois	*I Know What You Did Last Summer*	Story of a group of teenagers who kill a young boy on a bicycle during a drinking and driving accident and make a pact not to tell anyone; great for prediction; advanced read-aloud; suspense
Flewellyn, V. S.	*Poetically, Just Us*	Good collection of multicultural poetry; both boys and girls enjoy it
Gallo, Don	*Connections*	Anthology of short stories for young adults
Greenfield, Eloise	*Honey, I Love*	Collection of multicultural poetry; great language for read-alouds
Hill, Elizabeth Starr	*Evan's Corner*	Children's story about a boy who lives with his large family in a small apartment as he tries to find a space of his own; multicultural
Hunt, Irene	*The Lottery Rose*	Story about Georgie, a physically abused young boy who cannot read; realistic fiction; intermediate read-aloud
Jordan, Michael	*I Can't Accept Not Trying*	Motivational read-aloud about goal setting, failure, and success
Levine, Ellen	*Freedom's Children*	Collection of short stories experienced and told by young civil rights activists; history connections
Lionni, Leo	*Frederick*	Children's story about inner strength
Lobel, Arnold	*Fables*	Beautifully illustrated, one-page fables; great read-aloud
Medearis, Angela Shelf	*Skin Deep*	Collection of poetry appropriate for older grades in middle school; well liked by both girls and boys; multicultural; very realistic subject matter
Miller, Marvin	*You Be the Jury Courtroom II*	Brief fictional accounts of courtroom cases; comes with illustrations of evidence; good for teaching using text as source of information, rereading for clues in text
Myers, Walter Dean	*Fast Sam, Cool Clyde, and Stuff*	Humorous and poignant adventures of a group of young friends in New York City who decide to join together and have a club ;that looks out for each other on issues ranging form basketball to the first kiss; intermediate read-aloud
Myers, Walter Dean	*Scorpions*	Story of Jamal, a young boy living in New York City and being pressured to join his older brother's gang; realistic fiction; intermediate read-aloud; great action
Oppenheim, Shulamith	*The Lily Cupboard*	A children's story that addresses the Holocaust
Paterson, Katherine	*The Great Gilly Hopkins*	Humorous and poignant tale of a young girl who has been kicked out of numerous foster homes and her adjustment to her latest home; she fantasizes the return of her mother and has to face a hard reality at the end of the book; intermediate read-aloud
Philbrick, Rodman	*Freak the Mighty*	Humorous account of a friendship between Max, an LD student, and Kevin, a genius who is physically handicapped; good adventure; suspense; intermediate read-aloud
Polacco, Patricia	*The Keeping Quilt*	A children's story about a quilt that contains family heritage; history connections

Ringold, Faith	*Tar Beach*	A children's story about a young girl who tells her dream of flying above the world to end her family's troubles; gorgeous illustrations; based on an actual story quilt created by the author; history connections
Schwartz, Alvin	*Gold and Silver, Silver and Gold*	Funny folktales and tall tales; good for introducing genre and humor in writing or just a fun read-aloud; beginning read-aloud
Scieszka, Jon	*The Good, the Bad, and the Goofy*	Hilarious story about the time-traveling trio and their adventures back in the Wild West; short chapters; illustrations; history connections; beginning read-aloud
Scieszka, Jon	*Knights of the Kitchen Table*	Another book in the series of the time-traveling trio; this time they travel back to the time of King Arthur; short chapters; illustrations; very humorous; history connections; beginning read-aloud
Shreve, Susan	*The Flunking of Joshua T. Bates*	Humorous story of a young boy who flunks third grade and how he deals with stress of retention and the school bully; short chapters; illustrations; beginning read-aloud
Shreve, Susan	*Joshua T. Bates Takes Charge*	Sequel to *The Flunking of Joshua T. Bates;* Joshua deals with the school nerd claiming him as his best friend, and triumphs over the school bully; illustrations; short chapters
Sloane, Paul	*Lateral Thinking Puzzles*	Brainteasers
Soto, Gary	*Local News*	Anthology of short stories for young adults; Hispanic focus
Sparks, Beatrice, ed.	*It Happened to Nancy*	Diary of a teenage girl who is date-raped and contracts the AIDS virus; account of her illness, feelings about it, and her eventual death; serious subject matter; diary format; little action; advanced read-aloud
Spinelli, Jerry	*Who Put That Hair in My Toothbrush?*	Hilarious account of sibling rivalry; point of view switches after every chapter from the brother to the sister; beginning/intermediate read-aloud
Stock, Gregory	*The Kid's Book of Questions*	Collection of thought-provoking questions for kids; good for class discussions and writing prompts; food for thought
Swarthout, Glendon	*Bless the Beasts and the Children*	Realistic fiction; misfits being sent away to summer camp; advanced read-aloud
Taylor, Mildred	*The Friendship and The Gold Cadillac*	Two short stories about prejudice in the South; excellent history connection; poignant tales; illustrations
Volavkova, H., ed.	*I Never Saw Another Butterfly: Children's Drawings and Poems from Terezin Concentration Camp 1942–1944*	Collection of poetry and art from the children at Terezin
Wiesel, Elie	*Night*	Story of the author and his horrific experience in the Holocaust; mature content; advanced read-aloud
Zullo, A.	*Haunted Schools*	Collection of fictional short stories appropriate for read-aloud; great for introducing genre of suspense and prediction

Suggested Titles
for Independent Reading

Author's Name	Book Title	Available on Tape Y/N
Adoff, A.	*All the Colors of the Race*	N
Avi	*Something Upstairs*	Y
	S.O.R. Losers	Y
	Wolf Rider	Y
Babbitt, N.	*Tuck Everlasting*	Y
Barrett, P. A., ed.	*To Break the Silence*	N
Birdseye, T.	*Just Call Me Stupid*	Y
Blume, J.	*Are You There God? It's Me, Margaret*	Y
	Freckle Juice	N
	Just as Long as We're Together	N
	The One in the Middle Is a Green Kangaroo	N
	Otherwise Known as Shelia the Great	N
	Tiger Eyes	N
Buehner, C. and M. Buehner	*The Escape of Marvin the Ape*	N
Burton, T.	*The Nightmare Before Christmas*	N
Childress, A.	*Rainbow Jordan*	N
Christopher, M.	*Baseball Pals*	Y
	The Hit-a-Way Kid	Y
	Little Lefty	Y
Cooney, C.	*The Face on the Milk Carton*	Y
	Whatever Happened to Janie?	N
	The Voice on the Radio	N
Crichton, M.	*Jurassic Park—Junior Novelization*	N
Crutcher, C.	*Athletic Shorts*	Y
Cutler, J.	*No Dogs Allowed*	Y
Dahl, R.	*Charlie and the Chocolate Factory*	N
	James and the Giant Peach	N
	Matilda	Y
	The Witches	Y

Danziger, P.	*Amber Brown Is Not a Crayon*	N
	The Cat Ate My Gymsuit	N
Davis, J.	*Garfield at Large*	N
The Disney Company	*Disney's Beauty and the Beast*	N
	Disney's Hunchback of Notre Dame	N
	Disney's Pocahontas	N
Donnelly, J.	*The Titanic*	N
Dubowski, C.	*Camp Nowhere*	N
Duncan, L.	*Killing Mr. Griffin*	N
	Ransom	N
	The Third Eye	N
Durham, J.	*A New Life for Sarita*	N
Ferguson, D.	*Disney's Aladdin*	N
	Disney's The Lion King	N
Fleischman, S.	*Jim Ugly*	Y
Flewellyn, V. S.	*Poetically Just Us*	N
Gammell, S.	*Scary Stories—More Tales to Chill Your Bones*	N
Gardiner, J. R.	*Stonefox*	Y
George, J. C.	*Julie of the Wolves*	Y
	Shark Beneath the Reef	Y
	The Talking Earth	Y
Giovanni, N.	*Spin a Soft Black Song*	N
Greenfield, E.	*Honey, I Love*	N
Grimes, N.	*Meet Danitra Brown*	N
Hall, K., and L. Eisenberg	*101 Bossy Cow Jokes*	N
Handford, M.	*Find Waldo Now*	N
	Where's Waldo?	N
Haugaard, E.	*Princess Horrid*	N
Heide, F. P.	*The Problem with Pulcifer*	N
Henkes, K.	*Two Under Par*	Y
Hinton, S. E.	*The Outsiders*	Y
	Rumblefish	Y
	Taming the Star Runner	Y
	That Was Then, This Is Now	Y
Hurwitz, J.	*Class Clown*	Y
Isaacs, A.	*Swamp Angel*	N
Johnson, L.	*Dangerous Minds*	N
Koda-Dallan, E.	*The Tiny Angel*	N
Koningsburg, E. L.	*From the Mixed-Up Files of Mrs. Basil E. Frankweiler*	N
Krupinski, E., and D. Weikel	*Death from Child Abuse and No One Heard*	N
L'Engle, M.	*A Wrinkle in Time*	Y
Lester, J.	*To Be a Slave*	Y

McKissak, P. C.	*Mirandy and Brother Wind*	Y
Morrow, C.	*The Jellybean Principal*	N
Mead, A.	*Junebug*	Y
Medearis, A. S.	*Skin Deep*	N
Munsch, R. N.	*The Paper Bag Princess*	N
Myers, W. D.	*Darnell Rock, Reporting*	Y
	Scorpions	N
Paulsen, G.	*Canyons*	Y
	Hatchet	Y
	Nightjohn	Y
Pearce, Q. L.	*More Super Scary Stories for Sleep-Overs*	N
Peck, R. N.	*Soup in Love*	Y
Peters, J. A.	*The Stinky Sneakers Contest*	N
Potter, B.	*The Tale of Peter Rabbit*	N
	The Tale of Squirrel Nutkin	Y
	A Treasury of Mouse Tales	N
Prelutsky, J.	*The Dragons Are Singing Tonight*	Y
	Something Big Has Been Here	Y
Resnick, J.	*Original Fairy Tales from the Brothers Grimm*	N
Rosenber, L.	*Monster Mama*	Y
Sabin, F.	*Jesse Owens Olympic Hero*	Y
Sachs, B.	*Mountain Bike Madness*	Y
Sanderson, J.	*Buying Trouble*	N
Sansouci, R. D.	*Short and Shivery*	Y
Schwartz, A.	*Scary Stories to Tell in the Dark*	Y
	More Scary Stories to Tell in the Dark	N
	Scary Stories III	N
Scieszka, J.	*The Frog Prince Continued*	N
	The True Story of the Three Little Pigs	N
Selden, G.	*A Cricket in Times Square*	Y
Sendak, M.	*Where the Wild Things Are*	N
Sharmat, M. J.	*Genghis Khan—A Dog Star is Born*	N
Sharp, M.	*The Rescuers*	Y
Silverstein, S.	*Falling Up*	N
	A Light in the Attic	N
Simmons, A.	*Smoke*	N
Snyder, A.	*My Name Is Davy and I'm an Alcoholic*	N
Synder, Z. K.	*Witches of Worm*	Y
Sobol, D. J.	*More Two-Minute Mysteries*	N
Soto, G.	*The Skirt*	Y
Sparks, B., ed.	*Go Ask Alice*	Y
Stanley, D.	*Moe the Dog in Tropical Paradise*	N

Staples, S. F.	*Haveli*	Y
	Shabanu	Y
Steck-Vaughn Company	*Steck-Vaughn Mystery, Adventure, and Science Fiction Set*	N
Steig, W.	*The Real Thief*	Y
Stine, J. B.	*How to Be Funny*	N
Stine, R. L.	*Bad Dreams*	Y
	Beach Party	Y
	Blind Date	N
	The Dare	Y
	The Dead Girlfriend	N
	Double Date	Y
	The New Boy	Y
Taylor, M.	*Mississippi Bridge*	N
	The Road to Memphis	N
	Roll of Thunder, Hear My Cry	Y
	Song of the Trees	N
Taylor, T.	*Tuck Triumphant*	Y
Thaler, M.	*The Teacher from the Black Lagoon*	N
Van Leeuwen, U.	*Dear Mom, You're Ruining My Life*	N
Voirst, J.	*Alexander and the Terrible, Horrible, No Good, Very Bad Day*	N
	Alexander, Who Used to Be Rich Last Sunday	N
Wachter, O.	*Sex, Drugs, and AIDS*	N
Weiss, E., and M. Friedman	*The Curse of the Calico Cat*	N
White, E. B.	*Charlotte's Web*	Y
Wilcox, C.	*Mummies and Their Mysteries*	N
Williams, L.	*The Little Old Lady Who Wasn't Afraid of Anything*	Y
Williams, M.	*The Velveteen Rabbit*	N
Williams-Garcia, R.	*Like Sisters on the Homefront*	N
Wolff, V. E.	*Make Lemonade*	N
Wood, A.	*King Bidgood's in the Bathtub*	N
	The Napping House	N
	Rude Giants	Y
Wood, N.	*Dancing Moons*	N
Woodson, J.	*I Hadn't Meant to Tell You This*	N
Yep, L.	*The Rainbow People*	Y

Professional References

Allen, J. 1995. *It's Never Too Late: Leading Adolescents to Lifelong Literacy.* Portsmouth, NH: Heinemann.

Allen, J., and K. Gonzalez. 1996. Step by Step: Learning in Many Voices. In *Meeting the Challenges: Stories from Today's Classrooms,* ed. M. Barbieri and C. Tateishi. Portsmouth, NH: Heinemann.

Allington, R. 1984. Policy Constraints and Effective Compensatory Reading Instruction: A Review. Paper presented at the 29th annual meeting of the International Reading Association (May 6–10, 1984, Atlanta, GA). ED 248456.

Armbruster, B. B., and T. H. Anderson. 1980. *The Effect of Mapping on the Free Recall of Expository Text.* Tech. Rep. No. 160. Urbana, IL: University of Illinois, Center for the Study of Reading.

Anderson, R. C., E. H. Hiebert, J. A. Scott, and I. A. G. Wilkinson. 1985. *Becoming a Nation of Readers: The Report of the Commission on Reading.* Washington, DC: The National Institute of Education, U. S. Department of Education.

Atwell, N. 1987. *In the Middle: Writing, Reading, and Learning with Adolescents.* Portsmouth, NH: Boynton/Cook.

Bolton, F., and D. Snowball. 1993. *Ideas for Spelling.* Portsmouth, NH: Heinemann.

Bridges, L. 1995. *Assessment: Continuous Learning.* York, ME: Stenhouse.

Britton, J. 1970. *Language and Learning.* Harmondsworth, Middlesex, GB: Penguin.

Brown, C. S. 1994. *Connecting with the Past: History Workshop in Middle and High Schools.* Portsmouth, NH: Heinemann.

Brown, H., and B. Cambourne. 1990. *Read and Retell.* Portsmouth, NH: Heinemann.

Brozo, W. G., and M. L. Simpson. 1995. *Readers, Teachers, Learners: Expanding Literacy in Secondary Schools.* New York: Macmillan.

Butler, D., and T. Liner. 1996. *Rooms to Grow: Natural Language Arts in the Middle School.* Durham, NC: Carolina Academic Press.

Cambourne, B. 1988. *The Whole Story: Natural Learning and the Acquisition of Literacy in the Classroom.* New York: Scholastic.

Canfield, J., and H. C. Wells. 1994. *100 Ways to Enhance Self-Concept in the Classroom.* Boston: Allyn and Bacon.

Chambers, A. 1996a. *The Reading Environment: How Adults Help Children Enjoy Books.* York, ME: Stenhouse.

———. 1996b. *Tell Me: Children, Reading, and Talk.* York, ME: Stenhouse.

Clay, M. 1989. Involving Teachers in Classroom Research. In *Teachers and Research: Language Learning in the Classroom,* ed. G. S. Pinnell and M. L. Matlin. Newark, DE: International Reading Association.

Coles, R. 1989. *The Call of Stories: Teaching and the Moral Imagination.* Boston: Houghton Mifflin.

Crowley, P. 1995. Listening to What Readers Tell Us. *Voices from the Middle* 2 (2): 11.

Ernst, K. 1993. *Picturing Learning: Artists and Writers in the Classroom.* Portsmouth, NH: Heinemann.

Fader, D., J. Duggins, T. Finn, and E. McNeil. 1976. *The New Hooked on Books.* New York: Berkley.

Farr, B. P., and E. Trumbull. 1997. *Assessment Alternatives for Diverse Classrooms.* Norwood, MA: Christopher-Gordon.

Fielding, L. C., P. T. Wilson, and R. C. Anderson. 1986. A New Focus on Free Reading: The Role of Trade Books in Reading Instruction. In *Contexts of Literacy,* ed. T. E. Raphael and R. Reynolds. New York: Longman.

Freire, P. 1970. *Pedagogy of the Oppressed.* New York: Seabury.

Gardner, H., and T. Hatch. 1989. Multiple Intelligences Go to School: Educational Implications of the Theory of Multiple Intelligences. *Educational Researcher,* November. 18: 4–10.

Gibbs, J. 1994. *Tribes: A New Way of Learning Together.* Santa Rosa, CA: Center Source Publications.

Hansen, J. 1981. The Effects of Inference Training and Practice on Young Children's Reading Comphrension. *Reading Research Quarterly* 16:391–417.

Henning-Stout, M. 1994. *Responsive Assessment: A New Way of Thinking About Learning.* San Francisco: Jossey-Bass.

Johns, J. 1993. Strengthening Your Reading Program: What to Look For. *Reading TODAY,* August/September. 2 (1): 13–15.

Johnson-Laird, P. N. 1983. *Mental Models.* Cambridge, MA: Harvard University Press.

Kaywell, J. 1993. *Adolescents at Risk: A Guide to Fiction and Nonfiction for Young Adults, Parents, and Professionals.* Westport, CT: Greenwood.

Keefe, C. H. 1996. *Label-Free Learning: Supporting Learners with Disabilities.* York, ME: Stenhouse.

Kirby, D., and T. Liner. 1987. *Inside Out: Developmental Strategies for Teaching Writing.* Portsmouth, NH: Heinemann.

Kirby, D., T. Liner, and R. Vinz. 1988. *Inside Out: Developmental Strategies for Teaching Writing.* 2d ed. Portsmouth, NH: Boynton/Cook.

Kohl, H. 1991. *I Won't Learn from You: The Role of Assent in Education.* Minneapolis, MN: Milkweed Editions.

Kohn, A. 1993. Choices for Children: Why and How to Let Students Decide. *Phi Delta Kappan* 75 (1): 8–16, 18–21.

Krogness, M. 1995. *Just Teach Me, Mrs. K.* Portsmouth, NH: Heinemann.

Lamott, A. 1994. *bird by bird: Some Instructions on Writing and Life.* New York: Pantheon.

Langer, J. A. 1981. From Theory to Practice: A Prereading Plan. *Journal of Reading* 52 (2): 152–56.

Langer, J. A., and A. N. Applebee. 1987. *How Writing Shapes Thinking: A Study of Teaching and Learning.* Urbana, IL: National Council of Teachers of English.

Mandler, J. M., and N. S. Johnson. 1977. Remembrance of Things Passed: Story Structure and Recall. *Cognitive Psychology* 9: 111–51.

McKeown, M., I. Beck, G. Sinatra, and J. Loxterman. 1992. The Contribution of Prior Knowledge and Coherent Text to Comprehension. *Reading Research Quarterly* 27: 79–93.

Mooney, M. 1988. *Developing Life-long Readers*. Wellington, NZ: Learning Media, Ministry of Education.

———. 1990. *Reading to, with, and by Children*. Katonah, NY: Richard C. Owen.

Morrow, D. G. 1985. Prominent Characters and Events Organize Narrative Understanding. *Journal of Memory and Language* 24: 304–19.

Murray, D. M. 1996. *Crafting a Life in Essay, Story, Poem*. Portsmouth, NH: Boynton/Cook.

Nagy, W. E., P. A. Herman, and R. C. Anderson. 1985. Learning Words from Context. *Reading Research Quarterly* 20: 233–53.

Nell, V. 1988. *Lost in a Book: The Psychology of Reading for Pleasure*. New Haven, CT: Yale University Press.

Newman, J. M., and S. M. Church. 1990. Myths of Whole Language (Commentary). *The Reading Teacher* 44 (1): 20–26.

Noble, C. 1992. *The Power of Goals,* ed. P. Anderson. Lombard, IL: Celebrating Excellence.

Ohanian, S. 1994. *Who's in Charge? A Teacher Speaks Her Mind*. Portsmouth, NH: Boynton/Cook.

Ogle, D. M. 1986. K-W-L: A Teaching Model That Develops Active Reading of Expository Text. *Reading Teacher* 39: 564–70.

Parsons, L. 1991. *Writing in the Real Classroom*. Portsmouth, NH: Heinemann.

Pearson, P. D., and D. D. Johnston. 1978. *Teaching Reading Comprehension*. New York: Holt, Rinehart & Winston.

Pennac, D. 1994. *Better Than Life*. Toronto, Canada: Coach House.

Phelan, P., ed. 1996. *High Interest—Easy Reading: An Annotated Booklist for Middle School and Senior High School*. 7th ed. Urbana, IL: National Council of Teachers of English.

Pinnell, G. S., and M. L. Matlin, eds. 1989. *Teachers and Research: Language Learning in the Classroom*. Newark, DE: International Reading Association.

Plain Talk About Learning and Writing Across the Curriculum. 1987. Commonwealth of Virginia: Department of Education.

Readence, J. E., T. W. Bean, and R. S. Baldwin. 1985. *Content Area Reading: An Integrated Approach*. 2d ed. Dubuque, IA: Kendall/Hunt.

Rief, L. 1991. *Seeking Diversity: Language Arts with Adolescents*. Portsmouth, NH: Heinemann.

Rohnke, K., and S. Butler. 1995. *Quicksilver: Adventure Games, Initiative Problems, Trust Activities and a Guide to Effective Leadership*. Dubuque, IA: Kendall/Hunt.

Roller, C. M. 1996. *Variability Not Disability*. Newark, DE: International Reading Association.

Rosenblatt, L. M. 1976. *Literature as Exploration*. New York: Modern Language Association of America.

Rothman, R. 1995. *Measuring Up: Standards, Assessment, and School Reform*. San Francisco: Jossey-Bass.

Rumelhart, D. E. 1977. Understanding and Summarizing Brief Stories. In *Basic Processes in Reading: Perception and Comprehension,* ed. D. LaBerge and S. J. Samuels. Hillsdale, NJ: Erlbaum.

Sanford, A. J., and S. C. Garrod. 1981. *Understanding Written Language*. New York: Wiley.

Schlechty, P. C. 1990. Reform in Teacher Education: A Sociological View. Monograph. Washington, DC: American Association of Colleges for Teacher Education. ED 332981.

Schwartz, L. S. 1966. *Ruined by Reading*. Boston: Beacon Press.

Shaw, V., with S. Kagan. 1992. *Communitybuilding in the Classroom*. San Juan Capistrano, CA: Kagan Cooperative Learning.

Smith, F. 1988. *Joining the Literacy Club: Further Essays into Education*. Portsmouth, NH: Heinemann.

Smith, J. W. A., and W. B. Elley. 1994. *Learning to Read in New Zealand*. Katonah, NY: Richard C. Owen.

Spear, K. 1988. *Sharing Writing: Peer Response Groups in English Classes*. Portsmouth, NH: Boynton/Cook.

Steffey, S., and W. Hood, eds. 1994. *If This Is Social Studies, Why Isn't It Boring?* York, ME: Stenhouse.

Steinberg, L. 1993. *Adolescence*. New York: McGraw-Hill.

Stover, L. T. 1996. *Young Adult Literature: The Heart of the Middle School Curriculum*. Portsmouth, NH: Boynton/Cook.

Taba, H. 1967. *Teacher's Handbook for Elementary Social Studies*. Reading, MA: Addison-Wesley.

Tharpe, R., and R. Gallimore. 1988. *Rousing Minds to Life: Teaching, Learning and Schooling in Social Context*. Cambridge, GB: Cambridge University Press.

Thorndyke, P. W. 1977. Cognitive Structures in Comprehension and Memory of Narrative Discourse. *Cognitive Psychology* 9: 77–110.

Tunnell, M. O., and R. Ammon, eds. 1993. *The Story of Ourselves: Teaching History Through Children's Literature*. Portsmouth, NH: Heinemann.

Valencia, S. 1994. Authentic Assessment in Classrooms. In *Authentic Reading Assessment: Practices and Possibilities,* ed. S. W. Valencia, E. H. Hiebert, and P. P. Afflerback. Newark, DE: International Reading Association.

van Dijk, T. A., and W. Kintsch. 1983. *Strategies for Discourse Comprehension*. New York: Academic Press.

Vygotsky, L. S. 1978. *Mind in Society: The Development of Higher Mental Processes*. Cambridge, MA: Harvard University Press.

Wells, M. C. 1996. *Literacies Lost: When Students Move from a Progressive Middle School to a Traditional High School*. New York: Teachers College Press, Columbia University.

Wiggins, G. P. 1993. *Assessing Student Performance: Exploring the Purpose and Limits of Testing*. San Francisco: Jossey-Bass.

Wright, J. 1995. Not Just Words on a Page: Kids, Parents and Teachers Learning About Reading Together. *Voices in the Middle* (2): 2, 21–28.

Zemelman, S., H. Daniels, and A. Hyde. 1993. *Best Practice: New Standards for Teaching and Learning in America's Schools*. Portsmouth, NH: Heinemann.

Literary References

Aardeam. 1975. *Why Mosquitoes Buzz in People's Ears.* New York: Puffin Pied Piper.

Adoff, A. 1982. *All the Colors of the Race.* New York: Beechtree.

Anderson, P., ed. 1992. *The Power of Goals.* Lombard, IL: Celebrating Excellence.

Angelou, M. 1970. *I Know Why the Caged Bird Sings.* New York: Random House.

———. 1986. *Poems.* New York: Bantam.

Avi. 1984. *S.O.R. Losers.* New York: Avon Camelot.

———. 1986. *Wolf Rider.* New York: Aladdin.

———. 1988. *Something Upstairs.* New York: Avon Flare.

Babbitt, N. 1975. *Tuck Everlasting.* Toronto: HarperCollins Canada.

Barrett, P. A., ed. 1986. *To Break the Silence.* New York: Dell.

Baum, L. F. 1985. *The Wizard of Oz.* New York: Scholastic.

Beals, M. P. 1995. *Warriors Don't Cry.* New York: Archway.

Bellairs, J. 1973. *The House with a Clock in Its Walls.* New York: Puffin.

Bennet, J. 1987. *Noisy Poems.* New York: Oxford University Press.

Birdseye, T. 1993. *Just Call Me Stupid.* New York: Puffin.

Blume, J. 1970. *Are You There God? It's Me, Margaret.* New York: Dell.

———. 1971. *Freckle Juice.* New York: Dell.

———. 1972. *Otherwise Known as Sheila the Great.* New York: Dell Yearling.

———. 1981. *The One in the Middle Is a Green Kangaroo.* New York: Dell.

———. 1982. *Tiger Eyes.* New York: Bantam Doubleday Dell Books for Young Readers.

———. 1987. *Just as Long as We're Together.* New York: Dell.

Branden, N. 1995. *Nathaniel Branden's Little Blue Book of Self-Esteem.* New York: Barnes & Noble.

Bridwell, N. 1990. *Clifford's Happy Day.* New York: Scholastic.

———. 1994. *Clifford's Big Book of Stories.* New York: Scholastic.

Brown, H. J., Jr. 1991. *Life's Little Instruction Book.* Nashville, TN: Rutledge.

Buehner, C., and M. Buehner. 1992. *The Escape of Marvin the Ape.* New York: Trumpet Club.

Burton, T. 1993. *The Nightmare Before Christmas.* New York: Hyperion.

Canfield, J., and M. Hansen. 1993. *Chicken Soup for the Soul: 101 Stories to Open the Heart and Rekindle the Spirit.* New York: Berkeley.

———. 1995. *The Aladdin Factor.* New York: Berkeley.

Childress, A. 1981. *Rainbow Jordan.* New York: Avon.

Christopher, M. 1959. *Little Lefty.* New York: Little, Brown.

———. 1984. *Baseball Pals.* New York: Little, Brown.

———. 1988. *The Hit-a-Way Kid.* New York: Little, Brown.

Coerr, E. 1977. *Sadako and the Thousand Paper Cranes.* New York: Dell Yearling.

Conly, J. L. 1993. *Crazy Lady.* New York: HarperTrophy.

Cooney, C. 1990. *The Face on the Milk Carton.* New York: Bantam.

———. 1993. *Whatever Happened to Janie?* New York: Bantam Doubleday Dell.

———. 1996. *The Voice on the Radio.* New York: Delacorte.

Crichton, M. 1993. *Jurassic Park—Junior Novelization.* New York: Putnam.

Crutcher, C. 1986. *Running Loose.* New York: Bantam Doubleday Dell Books for Young Readers.

———. 1992. *Athletic Shorts.* New York: Bantam Doubleday Dell Books for Young Readers.

Cusick, R. 1990. *Teacher's Pet.* New York: Scholastic.

Cutler, J. 1992. *No Dogs Allowed.* Toronto: HarperCollins Canada.

Dadey, D., and M. Jones. 1990. *Vampires Don't Wear Polka Dots.* New York: Scholastic.

Dahl, R. 1964. *Charlie and the Chocolate Factory.* New York: Knopf Books for Young Readers.

———. 1983. *Revolting Rhymes.* New York: Bantam Skylark.

———. 1985. *The Witches.* New York: Puffin.

———. 1988a. *James and the Giant Peach.* New York: Puffin.

———. 1988b. *Matilda.* New York: Puffin.

Dakos, K. 1990. *If You're Not Here, Please Raise Your Hand.* New York: Simon and Schuster Books for Young Readers.

Danziger, P. 1974. *The Cat Ate My Gymsuit.* New York: Dell.

———. 1994. *Amber Brown Is Not a Crayon.* New York: Putnam.

Davis, J. 1980. *Garfield at Large.* New York: Random House.

DeFelice, C. 1990. *Weasel.* New York: Macmillan.

———. 1994. *Lostman's River.* New York: Camelot.

DeGross, M. 1994. *Donovan's Word Jar.* New York: HarperCollins.

de Spain, P. 1993. *Thirty-Three Multicultural Tales to Tell.* Little Rock, AR: Angel House Publishers.

Dickens, C. 1976. *Great Expectations.* New York: Penguin Books.

Disney's The Little Mermaid. 1990. New York: Penguin Books.

Disney's Beauty and the Beast. 1991. New York: Penguin Books.

Disney's Pocahontas. 1995. New York: Penguin Books.

Disney's The Hunchback of Notre Dame. 1996. New York: Penguin Books.

Donnelly, J. 1987. *The Titanic.* Orlando, FL: Harcourt Brace.

Dorris, M. 1996. *Sees Behind Trees.* New York: Hyperion Children's Books.

Draper, S. M. 1994. *Tears of a Tiger.* New York: Aladdin.

Dubowski, C. 1994. *Camp Nowhere.* New York: Hyperion.

Duncan, L. 1973. *I Know What You Did Last Summer.* New York: Pocket.

———. 1978. *Killing Mr. Griffin.* New York: Dell.

———. 1984. *The Third Eye.* New York: Dell.

———. 1990. *Ransom.* New York: Bantam Doubleday Dell Books for Young Readers.

Dunning, S., et al. 1995. *Reflections on a Gift of Watermelon Pickle.* Glenview, IL: Scott Foresman.

Durham, J. 1971. *A New Life for Sarita.* New York: Scholastic.

Feelings, T., and E. Greenfield. 1981. *Daydreamers.* New York: Dial.

Ferguson, D. 1992. *Disney's Aladdin.* New York: Penguin Books.

———. 1994. *Disney's The Lion King.* New York: Penguin Books.

Fleischman, S. 1992. *Jim Ugly.* New York: Dell.

Flewellyn, V. S. 1990. *Poetically Just Us.* St. Paul, MN: Parker Initiatives.

Frank, A. 1993. *The Diary of Anne Frank*. Orlando, FL: Harcourt Brace.

Gallo, D. 1987. *Visions: Nineteen Short Stories by Outstanding Writers for Young Adults*. New York: Dell.

———. 1989. *Connections*. New York: Laurel Leaf.

Gallo, D. R., ed. 1993. *Join in Multiethnic Short Stories*. New York: Bantam Doubleday.

Gammell, S. 1991. *Scary Stories—More Tales to Chill Your Bones*. New York: HarperCollins.

Gardiner, J. R. 1980. *Stonefox*. New York: HarperTrophy.

George, J. C. 1972. *Julie of the Wolves*. New York: HarperCollins.

———. 1983. *The Talking Earth*. New York: HarperCollins.

———. 1989. *Shark Beneath the Reef*. New York: HarperTrophy.

Giono, J. 1954. *The Man Who Planted Trees*. White River Junction, VT: Chelsea Green Publishing.

Giovanni, N. 1971. *Spin a Soft Black Song*. Toronto: HarperCollins Canada.

Grahame, K. 1967. *Wind in the Willows*. New York: Lancer.

Greene, B. 1991. *The Drowning of Stephan Jones*. New York: Bantam.

Greenfield, E. 1978. *Honey, I Love*. New York: Trumpet Club.

Grimes, N. 1994. *Meet Danitra Brown*. New York: Trumpet Club.

Hall, K., and L. Eisenberg. 1989. *101 Bossy Cow Jokes*. New York: Scholastic.

Handford, M. 1988a. *Find Waldo Now*. New York: Little, Brown.

———. 1988b. *Where's Waldo?* New York: Little, Brown.

———. 1989. *The Great Waldo Search*. New York: Little, Brown.

Haugaard, E. C. 1990. *Princess Horrid*. New York: Random House.

Hayden, T. 1981. *One Child*. New York: Avon.

———. 1996. *The Tiger's Child*. New York: Avon.

Heide, F. P. 1982. *The Problem with Pulcifer*. New York: Mulberry.

Henkes, K. 1987. *Two Under Par*. New York: Greenwillow.

Highwater, J. 1977. *Anpao*. New York: HarperCollins.

Hill, E. 1993. *Evan's Corner*. New York: Puffin.

Hinton, S. E. 1967. *The Outsiders*. New York: Dell.

———. 1971. *That Was Then, This Is Now*. New York: Dell.

———. 1975. *Rumblefish*. New York: Dell.

———. 1988. *Taming the Star Runner*. New York: Dell.

Hunt, I. 1970a. *No Promises in the Wind*. New York: Berkley Books.

———. 1970b. *The Lottery Rose*. New York: Tempo Books.

Hurwitz, J. 1987. *Class Clown*. New York: Scholastic.

Isaacs, A. 1994. *Swamp Angel*. New York: Trumpet Club.

Johnson, L. 1995. *Dangerous Minds*. New York: St. Martin's.

Jordan, M. 1994. *I Can't Accept Not Trying*. New York: HarperCollins.

Koda-Dallan, E. 1991. *The Tiny Angel*. New York: Workman.

Koningsburg, E. L. 1973. *From the Mixed-Up Files of Mrs. Basil E. Frankweiler*. New York: Bantam Double Day Books for Young Readers.

Krupinski, E., and D. Weikel. 1986. *Death from Child Abuse and No One Heard*. Winter Park, FL: Currier Davis.

Kuller, A. M., ed. 1988. *Readings from the Hurricane Island Outward Bound School*. Hurricane Island, ME: Hurricane Island Outward Bound School.

L'Engle, M. 1972. *A Wrinkle in Time*. New York: Dell.

Lester, J. 1968. *To Be a Slave*. New York: Scholastic.

Levine, E. 1993. *Freedom's Children*. New York: Avon.

Lionni, L. 1967. *Frederick*. New York: Trumpet Club.

Lobel, A. 1980. *Fables*. New York: HarperTrophy.

London, J., ed. 0000. *Thirteen Moons on a Turtle's Back: A Native American Year of Moons*. New York: Putnam.

Lowry, L. 1990. *Number the Stars*. New York: Bantam Doubleday Dell Books for Young Readers.

———. 1993. *The Giver*. New York: Bantam Doubleday Dell Books for Young Readers.

MacCracken, M. 1976. *Lovey—A Very Special Child*. New York: Dutton.

Matas, C. 1993. *Daniel's Story*. New York: Scholastic.

McCall, N. 1994. *Makes Me Wanna Holler: A Young Black Man in America*. New York: Random House.

McCammon, R. 1991. *Boy's Life*. Seattle, WA: PB Publishing.

McKissak, P. C. 1988. *Mirandy and Brother Wind*. New York: Trumpet Club.

Morrow, C. 1994. *The Jellybean Principal*. New York: Random House.

Mead, A. 1995. *Junebug*. New York: Bantam Doubleday Dell Books for Young Readers.

Medearis, A. S. 1995. *Skin Deep*. New York: Macmillan Books for Young Readers.

Miller, M. 1989. *You Be the Jury Courtroom II*. New York: Scholastic.

Munsch, R. N. 1980. *The Paper Bag Princess*. Buffalo, New York: Annick.

Myers, W. D. 1975. *Fast Sam, Cool Clyde, and Stuff*. New York: Puffin.

———. 1988. *Scorpions*. New York: HarperKeypoint.

———. 1994. *Darnell Rock, Reporting*. New York: Dell Publishing.

Nash, O. 1985. *Custard & Company*. New York: Little, Brown.

Oppenheim, S. L. 1992. *The Lily Cupboard*. New York: HarperCollins.

Paterson, K. 1987. *The Great Gilly Hopkins*. New York: HarperCollins.

Paulsen, G. 1987. *Hatchet*. New York: Puffin.

———. 1990. *Canyons*. New York: Bantam Doubleday Dell Books for Young Readers.

———. 1993. *Nightjohn*. New York: Delacorte.

Pearce, Q. L. 1995. *More Super Scary Stories for Sleep-Overs*. Los Angeles: Lowell House Juvenile.

Peck, R. N. 1972. *A Day No Pigs Would Die*. New York: Dell.

———. 1992. *Soup in Love*. New York: Dell.

Peters, J. A. 1992. *The Stinky Sneakers Contest*. Boston: Little, Brown.

Philbrick, R. 1993. *Freak the Mighty*. New York: Scholastic.

Polacco, P. 1993. *The Keeping Quilt*. Columbus, OH: Varsity Reading Services.

Potter, B. 1988. *The Tale of Squirrel Nutkin*. New York: Penguin.

———. 1991. *The Tale of Peter Rabbit*. Avenel, NJ: Derrydale.

———. 1995. *A Treasury of Mouse Tales*. Avenel, NJ: Derrydale.

Prelutsky, J. 1990. *Something Big Has Been Here*. New York: Scholastic.

———. 1993. *The Dragons Are Singing Tonight*. New York: Scholastic.

Resnick, J. 1991. *Original Fairy Tales from the Brothers Grimm*. New York: Derrydale.

Ringold, F. 1991. *Tar Beach*. New York: Crown Books for Young Readers.

Rosenber, L. 1993. *Monster Mama*. New York: Trumpet Club.

Sabin, F. 1986. *Jesse Owens Olympic Hero*. New York: Troll.

Sachs, B. 1994. *Mountain Bike Madness*. New York: Random House.

Sanderson, J. 1995. *Buying Trouble*. Austin, TX: Steck-Vaughn.

Sansouci, R. D. 1987. *Short and Shivery*. New York: Bantam Doubleday Dell Books for Young Readers.

Schwartz, A. 1981. *Scary Stories to Tell in the Dark*. New York: HarperTrophy.

————. 1984. *More Scary Stories to Tell in the Dark*. New York: HarperTrophy.

————. 1988. *Gold and Silver, Silver and Gold*. Toronto: HarperCollins Canada.

————. 1989. *Scary Stories III*. New York: HarperTrophy.

Scieszka, J. 1989. *The True Story of the Three Little Pigs*. New York: Viking.

————. 1991. *The Frog Prince Continued*. New York: Trumpet Club.

————. 1992a. *Knights of the Kitchen Table*. New York: Puffin.

————. 1992b. *The Good, the Bad, and the Goofy*. New York: Puffin.

Selden, G. 1960. *A Cricket in Times Square*. New York: Dell.

Sendak, M. 1963. *Where the Wild Things Are*. New York: HarperTrophy.

Sharmat, M. J. 1994. *Genghis Khan—A Dog Star Is Born*. New York: Random House.

Sharp, M. 1959. *The Rescuers*. New York: Little, Brown.

Shreve, S. 1984. *The Flunking of Joshua T. Bates*. New York: Random House.

————. 1993. *Joshua T. Bates Takes Charge*. New York: Random House.

Shuler, L. 1989. *She Who Remembers*. New York: Dutton Books.

————. 1993. *Voice of the Eagle*. New York: NAL/Dutton.

Silverstein, S. 1981. *A Light in the Attic*. New York: HarperCollins.

————. 1996. *Falling Up*. New York: HarperCollins.

Simmons, A. 1995. *Smoke*. Austin, TX: Steck-Vaughn.

Sloane, P. 1992. *Lateral Thinking Puzzles*. New York: Sterling.

Snyder, A. 1977. *My Name Is Davy and I'm an Alcoholic*. New York: Signet Vista.

Snyder, Z. K. 1972. *Witches of Worm*. New York: Dell.

Sobol, D. J. 1971. *More Two-Minute Mysteries*. New York: Scholastic.

Soto, G. 1993. *Local News*. New York: Scholastic.

————. 1994. *The Skirt*. New York: Dell.

Sparks, B., ed. 1971. *Go Ask Alice*. New York: Avon Flare.

————. 1994. *It Happened to Nancy*. New York: Avon Flare.

Spinelli, J. 1984. *Who Put That Hair in My Toothbrush?* New York: Little, Brown.

Stamper, J. B. 1988. *101 Super Sports Jokes*. New York: Scholastic.

Stanley, D. 1992. *Moe the Dog in Tropical Paradise*. New York: Putnam.

Staples, S. F. 1991. *Shabanu*. New York: Random House.

————. 1993. *Haveli*. New York: Random House.

Steig, W. 1973. *The Real Thief*. Toronto, Canada: HarperCollins Canada.

Stine, J. B. 1978. *How to Be Funny*. New York: Scholastic.

Stine, R. L. 1986. *Blind Date*. New York: Scholastic.

————. 1992a. *Beach Party*. New York: Scholastic.

————. 1992b. *The Dead Girlfriend*. New York: Scholastic.

————. 1994a. *The New Boy*. New York: Scholastic.

————. 1994b. *The Thrill Club*. New York: Pocket.

————. 1994c. *Bad Dreams*. New York: Pocket.

————. 1994d. *Double Date*. New York: Pocket.

————. 1994e. *The Dare*. New York: Pocket.

Stock, G. 1988. *The Kid's Book of Questions*. New York: Workman.

Swarthout, G. 1970. *Bless the Beasts and the Children*. New York: Pocket.

Taylor, M. 1976. *Roll of Thunder, Hear My Cry*. New York: Trumpet Club.

————. 1978. *Song of the Trees*. New York: Bantam.

————. 1987. *The Friendship and the Gold Cadillac*. New York: Dial Books for Young Readers.

————. 1990. *Mississippi Bridge*. New York: Bantam Skylark.

————. 1991. *Let the Circle Be Unbroken*. New York: Puffin.

————. 1992. *The Road to Memphis*. New York: Puffin.

Taylor, T. 1991. *Tuck Triumphant*. New York: Avon.

Thaler, M. 1989. *The Teacher from the Black Lagoon*. New York: Scholastic.

Thomas, J. C., ed. 1990. *A Gathering of Flowers*. New York: HarperKeypoint.

Tracy, B. 1995. *Brian Tracy's Little Silver Book of Prosperity*. New York: Barnes & Noble.

Van Leeuwen, U. 1989. *Dear Mom, You're Ruining My Life*. New York: Dial.

Viorst, J. 1972. *Alexander and the Terrible, Horrible, No Good, Very Bad Day*. New York: Macmillan.

———. 1978. *Alexander, Who Used to Be Rich Last Sunday*. New York: Macmillan.

Volavkova, H., ed. 1993. *I Never Saw Another Butterfly: Children's Drawings and Poems from Terezin Concentration Camp 1942–1944*. New York: Shocken.

Wachter, O. 1987. *Sex, Drugs, and AIDS*. New York: Bantam.

Weiss, E., and M. Friedman. 1994. *The Curse of the Calico Cat*. New York: Random House.

White, E. B. 1952. *Charlotte's Web*. New York: Harper and Row.

Wiesel, E. 1960. *Night*. New York: Bantam.

Wilcox, C. 1993. *Mummies and Their Mysteries*. New York: Scholastic.

Williams, L. 1986. *The Little Old Lady Who Wasn't Afraid of Anything*. New York: Trumpet Club.

Williams, M. 1975. *The Velveteen Rabbit*. New York: Dell.

Williams-Garcia, R. 1995. *Like Sisters on the Homefront*. New York: Dutton Children's Books.

Winokur, J., ed. 1986. *W.O.W.: Writers on Writing*. Philadelphia, PA: Running Press.

Wolff, V. E. 1993. *Make Lemonade*. New York: Scholastic.

Wood, A. 1984. *The Napping House*. New York: Harcourt Brace.

———. 1985. *King Bidgood's in the Bathtub*. Orlando, FL: Harcourt Brace.

———. 1993. *Rude Giants*. New York: Trumpet Club.

Wood, N. 1995. *Dancing Moons*. New York: Doubleday.

Woodson, J. 1994. *I Hadn't Meant to Tell You This*. New York: Bantam Doubleday.

Yep, L. 1989. *The Rainbow People*. New York: HarperCollins.

Yolen, J. 1992. *Briar Rose*. New York: TOR.

Zullo, A. 1996. *Haunted Schools*. New York: Rainbow Bridge.

Index